THIS WAY TO THE APOCALYPSE: THE '60'S

BY SIDNEY BERNARD

THIS WAY TO THE APOCALYPSE: THE '60'S
BY SIDNEY BERNARD

Introduction by
Seymour Krim

THE SMITH
by arrangement with
Horizon Press
New York
1969

The majority of the articles, essays and reviews published in this volume
have appeared in periodicals, to whose editors I make grateful acknowledge-
ment, as follows: *Cheetah, Commonweal, Cultural Affairs, Dude, Escapade,
Evergreen Review, Gent, Literary Times, The Morningsider, The Nation,
National Observer, New York Element, New York Herald Tribune Magazine, Nugget, Pictorial Living, Ramparts, The Realist, Rogue,* and *The
Smith.*

CONTENTS

1 Hip Yip Hurrah

2 Of Crows, Toads & Crocodiles

3 Literary Decathlon

4 Four Arts

Film:

Theater:

Galleries:

5 Manhattan Descants

6 Lunalude & Londinium Day

Introduction

Best pieces Bernard no one covering N.Y. day beat him crisp sharpshooting buzzy graphic how skip lip abyss last five year. Certain hundreds New Yorkers see wildhaired solitary reporter kibitzing streets Manhattan track his kind story, Columbia U. zagdown East Village shootup Lincoln Center travel arabeast Art Student's League, mythman Sid much part scene events writes. His town if ever town belong one eight millionth anybody belong lionhearted judah snooper. Like newest radical farout urban spaceman, kind Bernard drawn gets excited writing, manic faith kept self going when couldn't pull chickenshit sale 350-word filler pay rent West Side room buy girl normal preballing meal nothing. Now 50, maybe secret year two over under, has infinite namechanged past work city newsagency legman, publicity flack, girlie-mag contributor, part-time bookshop salesman, Post Office hustle Christmas, long tunneling background ultimate value only Bernard private eye know mutely. Others seemed usual history grimy failure, down-at-heels hanging on, what happened to that novel, Sid?, what about that play?, but all while Bernard sopping city street by touch by zeitgeist until Viet prolonged rot Yippee! resistance call him twinkling center overlooked man met destiny.

From death Jack Kennedy latest confrontation Fillmore East themes out on street now match experience hoard within, hope joy apocalypse poetics new politics gurus hips flips allofit, all natural pie him after post-Army 15 years knocking round being knocked down other world fading. Where fantastic freaky Sid get energy, haunting city Weegeelike every night twilight 4 AM, talking speed rappers under table Gem's Spa sidewalk Second Ave. nothing stronger Nescafé, lecturing advising arguing New Kids befriending, half dozen opinions every subject innocence and unhostility? Mines it out self turned on at body's midcentury seemingly inexhaustible, covers daily makes immediate notes chopping out leads paras spec only freelance shoelace anxiety works till foggy, bad eye clouding, again next day next because fiend work only thing true got. Possessions? Small room typewriter files phone 17 books (ton magazines newssheets) plenty paper stamp. Cautious change subway coffee and. It. Fearless freebee manipulator alert gatecrasher bearder famous bullshitter unfamous takes bouncing shoulder-length whitelocks around city like raunch Santa Claus finds no scene door uncharmed him grows time not recede example all.

Occasionally some gaudy once-style now hollow "boffo" other *Variety*-type locution stick prose like chewingum, reminder flocking schlocking days smartaleck streets, flashy rhinestone wordgraft hope make quick sale *Swank, Escapade, Cavalier, Dude, Gent*; family tell him monthly dinner home look bum Christ got to pull yard ($100) piece pitch it sideways slyways past gay editor clean self up—but other streets' lingo heard now then small strident overall gives N.Y. authenticity even Bernie's stick. Mind underneath clear shrewd observant resiliant manly rarely lies self others no piece faked written tightly bitely too. Range quickshifting city Yevtushenko to L. Rivers boxer Benny Paret Fuggers Muggers Bill Burroughs P.E.N. benefits riots shout-ins Tulibergs, invaluable record new underground action Manhattan. Sid might wiser debatable early stuff cut sacrifice miniature goodies tight focus Left-hippie-anarchotopian doings has in palm skull with only few rivals Nicholas von Hoffman John d'Wilcock John Garabedian late Don McNeill—all newcomers—none bringing earned perspective marching 30s all way spacedout 60s. Could made even nower pertinent statement possibly new materials only but SB much saved up—theater music cinema painting participating, guy's zest equals grepsi Pepsi—earnest want show public, self, no flash this morning's pop pan. Yet all said done it Sidney Bernard reality reporter, independent journalist, credit conscience human newsprofession, whose book is; here frustrated critic musician painter actor fictionist revolutionary all come together significant contemporary persona writer-reporter mutually bottling history on spot, all Sids rolled one catch it with net woven words years waiting. What lesson now nameless would-be Important Writer Types used condescend Sid, wanted be Tolstoy fuck journalism, this clean bright record from man form made by each both our age unlike other new true fit.

Seymour Krim
Granada, Spain
August 1969

Author's Foreword

A book of pieces is a collage of the author's times, vivid to the extent that it is a litmus of some of the reader's times as well. One characteristic of our times is the almost ruthless demand for brevity, for quick takes of experience that must be packaged in the supermarketed (and superheated) milieu of the dailies, slick weeklies and ahead-of-the-event monthlies. There is no virtue in this, except perhaps the virtue of quick reflexes in a time of stormy change.

In the past decade — and the decade of the 1960s is what this volume covers — the storms in the US have been storms of assassination, of youth in generational and political rebellion, of black challenge to white ingrainedness, of new styles on the culture front that mock — and tear away at — the bloat of what we've had. The book touches on all these areas, and here and there goes its own way toward what I'd suppose was the interstices of these areas. In form the pieces are mostly in the "short-takes " category, but it would be false modesty for me not to say that I saw — and wrote — them short because of my own chemical response largely, and not because of a need to bring them in brief for market.

The writing is primarily journalistic, but of a personal kind that attempts to add density, color and fresh observation to any and all experience I'm involved in. To the extent that I have a "writer's credo," I would say that I believe writing should not be a commercial thing, an exchange of "x" number of words crafted on a fast-moving typewriter for "x" amount of loot, but rather a personal testament of the author that clues the reader to his (the author's) rages and outrages, humors and distempers. The writer worth his salt is a man in search of, in a sense, Thoreau's "better mousetrap"; the latter being a clean metaphor for excellence, and for art, in one's workaday routine. James Agee and Thomas Merton are two writers I can think of for nonfiction who score for me. As to one small note of self-assessment, I would say there's always a hole in my work, where my best should be. And I try to narrow that hole. Fitfully, nervously, rarely easily, and almost every day.

Sidney Bernard
July, 1969

1 Hip Yip Hurrah

The Liberation of Fillmore East by Up Against the Wall Motherfuckers, Yippies, Hippies, Spades and other East Side Militants who Cracked Damn Near a Boxful of Eggs but Couldn't Make the Revolutionary Omelette.

The lower east side, with St. Mark's Place as umbilical, is a freak Siamese whose two faces are at war. One face is the hedonist grin of the spenders, tourists with bread mostly, who trot down to such places as the plush new McGregor's Garage eatery, the many boutique shops, the Electric Circus caravansary, and Ratner's where you can get Lindy's cheese cake at Lindy's prices. The other face is the angry scowl of the militants, Motherfuckers on the prowl from their East Fourth commune mini-headquarters, Yips and hippies moving around and laying barrages of laughing gas over the area, and the poets-painters-moviemakers who see the turf for what it is — a high-octane ethnic mix in a near-disaster area that's also one of the most radically engagé spots in the nation.

Heart of the Siamese is the Fillmore East, former Loew's showplace made over by a fast-running promoter named Bill Graham into a money-making dome of rock. What puts Fillmore at the center is the ability to draw hot flashes of green into the area, mostly from middle-class kids who come by for the rock doings weekends from squarest of square places like Long Island, Scarsdale and other points on the money compass. Oddly enough, the influx of good-time-seekers has caused rising tension. The result has been a face-off, protracted and menacing, between the militants and Graham.

It began at a Fillmore benefit for Columbia S.D.S. On stage was the Living Theatre, among other groups, and Julian Beck and Company found themselves smack in the middle. Actually, it was a "made" scene for Living Theatre, local tension and Living's own guerrilla stance being like keg joined to lit fuse. While L-T was performing half-dozen Motherfuckers, wearing dark shades and leather jackets, had kaplunked themselves on stage and were breathing fire into the mikes. In a kind of Black Panther shorthand, impaired only a little by a whitey inflection, they gave their ultimatum: "Bill Graham, you've sucked the neighborhood of its last buck, unless you give us this space to do our thing. Once a week — every week — we want this space."

The challenge was scary, and electrifying. Soon knots of angry people were on stage, many of them running hard on an adamant Bill Graham. The bone of contention was not so much free space, which Graham had agreed to in principle, but on how the "contract" was to be signed. Motherfuckers and Graham kept swapping mikes and chewing that bone. M-Fs: "You don't *give* us this space, we're *taking* it." Graham: "You take nothing that's *mine* to give, only over my dead body!" Walpurgis Night on the east side, with aisle-charging chorus of hundreds tasting free-Fillmore like honey on the tongue, and threats of bike chains and *burn the place down* waiting in the wings. Then, at about three in the morning, a glimmer of a positive solution. Largely it was the charisma (read, beautiful and forceful pleas) of Julian Beck and two or three of his company that showed the way. Graham said he'd agree to free Wednesday nights, foot the bill for ushers and lights, get together with community spokesmen on programs. The stalemate appeared to be over.

The next Wednesday night — this was back in October — saw the opener of an unprecedented event for the east side; a large commercial theater, partly due to management's sense of neighborhood equity in the matter, and partly due to a hanging threat of boycott or worse if it didn't, had thrown open its doors to the community, with no veto over who would appear on stage. It was as if having the space — the long cavern of 2,700 seats, dimly banked lights, and stage — to be together in was as vital as water from their taps. Flyers had announced the free evening and the turnout was a Second Avenue gala of long-haired youth, activists who whiffed Fillmore's air and thought they smelled revolutionary Bolshoi, rock devotees who were more into the Fugs than say Simon and Garfunkle, Tompkins Square barrio kids wearing Che berets, Panthers with a loose stride who were there to keep Graham (and maybe even the M-Fs) honest, street theater and rock groups homing in on a very live vibration.

Others pouring in were the uptown press, TV camera crews, people with recorders slung over shoulders, all on the trail of what looked like a confrontation story, and all more or less straight, who easily outnumbered the reporter-camera teams from East Village Other, the Village Voice, New York Free Press, and Rat. Local militants, along with M-Fs who picked up the cry, immediately called for a ban on the "bourgeois press." It was a seesaw issue ("What do we do with the Village Voice?" someone needled) and the ban never took, but the threat put a momentary tinge of pink, from embarrassment more than news fright, into the cheeks of one young lady from CBS. The program beginning at 7 p.m. was long and consisted of stretches of rock music, lots of rapping from the stage on TPF police tactics, the need for red-band community defense, Graham's and the Fillmore's "commercial bullshit," and an overall feeling of exhilaration that could be read as : "Takeover for the love of us all." There was also some uneasiness, brought on by a slippage back to rhetoric, the barricades rhetoric of the previous week. Motherfuckers, ad infinitum: "Dig, we *took* the Fillmore! Graham gave us nothing!" And from others, more observers than gut participants: "Okay, you took the Fillmore. Now on with the show."

All told there have been five or six evenings of liberated Fillmore, the script pretty much the same each time. A lavaflow of rock-and-rap, and then, at about the midpoint, a drift to "What do we do now?" The peak or bustout evening was December 26, during the good-will-to-man season. On that night there was a special treat, Elektra-sponsored and first New York appearance of a stormy quintet known as MC-5 (for Motor City), a group in from Detroit where they had shovelled some very hot rock coals. The persona and musical style of MC-5 — call them a hair of the dog crossbreed of Fugs and Doors — was gaited perfectly for the joy-hungry crowd that showed up. The five took their stance on stage, which had a backdrop of two huge American flags, and they proceeded to stone the audience with rock bon bons like: "The Motor City's burning baby/There ain't a thing that you can do." Kids were charging the aisles, in outbursts of pure energy release. Other couples were dry-hugging in their seats. And though the militants were quiescent for the moment, there was a kind of smoldering anger in the air even so.

Suddenly — and no one seems sure how it happened — a flash attack with bike chain on Bill Graham, who suffered broken nose and bloodied face. In the melee that followed, one usher got his arm broken, another person was stabbed, the MC-5 was molested trying to leave the stage, equipment was stolen, projection screen slashed and theater seats destroyed. Liberated Fillmore, ending in a bummer.

A sort of community Thermidor has set in, since. Graham has charged the M-Fs (and it's his mildest word) with "irresponsibility." The Up Against the Wallers countered with dire threats and called Graham a "cop out." A shafting double-entendre was no doubt intended, for Graham has been given the knock, by his opponents, of a too-cushy relationship with police. Efforts to reach a compromise — the very word seems like the coinage of a stutterer in a den of bloodlusty shouters — are going on with Graham making an offer to underwrite any "constructive, realistic and lawful program" the community might come up with, short of a return to the Fillmore. And while some feel this is a fair offer, the M-Fs and other militants are scornful, one of them labelling Graham's bid: "The Fillmore-Nixon Legal Hype." The militants insist that the community will do its thing in the main arena only, or else. Deponents rest, glaring hard at one another.

Over the same period, there were two Fillmore benefits, and incidents therein, that point up the near-hemophilic nature of east side's political blood lust. At an affair for the weekly Guardian, mainspeaker Rap Brown warned he'd quit the stage, if the catcalling didn't stop. To some in the large audience, Brown's warning must have smacked of temperament (" It's bourgeois to carry on so, Rap ") or worse, and they weren't buying it. And so Brown did exactly that, majestically walking off stage after a mere two rounds or so, or about six minutes. At a later benefit, this one for the New York Free Press, Norman Mailer seemed to be clubfighting his way for the distance, when someone from the packed orchestra floor threw him a low one: "Who the fuck is Norman Mailer!" Generation-gap or no, the gritty and tightly-vested Mailer, lugging a good 20-pounds over his best weight, shot back in a flurry, beginning with the jab: "Who the fuck are we *all*. That's the mystery." He then paced off to the wings. The time was about midway of the ninth round, or 25 minutes or so from his openers. (There are no between-round pauses at the Fillmore.)

A good guess can be made why Mailer never finished his peroration, which was on "Who Is the Enemy?" He had made it clear that he wasn't going to talk "on the Pentagon, Vietnam, J. Edgar Hoover, and the rest. We know all about those." The enemy he wanted to talk about — always implied but never quite spelled out — was right out there among them, seemingly the miasmic uptightness and self-destructiveness coming from the left's own ranks. And the audience wasn't buying that, either. What they did buy, earlier that evening, was the Fugs's rendition of a new rock number, the group's own "4 Minutes to Twelve And There's a Madman at the Wheel." It was a premiere, offered in their set before Mailer's arrival, and aimed like an arrow at the inaugural only a fortnight away. And the Fugs went at it — went after the "new" White House dispensation — with a kinetic frenzy that reached, if not the upper floors of the Pierre Hotel, where the President-elect was doing *his* thing, then surely to the far walls of Fillmore's balcony. The audience bought that, with high-pitched demonstrative pleasure.

Congeries of bothersome questions float by. Questions on tactical posture, real or token change, militancy as means or ends, rhetorical overkill, switch or fight. Some of the psychological, and political, sidewinders of free-Fillmore nights.

1969

Lion Coming Down

The weeklong seizure of Columbia University by rebellious students was not so much the days and nights of the long knives as the days and nights of the crepe paper arm bands. In the around-the-clock ebb and flow, hardly a person did not display one or another of the many colored arm bands, worn high on the sleeve like so many tourniquets of belief, an assortment that symbolized a complex of differing views as well as the almost hour-by-hour shift in tactics. Red for the S.D.S. and Afro-American activists, white for the faculty that distinguished itself by a body-on-the-line concern, blue for the one-thousand or so (out of a student body of 17,500) conservative "jocks" who opposed the sit-ins, green for a fast-growing number of students and faculty who advocated no punishment for the embattled ones, and black for those who mourned the bloodshed and condemned the Kirk administration.

For an urban campus with a persona of coolness, the events were unprecedented explosions of pent-up passions. They cut across every level of consciousness — from the mandarin oriented trustees and administration to the concerned faculty to the wave-making and wave-stopping students to the alert and boiling community forces to the Mayor and his cops. Taking them in the order named, trustees and the administration of Grayson Kirk and David B. Truman were shaken from their long-standing icy distance to the need of both community and students. Faculty in large number were rejecting a play-it-safe role, said role fed by the rewards of good salary, tenure and career prestige. The students were acting out the 1968 campus drama — a political happening whose various parts might have been scripted by such as Stokely Carmichael, Professor Herbert Marcuse, Che Guevara, a little of Mao, a little of the Fugs, a little of William Buckley. The black community of West Harlem saw the Morningside gym project as an $11-million stigma of white pushiness. As for the Mayor and the police — rage against the police could hardly be overstated, and if the Mayor was not exactly happy over the fact that the police blew it, he still was not about to be given high marks for a liberalist stance.

A daily report of the brave acts would make a volume — and conversely, a report of the mean acts would barely make a chapbook. First and perhaps most decisive of the brave was the faculty picket line around Low Library, which was set up as a physical barrier against police or jockey attempts to bust the sit-ins. It was mostly a silent line, holding its ground day and night, a changing guard of tired profs and junior faculty whose one aim was defense. And when the police bust came — in a kind of darkly-mantled set of maneuvers at an hour when Harlem was asleep — the faculty was not absent in terms of clubbed bodies, paddy wagon rides and police bookings. Another brave act was the march across College Walk of fifty or so black and white youths, who were hefting baskets of food and chanting *food food food*. They climbed Low's wide stairs and made a half U turn for the building's west facade, where they soon became embroiled with jocks who vowed they would starve out the rebels. A few scuffles and bloody noses later, and the food bearers took to the air, lobbing sandwiches and fruit over the heads of the jocks, to the waiting and sometimes fumbling hands of the hungry rebels. (Friendly shouts of "Call in Sid Luckman!" and the like.) And from the opposing side — the anxious Business School member dressed in proper suit, shirt and tie who popped up everywhere on campus. He was conducting his own rump meetings — a sort of floating minority of one who brought down fire and brimstone on the sit-ins in the form of, as one of his proposals had it, "A suit against the S.D.S. and the Afro-Americans for $300,000 a day for every day they've forced us to miss class." He asked for signatures and got boos. Came one response, "You'll need a Philadelphia lawyer for that one."

The cult of personality, for sure, is one course they don't teach at Columbia. Still there were certain individuals — mostly from the faculty — who got into the spotlight, by dint of word and deed that caught on with the campus. One of them was Rabbi Bruce Goldman, adviser to students, who played a sort of odd man in, avid in his appeals to keep things cool, but at the same time, total in his identity with the main student demands. Goldman is 32, but looked older, not so much harassed in body, as creased a little in soul, with concern. He was among those slugged by police, and wore on his forehead that unique medal of Columbia's sit-in week, what might come to be known as the Bandaid Chevron of the Bust. Of medium height and a little paunchy, beard trimmed neatly to a point, small lively eyes that revealed alternating moods of seriousness and humor, Rabbi Goldman roamed the campus at all hours of day and night, making contact. ("I asked three students how to spell coalition" — the jocks called themselves the Majority Coalition — "so they held a brief conference and then gave me their answer.") Another was Prof. Eric Bentley, the Brechtian — perhaps the archetype of what the students most want — a teacher who relates himself, beyond the books of his trade, to the relevant issues of the time. And to the need for change — which Bentley diagrammed at campus rallies and among the faculty, using the McMillin stage or St. Paul's chapel as kinds of barricades against musty views. His words were barbed, his thrusts needling and satiric. All in all his performances were not unlike Brechtian set pieces on the academy, right down to the burst of thinning hair combed downward on his forehead.

And the avuncular Prof. Quentin Anderson, of the English Department, in his ad lib sessions with students at the sun dial. Burly, tweedy, pipe-smoking — and fiftyish. The avuncular part, a thinly-disguised put on, seen through by the way his voice would suddenly change — it would take on timbre, and authority, as he'd comment on some new flyer that was handed to him. A flyer, say, that the pro-sit-ins professor and students weren't about to buy, whereupon Prof. Anderson would take the flyer apart point by point, in a style of address far from avuncular, and with sidewinders like: "The average American is a Hamlet in a supermarket. To buy or not to buy, that is the question." And there was Prof. Lionel Trilling — sallow and unsmiling, eyes rimmed darkly with worry, spare body leaning a little into the books he carried, looking for all the world, and with a lot of sorrow, as if he would never find his scholarly grail of a middle ground between, say, humanism and establishmentarianism. And there were more such spotlighted figures, but none were about to be dragged into the personality-cult phase. Kicking, screaming or otherwise. Not on the Morningside campus, anyway.

Participatory democracy — call it campus meeting with mental muscle — was marathon in form, political cram course in content. Take the scene outside St. Paul's chapel, several hours after the police bust. About 200 students were marking time on the small redstone quadrangle while an important meeting was going on inside with some 400 senior faculty and administration high brass including President Grayson Kirk and Vice President David T. Truman. Two key issues were the police violence and amnesty for the sit-ins. The students — two or three had hobbled over with casts on their legs — were naturally curious. And more than curious. They shouted in cadence: "Kirk must go!" "Kirk must go!" They displayed the V sign, that pumping motion of index and third fingers that was the leit motif of sit-in week. As the shouts grew louder, a teacher came off St. Paul's portico, announced he was junior faculty, (and thus was excluded from the meeting inside), and pleaded with the students for silence. He told them: "I'm with *you*, but I feel it's wrong to do it this way." Some quieted down, others demurred. He went on: "Give them a chance to talk. After that, you'll see what you'll see."

One of the sit-in students, still fresh after some hours in the lockup, popped forward and called for a vote. They rapped for a while and then took a show of hands. A good majority favored the teacher. And so it began. They were off and running in search of the right tactic, the tactic that would give weight to numbers and thrust to conviction. They sat down — this too was voted on — in a tight-squeeze lotus position and, after a myriad of proposals and discussions, it was agreed that they'd greet the professors and administration brass, when the latter groups came out of the meeting, with a stance of total silence. The students opened a passage of no wider than 6 feet, which ran from portico to quadrangle's end, itself a distance of 70 feet or so. The "escape" was thus cordoned off and could be negotiated only through their own seated, silent ranks. They waited, several in the meantime rising and giving witness to the early-morning confrontation with the police. A light rain began to fall. Sections of newspapers were passed around, and within minutes the two seated blocks of students were half hidden by canopies made out of, in the main, sheets from dozens of *New York Timeses,* whereupon a slightly wetted down but still pretty Barnard girl quipped: "Newsproof but not waterproof." About a half-hour later, and some two hours after the students first gathered, the meeting inside St. Paul's ended. As the professors and administration people came out in the open, nearly all of them registered surprise, a surprise that changed rather quickly — and almost uniformly — into a kind of passive and eyes-straight-ahead anonymity, as each walked past the two blocks of seated, silent and waterlogged students. But the scatterings of V's — from maybe one prof in five — in response to the sea of student V's, seemed no small affirmation of the sit-in cause.

Except at schools, other college campuses and the Harlem area, there was little cheer in the outer New York community for Columbia. The *Times* blasted the S.D.S. in daily editorials. Phrases like "the nightmare of disintegration" and "the youthful junta" and "tactics of a reckless minority" were parts of a catchall threnody on an agenda of revolution that, in perfect candor, existed more in the minds of the editorial writers than on campus. Roasted over the editorial coals were sit-in leaders like S.D.S.'s young Mark Rudd, a mild-looking engine of campus radicalism who may or may not aspire to the role of a

"Red Rudi" Dutschke, but who in any case was too busy with nuts and bolts of daily tactics to answer the press charge. More serious were the media charges that "Maoists" had come in and might even have taken over — meaning people like Carmichael, Rap Brown and Tom Hayden. Such charges were as vague as they were loaded. The media seemed to be addressing itself to readers and TV watchers who presumably would go chill at any mention of the name Mao. (Like the drag on a cigarette, the Chinese Dragon menace is a hard habit to break.) But people on campus saw the Mao thing differently, that is, they saw Carmichael and Company's presence as far more a case of observing the events than of leading them.

Any way they played it, the show was and is an all-Columbia one, with the persona of coolness all but hidden for now by hot poultices of change, or so the over 700 arrests and dozens of police-gift beatings would seem to foretell. Roar lion roar is what Columbia is doing for real — at least in so far as the lion did come down from its pedestal, and did act on the needs of students, faculty, community and the larger American landscape. The short term needs that were sparked by the sit-ins — such as elimination of the gym, withdrawal of Columbia from IDA (Institute of Defense Analyses), and amnesty for all who were involved, which would include that the administration makes no criminal trespass charges against the students. And the long term needs — such as greater faculty and student voice in running the university, the priority of human values in dealing with Harlem and other communities, and an end to trustee power in so far as it is an absentee power. The rest is far from silence.

1968

Sane: Norman Thomas

The aging, near-blind and very alive Norman Thomas slowly made his way to the podium microphone at Madison Square Garden. It was late. The long program had included nearly a dozen speakers, a pageant where the Bread and Puppet Theatre pantomimed some of the horrors of the Vietnam war, a rousing 15 minutes of song by Pete Seeger, and one or two set pieces (such as a collection) that are endemic to large rallies. Thomas was last speaker of the evening, an evening arranged by SANE to voice demands that we end the war in Vietnam now, and an evening that at its height had drawn close to 20,000 into the huge arena, with an overflow of 500 more who remained in the outer lobby while the proceedings were piped from the podium. As Thomas got ready to speak, the audience which by then was down to a bare third, rose as one person to greet him. They kept up the demonstration, and Thomas in his old pro style tried to shortcircuit them into silence, and was able to do so only after the announced that he wanted the remaining minutes for words of action not cheers, words that would be "A dialogue between myself and the President, and through me, between you of the audience and Lyndon Johnson."

Norman Thomas peered out at the near and far reaches of the Garden, his unseeing eyes in his fine chiseled head taking on the piercing directness of a laser beam, and for the next 15 minutes or so Thomas addressed himself to President Johnson in words of conscience, moral fervor, occasional darts of humor and point-by-point dissent on Vietnam that had the audience very nearly honed to a glimmer of hope for change in our policy. The intuitive sense was that if this ancient (he is past 80) has been with us for so long; and has been part of so much that was good — like the FDR years, the early Marshall Plan; and has fought and helped change the bad — like the Joe McCarthy days; then surely his very survival, and his still robust presence on this night, was vital and inspiring witness. In a short 15 minutes, Norman Thomas seemed to epitomize the thrust and passion of the huge rally — and his identification with the youth ("I tell you that not many of the young people here tonight will live to see my years — and that is an understatement — if our leaders do not change their course") touched the audience with the chill and grandeur of an Isaiah.

There had been a quilting-bee of speeches — black for despair, red for the bloodshed, purple for the mock optimism of government pronouncements, and bright pastels for hope. Besides Norman Thomas, some others who spoke were I. F. Stone who did a series of barbed explications of White House and Pentagon policy ("What we need in Washington, and I hope IBM is listening, are computers that can blush . . ."); Floyd McKissick who said civil rights battles and Vietnam withdrawal are two sides of the same coin ("Black folks and poor folks are fighting the war . . ."); Jules Feiffer who did a takeoff on the President's peace-or-bombs syndrome, using a Johnson City drawl and draw all the way; and Professor Gunnar Myrdal who had flown in from Sweden to read a lengthy analysis of U.S. policy, one which showed that policy to be mired in contradiction. Rev. William Sloan Coffin, Jr. and actor Ossie Davis took turns as chairman.

The rally was salted with lighter moments—as when a SANE cheering squad of 24 lively and youthful boys and girls, the latter decked out in Danskins, minis and tight sweaters, would race to the front of the podium after each speaker had concluded and do a jumping locomotive cheer (such as "M-C-K-I-S-S-I-C-K"). While some resisted the gymnastic capers, no doubt on the premise they were too close a parody of every Siwash U. on Saturday afternoon TV, the cheering squad did lend a grace note of playful enthusiasm. The note on youth was strong in the audience, too—with hundreds of young couples from schools, the arts and businesses co-mingling with an older spectrum (teachers, people from show business and the arts, activists from various political clubs, etc.) in a hands-across-the-generations compact, thus sandbagging at least for the evening the "Never trust anyone over 25" canon of the new left. Others who drew cheers were a group of several hundred from Veterans for Peace, and a large block of 5,000 trade unionists from the Fur Workers, Amalgamated Clothing, Hotel, Furniture, United Auto, Brewery and Department Store Employees. And outside the Garden there were two groups of counter-rally pickets — hawks of the superleft called "Sparticists" who shouted for unstinting N.L.F. victory, and hawks of the far right from the National Renaissance Party who merely wanted a little more conscientious bombing of Hanoi.

One went to the rally with the feeling that it was just another exercise in futility, only to have that change as the evening progressed to a firmer sense that it was more like an exercise in votes. The votes motif was borne out by the announcement that whereas the house was almost completely sold out, last year's SANE rally at the same place had drawn several thousands less. And the date of the rally was not without irony. December 8, or one day after the Pearl Harbor anniversary. Back then it was Hickam and the harbor — *our* Hanoi and Haiphong — that got the bursting bombs. For a day only.

1967

The Grand Central Bust

The Tactical Patrol Force is a kind of Praetorian Guard of the New York City police. They can't be told apart from the others except by the "TPF" brass initials on their coat collars — that and a reputation for swift action. Some would call TPF tactics "unsavory" as well, and that makes a difference too. And so, if you throw a TPFer at a hippie, you have a fairly predictable outcome: onesided violence. Moreover, when the battleground is Grand Central Terminal, you come upon a modern version of that ancient baiting game: lions versus Christians in the Roman Colosseum.

That was the scene, as several thousand youths gathered at the Terminal to celebrate the "spring equinox." It was Friday midnight — actually, two days after the constellation shift — and suburban travel was at a near-standstill. Called by the Youth International Party — an amalgam of hippies and activists who sprung a huge "life" convention at the time of the Democratic Party "death" convention in Chicago — the affair was coasting along in good order, when it was derailed suddenly by violence. The witness from outer space — the clear-eyed witness, with no Earthian hang-up to mar his view — would have had a good seat from which to judge the problem: *Who makes the violence.*

I arrived at the Terminal at 11:30, coming in through the main entrance at 42nd Street. My spot turned out to be advantageous — I was directly south of the circular information booth and domed clocks, from which area most of the activity radiated. Only ten feet to my left was the police command post — a loose cluster of high brass, detectives, uniformed police — and whatever leftovers. There was no sign of tension — rather, just the opposite. As the hippies swelled into the Terminal main room, the police were taking no action beyond that of keeping paths open for late commuters. It was "business as usual" — and the police, on the one or two occasions I was asked to move, had put it to me in a formal: "Sir, would you keep the aisle open . . ."

The pattern was pretty well set — both for police and celebrants. At about 12:30 the crowd reached its height — three or four thousand in a tight squeeze of two main groups that swayed, danced and sang. Balloons popped up everywhere, as many in both circles played a kind of netless volleyball game. Attention was focused on the information booth. Here several of the more active were doing their thing — and it was clear that their chants, shouts and slogans were taking on a more overtly political hue. The "Hell no, we won't go!" number got a big play, as did the burning of dollar bills (whether real or stage money, it was hard to tell), and the yips for peace. A fist fight had broken out, smack in the middle of one tight circle, and three or four cops charged in and ended it. It was a harmless flurry at worst — throwing a punch in that kind of body-crush was about as effective as trying to kayo a bag of cement.

What, then, caused the change? From a groovy, loosely spontaneous happening, one minute — to a club-swinging, bloody mess the next? The consensus of police, hippie leaders and press seemed to agree on two or three factors. One was the vandalizing of the clocks

— the removal, that is, of two minute hands, from two of the four clocks. Another was the explosion of two cherry bombs — or maybe they were little old Chinese half-inchers — which came about 40 minutes apart, and which rent the vaultlike Terminal with a kind of teasing, instantaneous crack of doom. (After which, laughs.) A third was the breaking of glass — some said from a ticket booth, others said from a partition. And yet none of these incidents was the touch-off. If anything they seemed like mere ripples on the broad tides of fun and they were absorbed pretty near in an opera bouffe style.

That leaves one other possible cause, mentioned by none. Among the dozen or so who had lofted themselves to clock level — and could thus lay claim to a kind of tight extraterritoriality — there were two young men who held cheese-cloth signs, which they attempted to unfurl now and then. Footing was rather awkward, and they didn't entirely succeed at first. When one of them did finally make it — and then only for seconds — the sign he unfurled brought on a low hum, and some cheers of approval. The message was in red paint, and there were two handprints in black. The sign read: "UP AGAINST THE WALL MOTHER FUCKER." The young man was white, possibly Latin. He broke out in an ear-to-ear grin of triumph. His face and brow — topped by a narrow braid of beads — went pale from the effort. He fluttered the sign once, twice. And then collapsed it against his chest, as he began to lose his balance. Several hands reached up to hold him, and the crowd gave him another quick cheer.

I looked over at the knot of police. Their reaction to the sign, and maybe to the crowd's response as well, was that of an icy disdain. The time was a little past one a.m. Hardnosed question: Did someone from the command flash the signal, just then? Moments later came the first police charge. The TPF — the Praetorians — came barreling into the 42nd Street entrance, 20 or more of them in a hefty wedge. And I for one got over to the wall fast. They hit for the outer circles, for those who were detached, and they picked off hippies left and right. High school kids and women included. More than likely, even a non-hippie or two. The TPF swung night-sticks freely. Many defended themselves, but caved in under the odds. (In some cases it was five-to-one.) The TPF was simply more efficient, and more full of group muscle. And in minutes flat their labor produced scores of bloody heads and noses, anguished cries and a general pandemonium all through the big hall.

Fifty-seven in all were arrested, and were forced into paddy wagons. But the cops never did close down the celebration, not entirely. A hard core of about 200 stood fast until 3:30 (even as some had had to run fast earlier to stay clear of TPF's clutches). Later they went to Sheep Meadow to yip up the sun. Meanwhile several of the arrested were treated at Bellevue for various injuries, at least two of a serious nature according to reports. All were arraigned the next day — a Sunday — on charges ranging from disorderly conduct to resisting arrest to obstructing traffic. Abbie Hoffman and Keith Lampe, two field reps of the YIP movement, charged the police with "No attempt at communication." Both had requested — two or three times — that the police allow them the use of the Department's bullhorns, to help control the crowds. Which even then left moot the problem of how to control the TPF. And no small problem it must be, at least in the view of one young man who was beaten and arrested, the young man who charged the TPF with "animalistic behaviour," "brutality" and "creephood."

Hardly seems likely the witness from outer space would have put it better, not even he. And an add to the lions-Christians note — FM radio station WBAI was a kind of Wailing Wall for the hippie oppressed. The kids trooped by WBAI's small redstone building, which is only three blocks from the Terminal, and they rapped for hours. A real live "Tell it like it is" session. They were red-eyed, and they were vivid. Light years beyond Hunt-Brink.

1968

The Big March

The canvas sign, rainsoaked and fading, spelled out in big block letters the words: EVEN PRINCETON. It was held waist high by three undergrads, with 20 or 30 more students and faculty behind them, as the group from the New Jersey ivy campus came into the United Nations Plaza. Behind the Princetons were other academic contingents bringing up the delayed rear. These were the last of a six-hour assembly and march, the Spring Mobilization to End the War in Vietnam, by far the greatest in numbers — police had estimated 125,000 — and most vocal in the two or three year history of protest over "this lousy war," as one speaker had called it. It was the by-now famous April 15th march.

Even the rain was welcome, in two senses. It came late in the huge meeting and march, around five-thirty p.m., and it helped clear the jammed plaza in a matter of minutes. This allowed an opening for the many thousands who were strung out for a mile or more from the main rally point for most of the afternoon, and who were now able to move into view of the speaker's stand at FDR Drive. They did so like the last yards of a marathon, sloshing through the gutter rivulets, wilting banners and signs held high. And they were greeted by the loudest cheers, coming from several hundred who ventured back into the plaza to see them — the rain seemed more a benediction than hindrance — as if the day's keen purpose wanted just this baptism from gray skies for a coda.

It was a day writ large not only in the number of paraders — but in the response of these tens of thousands to the running provocation of handfuls of pro-war barkers, obscenity shouters, egg and paint throwers. Up and down the line of march the latter ran, pumping their "Bomb Hanoi" and other banners in midair, croaking out accusations of disloyalty. And getting from the paraders, for all the hawkish fluff of the pro-war demonstrators' patriotism, a steady rebuke of coolness and laughter. The rebuke in the final sense of that most grassroots of actions, voting with your feet.

And wearing seven-league boots to get there, from places all along the Eastern Seaboard and inland — Portland, Maine; Providence, Rhode Island; Boston and Washington and Philadelphia; Chapel Hill, North Carolina. From as far west as Chicago, and from the Sioux reservation in South Dakota, a delegation of very original Redmen and squaws. All piling out of buses and trains, on this half-winter half-spring Saturday morning, making New York very much " the rest of America." They visited Automats and coffee shops and hotel lobbies in midtown, to freshen up or ease traveler's hunger in quick bursts of activity. And they gradually moved into Sheep Meadow (Fun City's very own reservation), visitors merging with the increasing thousands of New Yorkers some of whom had arrived at dawn. Pretty soon the atmosphere was as much carnival as political, many natives reprising some of the rites of the Easter Sunday Be-In at the same place. The offering of daffodils and buttons and food, group chanting of mantras, swift beating of bongos, poetry readings and folk singing from open trucks. It was the first joining in large numbers of the hippy divinity of Hare Krishna, and the engaged mood of conscience and protest over Vietnam.

On the southeast promontory, that hill that is fast becoming a chapel of political witness, the day's most serious act was taking place. Seventy young men gathered to burn their draft cards. They were joined by others on the spot, and some estimated that nearly two-hundred cards were burned. The card-holders sat or stood in clusters, and lit matches or cigarette lighters, or passed their cards up to a

31

youth who held a flaming coffee can. As the tiny cards caught fire, the owners began a chant of "Resist, resist." Girlfriends, wives and dozens of paraders joined in the cry. Most were of college age, and the card holders included bearded young men in knockdown kind of dress, as well as the more conservative in tweeds and ties. They were joined by a group of older men, including several veterans and the Rev. Thomas Hayes of the Episcopal Peace Fellowship. The scene drew a number of quick-shooting press photographers, and a covey of plainclothesmen — most of them in blue business suits — who wore in their lapels the tiny enamel triangle button of their trade. The plainclothesmen — whether Federal or local, it was hard to tell — were also present at a flagburning, which happened earlier, a flash incident that came and went with more surprise than shock, but which also provoked some verbal protest. Order was kept throughout, and the effect of the burnings was something less than an eyeball to eyeball confrontation.

The marchers stepped off a little past noon, with 70 or more Sioux in the lead, many in full regalia. The sight of the braves coming through the ravines and winding paths of the West Walk, with hundreds looking on from high boulders and outcroppings, gave a strange aura of a symbolic powwow, of Redmen coming to the Central Park lair of the white man, to show him the magic ways of peace. The paraders came out of the park at Fifty-ninth Street, where big sidewalk crowds had gathered. Most were silent watchers, crowds of the kind that would be window-shopping, or walking their dogs, or taking the park air — on a normal Saturday. But the long-look focusing of eyes, furrowing of brows and tautness of lips — these were details that spelled concern. Applause from behind the wooden barriers greeted the marchers here and there; and tentative jeers came from a few in response to the constant needling of the young hawks who ran up and down the line pumping their signs hard. Police — who might have broken their own record, with 3,000 uniformed in the line — had made five arrests, four of them from among the estimated 1,000 antiparade partisans.

From East Fifty-ninth the parade turned south into Madison Avenue. Here the stylish shops, boutiques and beauty salons tried to maintain a facade of business-as-usual. But even here the only real business was the parade, although the onlookers had thinned to clusters leaning on wooden barriers or standing on corners. One point of curiosity if not tension was the gracefully curving and arched windows of the graystone Gothic eminence that rises on Fiftieth and Fifty-first — the back sections of St. Patrick's Cathedral. All afternoon marchers and bystanders had been looking up at the windows, but there was no sign anyone was home. Now a group of nuns, teachers and students from Fordham University — near one hundred in all — marched past Fifty-first Street. They halted and then faced the windows. The Fordham group kneeled down in the street and made a silent prayer. They then stood up and in chantlike voice intoned, "Peace! Peace!" No one appeared at the windows. Further along, at Forty-seventh and Lexington, the Fordhamites and others had to run a gauntlet, not of silence, but of noisy jeers and — indeed — curses. The verbal blasts came from a group of around fifty, most of them teenagers, with a sampling of aging legionnaires, the latter displaying medals and potbellies in equal prominence. They were ringsiding from a 60 or 70 foot abutment — it rose 10 feet or so from the ground and ran parallel to an apartment building — and they had a decided separate-but-equal status all afternoon. One lanky youth, his cheeks drained white from shouting, ran along the stone rim, repeating the theme: "Homosexuals — never saw such a bunch of *homosexuals!*" The others leered and shouted agreement. It was from this corner building that two or three eggs were tossed, and there were five such incidents all day. One had caught, and added a new color to, the maroon and white Fordham standard. "They supply the eggs," someone mused, "and we make the peace omlette."

By two p.m. the main meeting site at the United Nations was two jammed phalanxes of people that formed an arrowhead with the speaker's stand at the apex — in total around 75,000. The feeder points were Hammarskjold Plaza and FDR Drive, both now locked tight to later arrivees. From an elevation of 200 feet or so, and in a gray overcast, a helicopter came buzzing back and forth. Stokely Carmichael of Snick had quipped over the microphone, " CIA's flyboys;" and from a parader came the topper, "LBJ's people prodder." The great crowd roared when Monsignor Charles Rice of Pittsburgh who was an early speaker of the dozen or more exclaimed: " Let's get out of there, and pay the Vietnamese an indemnity." The speeches were brief, except for the main one, by Martin Luther King, which Dr. King read from notes, and which lasted nearly 30 minutes. It was an oration delivered evenly, but in a voice by turns sorrowful, and packed with moral (and political) concern. The crowd gave off a kind of long wavelength of silence, broken now and then by applause, which had the effect of wavering drumrolls of hand clapping. Towards the end of his speech, when Dr. King strongly urged the need for organization and action, especially among students and youth, the audience burst out of its cathedral attention with loud expressions of assent. Later came the first light drops of rain and the crowd moved evenly out of the area; as they did so many among the backed up thousands came into the plaza, rather than break ranks and seek shelter. The last sodden yards seemed important, even if the meeting was over.

All day there had been shouts for "Black Power," for "Flower Power," for "Red (for Indian) Power" and — as the clouds opened — even for "Rain Power." What it all seemed to spell was "Vote Power."

1967

The Fugs vs Coca Cola

Dee jays avoid them. Editors find them a little hot, so they too avoid them. Two reasons why the Fugs, that Molotov cocktail of rock, have remained in relative obscurity. The article was bought by the entertainment editor of Diplomat, and scheduled for their January, 1967 issue. It was nixed by the editor, and never ran in Diplomat. Soon after, Diplomat folded. Rumor was that Metromedia, multimillion complex that published Diplomat, sank the magazine because it was becoming too controversial. Diplomat's all-China issue for one. Status then bought Diplomat's inventory, and once again the article sat around, this time for over a year. Obviously it was too controversial for Diplomat's and Status's jet-set orientation, and Status finally released the article back to me. Here in its original form, the article describes an early performance of the Fugs, a group that — if anything — is more incendiary than ever.

S.B.

Folkways Records has signed them up — they have performed in England and at Town Hall. These moderate scores have not affected — not by so much as a yawn — the quartet of East Village rock 'n' politics minstrels known as the Fugs. They are neither affected by the threat of suddenly accumulated green and fame, nor by the broadening field of assault-by-song that Folkways and future personal appearances outside their home base will surely bring. The Fugs are first and foremost *themselves* — a foursome that sizzles, like four lit and joined fuses on their way to making explosions in the audience's collective guts, as they go about the business of singing and rocking things like Coca Cola, Madison Avenue, tabloid sensationalism, *Time* Magazine, the draft board, bomb-Hanoi warriors, dope-raid shoeflies

34

(and more) some distance beyond the pale.

Home base and stage for the Fugs is a small 100-seat art gallery and theater called The Bridge, on St. Mark's Place, just east of Third Avenue, which itself has fostered more than a few pocket-size avant cultural explosions since its founding a little over one year ago. John Cage's "non"-music (so far out, not even critics can name it), happenings that combine dance, film and poetry into collages of a sharply experimental nature, off-beat (and to some) out-of-focus theater pieces, nightly screenings of 8- and 16-millimeter premieres from the film underground, were only part of a typical week's bag at The Bridge. It has made for the Fugs an ambiance of hot receptivity for their highly individual repertory.

On a recent Saturday midnight — which is favorite post time for both group and audience — I climbed the iron stairway that forms a kind of bridge from street to theater to catch the Fugs in one of their weekly shows. As on most Saturdays, the $1.50-admission house was sold out. Much of the under-20 audience was booted and coiffeured in the prevailing East Village mode — youthful rockers, in the main, with a good deal of churning dissent underneath the flowing hair, and on their very busy tongues. The midnight hour found them, however, less in a political-manifesto mood than in one of bantering anticipation. They seemed to half-laugh away most of the pieces of twisted, carbuncled lobby sculpture — those of them who stopped to look. The rest stood around — while the Fugs warmed larynxes, instruments and sound equipment on stage — and dropped hot tidbits from the civil rights and Vietnam fronts, or exchanged posies of Saturday-night courtship chatter. Soon the doors to the theater were opened, and the crowd filed in and seated themselves.

The four Fugs regulars — Ed Sanders (26), holding a battered tambourine; Tuli Kupferberg (at 38, the "dean"), doing practice toots on a toy saxophone; Vince Leary (23), tightening strings on his guitar; and Ken Weaver (24), settling himself behind his drums — were augmented by a guitar and piano duo, Pete Kearney (22) and Lee Crabtree (22). They all found places on the curtainless stage. Sanders, the group's pivot man cum raconteur, shambled to the mike, blowing into it for a sound test. He offered one or two cozy, friendly obscenities — the mike was live — and then jawed away softly off-mike with Kupferberg. The other performers were standing by like somnolent volcanos, ready to pour forth on Sanders' opening cue. (For its part, the audience was quietly settling in, waiting for the flow with backs tight up against seats.)

In dress and appearance the Fugs were, by Elvis Presley standards, graphically dishevelled. Sanders, tall, handsome and vinegar-eyed, wore a long, silver-colored Russian style tunic — on which was emblazoned, in sequins, the word "Fugs." His thick chestnut hair rode — or rather, cascaded — down from his crown, to the back of his neck. (That, and an 1890's droop-style mustache, too.) Medium-high boots, into which were stuffed the legs of tight chino pants, completed the outfit. All told he had the look of a faun with a little something extra — maybe dynamite — on his mind. Kupferberg, less spectacularly hirsute than Sanders, but with crescent black beard to make up for it, was outfitted in a gasoline attendant's American Oil jacket, with pants of a deep, shiny carmine-red hue. Where — or even why — he got the uniform was its own proper mystery. Both the color and the lofted liberty-torch emblem on the jacket gave his garb a Fourth-of-July look that was hard to beat. Not as tall as Sanders, and with a roguish play around his coal-jet eyes, Kupferberg gave the impression (the uniform aside, that was for American Oil to figure out) of a lapsed Hasidic post-graduate, momentarily lost on the road to a carnal orgy at the Mandelbaum Gate (either side). Ken Weaver in rumpled sweater and levis, with Smith Brothers beard hiding by three-quarters his (when off drums) quiescent good looks; guitarists Vince Leary and Pete Kearney, both more or less tall and stringy who, in dress and manner, suggested a city-country hybrid style; and pianist Lee Crabtree, all but hidden from view except for a chock-full of roaming hair all contributed to the sartorial mood of quirky independence.

The performance, if that's not too formal a word for it, began with Sanders doing a sort of recitative on a number called "Slum Goddess" which, he had promised, contained "dope, sex and pot." As in all his free-form introductions, which start out as sotto voce patter but gain depth as he goes along, the form was vaguely operatic. (Example: "She comes slithering to me on the eight-foot rug.") A leering echoing Kupferberg chimed Sanders' each line with a bass-baritone carnal zest of his own. The Fugs, in totality, went at the song with a rising, near-frenetic drive of sharp-twanging guitars, crashing, tambourine, and rumbling drums. And the audience was caged, in a sense, in a musical sound-effects chamber that seemed to reduce them, as at the opera, to a putty of satiated but happy passion. (Chorus: "There's not a chick in the world who's half as hip as she/ My swingin' little goddess from Avenue D/It's really very groovy to take her to a movie/Where we make it in the balcony.")

Next came "Coca Cola Douche," a song that Sanders, in his patter, had dedicated to Kenyon & Eckhardt. This *double-entendre* number, of pitchmanship transmuted into hyper-athletic love play, was typical of the Fugs' walloping style. "Coca Cola," with its jagged lyric line, matched by sharp ascending-descending phrasing, in the music, gave a kind of purgative aura to the moment. More so, with the lines themselves, such as: "My baby she fizzes & she fuzzes/ . . . Cause she makes that/Coca Cola douche . . ." And, if the first song (Goddess) was operatic, "Coca Cola" was—in its drollery and sardonic accent —more in the tone of Villonesque street minstrelsy; storming, by sex and satire, the Mad Avenue rampart.

With "Supergirl" (described by Sanders as "a tender ballad of the pubs") the Fugs completed one phase. After this there was a change of pace from couch to slit trench with a song called "Kill for Peace." A heated-up but controlled scorn marked Sanders' openers. We will now offer, "in the key of strafe them gooks in the rice paddy, daddy" and ". . . in the key of gook blood" were but two of his introductory capsules. Partisan identity (highly Vietnik) and sound volume both rose noticeably with "Kill." And the simple but sulphurous lyrics, sort of Gilbert and Sullivan with blood in the eye, were sung by Sanders and Kupferberg with a wild assortment of bodyrolls and gung-ho grimaces—all of which had the audience bucking in its seats. ("Kill Kill Kill for peace/Kill Kill Kill for peace/Near or/Middle or very far east/Far or near or very middle east.")

Later on, after what was announced as a "ten minute dope break," Sanders roused his youthful listeners (some of whom were going limp in the stretch) with two songs of a more personal style. One was an adaptation from William Blake's "Songs of Experience," the second from a Charles Olson poem. He did them solo, to soft guitar accompaniment. A poet of talent, Sanders practically honed the numbers across, giving them a poignance that—after the revved-up drollery and corrosiveness of some of the other songs—fell on the house like pellets of snow in moonlight. Moments later the Fugs were off and running again, this time with a piece of prurience to end all prurience, a ditty called "Dirty Old Man." The old man was touted by Sanders as the "Ex-jailbird-reprobate who hangs outside every high school exit . . ." And the Fugs drooled and twanged the lines out: "Hanging out by the/school yard gate/looking up every/dress I can/sucking wind/thru my upper plate/I'm a dirty old man . . . "

The finale was called "Nothing." This one could safely be described as the Fugs' nadir, a tribute to Everyman's every hope gone sour, a lament in extremis. "Monday nothing/Tuesday nothing/Wednesday and Thursday nothing/Friday for a change a little more nothing/

Saturday once more nothing . . ." An empty cornucopia. "January nothing/February nothing/March and April nothing . . ." The pink slip, with vacation coming up. "1966 nothing/1967 nothing/1968 and 1969 nothing . . ." An attack of VD, on the eve of marriage. "Montik garnisht/ Dienstik garnisht/Mitwòch un Donershtik garnisht . . ." A nuclear blast, with the UN in session. "Lunes nada/Martes nada/Miercoles y jueves nada . . ." And the Fugs howled it, keened it, lashed it out to a dissonant stropping of guitars, plunging piano and mayhem drums, with Sanders and Kupferberg writhing dead prone on stage at the finish. ("The beautiful spastic Fugs!" murmured one young lady to her escort. It seemed a good consensus wrap-up.)

Music and lyrics are pretty much a co-operative mix of Ken Weaver's, Ed Sanders' and Tuli Kupferberg's efforts, the last two being responsible for most of the lyrics. Sanders, besides, is publisher of a highly volatile, highly scatological and (in the opinion of almost all who've had their hands on it) highly entertaining little magazine whose title is a four-letter word followed by the word You. He distributes the magazine, past issues of which have contained the work of Robert Creeley, Lawrence Ferlinghetti and Charles Olson, among others, on a private basis only. Kupferberg, too, is a magazine publisher of an irregularly-produced format called "Yeah" whose motif is the obverse of a Sears Roebuck catalogue. "Yeah" is a sharply irreverent put-down of admanship in all its high, middle and low guises. And Sanders is wandering proprietor of a dark warren of a bookstore-cum-house den, specializing in poetry, poetry-erotica and political protest. His enterprise is called the "Peace Eye Bookstore" and is located in a tenement on deep East 10th Street. An example of his wry — and no doubt conscious — *chutzpah*, as well as the Fugs' hurry towards an overflowing schedule, is the "Wanted" sign in the bookstore's window: "Energetic, eager person to manage PEACE EYE BOOK-STORE. No narcs please. Excellent opportunity for young Sam Glick types . . ." The window also has a painted "Strictly Kosher" sign (in Hebrew); a symbol of the Eye of Horus (an Egyptian solar deity), and another sign, a kind of self-proclaimed heraldic notice: "Ed Sanders — book creep, grass cadet, fug poet, editor, squack-slarfer, madman, composer, and poon-scomp." (The words you don't recognize have no literal meaning.)

The germ of the Fugs was a literary bug. Back in March, 1966, Ed Sanders and Tuli Kupferberg were (in the latter's words) "unbending after a poetry-reading gig at the Le Metro." They had come to the nearby Dom (the St. Mark's Place bistro whose image is that of an expatriate corner for the younger literati, college hipster, et al, who refuse to "make the scene" at the more prosperous and touristy West Village). While listening to the loud, hypoed sound of the Dom's jukebox, Sanders was struck with the idea of using this kind of sound — with its sharpness and immediacy — as a kind of wrapper for a meaningful lyric, or even poem, as opposed to the "Cry me a river . . . yeah yeah yeah" kind that was coming over that night. He posed the idea for a new rock singing group to Kupferberg, and two or three beers later, they agreed that the name *had* to be the "Fugs" — on Kupferberg's theory that "fug" was a far more accurate capsule of what the new rock 'n' roll youth were groping for, than the hackneyed "cry" (and relatively cry-baby) lyric of most of the industry. No more than a day or two later they approached Steve Weber and Pete Stampfel, both of whom were active in the East Village jazz scene, playing guitar, and made Weber and Stampfel (who are no longer with the Fugs) the new group's "musical advisers." They premiered the Fugs soon after at the Peace Eye before a high-octane lit'ry assemblage including William Burroughs, Allen Ginsberg and Norman Mailer. Burroughs made an early exit ("We were not exactly," Kupferberg admits, "a finished product at that early stage") but most remained the full hour and expressed approval.

From the very start, it was clear to both that they had to have, along with the sharp sexual breakthrough, an equally sharp breakthrough of ideas. Tuli Kupferberg, born on the East Side and schooled at Townsend Harris and Brooklyn College puts it: "In a way, we thought of ourselves as a leap off the printed page and off the daily headline. Thus it can be seen that ideas were — and are — an important part of the Fugs' program. Nor is it solely a case of us 'living' and feeling the things we do — the emphasis we make on dissent and put-down. It is a pragmatic case of being able to reach the kids as well. The churned-up younger generation who are not in touch with parents, college dons, government leaders and paper intellectuals. They are not — repeat, *not* — in touch with that whole spectrum. And that leap of ours is a leap into the present, for these kids." And, he could have added, right into the nitty gritty of the establishment, as in Kupferberg's acidic hammer on the CIA man "Who can take the sugar from the sack/Pour in LSD and put it back . . ." The oldest of the Fugs is, after 38 years, still very much East Side. He lives in a clutter of spare, roughhouse furniture; books, magazines, politics broadsides, oddball music instruments, all gathered in a four-room apartment just above the Peace Eye Bookstore. He is divorced from his wife and has an 18-year-old boy who, he says, with an approving grin, "is a science freak with honors out of Erasmus Hall."

Ed Sanders, who got his feet wet — literally — as a political dissenter by going into the water off New London, Conn., in an attempt to stop a Polaris submarine launching, confesses that the Fugs are "anti-war, anti-creep, anti-repression." He says: "The real meaning of the Fugs lies in the term Body Poetry, to get at the frenzy of the thing . . . that is, to use the enormous technical proficiencies of modern poetry (as in Ginsberg, Robert Creeley, William Carlos Williams, Ezra Pound and Charles Olson) in musical presentation." And he talks of "eyeball kicks, Operation Sex Fiend and the psychedelic tenderness society . . . the hallucination of this culture of ours, which the Fugs want to capture in song." Sanders, who is a remarkable blend of Midwestern twangy candor and sharp young mover-shaker on the New York underground arts scene, spent his early years in Kansas City, Missouri. After a good deal of traveling with his oil-prospector father and "culture conscious" mother, who was a school teacher, he came to New York in 1960 (he met Kupferberg in '62) and pursued his own culture road — on the evidence, a hot and holy one. A classics major at N.Y.U., Sanders is author of *Poems from Jail* published by City Lights, which came out of his experience of trying to board the atomic sub, and prevent its going out to sea with its nuclear warheads. (A coast guard cutter ran him down and navy frogmen captured him before he could get on board.) He, his wife, and two young children live in a "non-toney" Gramercy Park apartment—Gramercy being the mostly wealthy northern-tier neighbor of the East Village.

The less-notorious Fugs (less not so much in a musical and talent sense, but in that they prefer a kind of gliding anonymity behind the big, thrusting wave Sanders and Kupferberg make) all have solid, if hardly ancient credentials of the East Side hip. Ken Weaver, single, 24, has a three-year Air Force hitch in his past; and he has been making "beautifully funky sound" (Sanders) on his drums for the Fugs and others since he came to New York from Texas a little over three years ago. Sanders is convinced not only of Weaver's genius on drums, but of his genius at wild, stunning and marathoning ratiocination on almost any subject. He speaks in awe of Weaver and poet Ted Berrigan zonking along in a poetry talk-out, with frequent Baudelairean asides, for eight straight hours one night. He credits Weaver with building the musical "spine" and taut, edgy rhythmic pattern the Fugs use. Lead-guitar Vince Leary is a Brooklyn transplant and a dramatic arts major at C.W. Post. Bass guitar Pete Kearney is an Ohioan who attended Fordham and N.Y.U. and worked in a bookshop before joining the group. Electric piano Lee Crabtree is from

Greenville, Mass., and majored in languages at Carleton College. All now reside on the East Side. There's a seventh and sometime member, 22-year-old John Anderson, bass guitarist and Yale student, who does a stand-in (when he can make it down from New Haven) on weekends. Anderson has been described as "half Yale, half Fug." The original quartet has been made open-ended, but Sanders now sees the Fugs as firming to a working sextet. They know their way around as many as forty musical instruments including exotics like sitar, autoharp, celesta, harpsichord, organ and Pan pipes. And there's a homemade skull-and-coffee-beans percussion doodad Kupferberg uses. Audiences invariably gasp on seeing that one.

The future? Ed Sanders is about to become his own Sam Glick of the rock 'n' politics revolution. Sanders says boldly, "We are shooting for the top . . . We have the sound, we have the content. A cannon-full of both. We see a whole new music evolving; a music away from grandstand stuff, from egotistical nit- and navel-plucking. Ours is a vital, personal, hardedge format. A musical forceps to the gut of America. To root out the phony, the drab, the puritanical and the bloody — all the heavy freightage that's been loaded down on us by polite, as well as evil, men. Song can help this along. And our kind of song will be listened to, accepted and *picked up*. So that in four years, at the outside, and maybe only in two — we expect to see the whole or major part of the pop music scene shattered and reformed by — if you'll pardon us the word — fuggery."

1966

Poetry Filibuster

It was an Eastern filibuster. Unlike the Southern kind, whose badmouthers usually empty the Senate, this one had them glued to the seats. The place was St. Mark's Church, on East Tenth Street. The time, a rainy Thursday evening, the holy Thursday of Easter. As the Eucharist ceremony came to an end, in the church's dimly lit parish room, the poetry crowds began to arrive. By the 9 start every one of the 200 or so folding chairs was occupied. It was only the beginning. They kept streaming in from the wet outdoors, for standing room at the back and side walls. By 9:15 the doors had to be shut. From then until the early-morning finis, it was a case of shuffling the early ones out, and shuffling the waiting ones in.

Moderator of the evening was Paul Plummer, a man of easy patience. Now he had his work cut out for him. Softly but firmly he would plead with the crowds: "Second set coming up. If you've heard the poets once, *please leave now.*" And he would plead with the poets, who used the church's kitchen as a sort of bullpen: "Only the cats who were announced can go on. How can I fit you *all* in?" But fit them all in, he did. Eighteen poets. "Names," lesser names, lyric poets, black-humor poets. All more or less igniters of the East Village explosion. Eighteen who sat before the small hand microphone and read from their work. Read with faces in heavy angular shadow, as the single spot cut the smoky atmosphere, an amber shaft that lit up the poets' pages in the otherwise dark hall.

Variety in audience, variety in poets. The former had the hallmark of youth. There were high-school seniors, hipped on the word, who caught the poets' lines greedily, like gulls at a fish-jamming. And young mothers — I counted a few — who were leaning into blanket-wrapped and dozing babies — even as they swayed to the lines. Lines from resident jinn Allen Ginsberg — part of a new work full of nostalgic play, dream-wake fantasy, paeans to bare-assed Chinese boys. Allen Ginsberg chopping them across like breakers, right hand shaped in a fist, first cutting the thick air like a baton. Lines, or staves, in a symphony of the great phallic O! And Carol Berge, dark, softly intense reader of dark, lyric lines — they had a curious aura of a hip Emily Dickinson. Armand Schwerner who read in mock scholarly tone, from a long poem full of nonsensical wit, a sort of explicating from ancient Egyptian tablets, as no scholar would dream of doing it. Jackson MacLow and his musical tool kit — a ram's horn, a zither, a triangle. He would read his lines, short teasers with punchy silences in between, and then go musical. Some Yom Kippur toots on horn, then back to reading. Some tingles on triangle . . . And so on.

And two Fugmen *cum* squack-slarfers, Ed Sanders and Tuli Kupferberg, they of the new Village minstrelsy, rippling poetic messages across on wires of highest voltage. Scathing lines on cornpone politics. In Vietnam, Mississippi and Washington. (Cry me a patriotic tune!) And Jerome Rothenberg, Harold Dicker, David Antin, Allan Planz, Peter Orlovsky; and Paul Blackburn, Allen, Katzman, Carl Arnold, Paul Erik Gorrin, Art Berger. And one or two more on the Late Late hour. Three long, long sets — ending on the near side of two, when the last of an estimated 500 quit the hall for the wet, tired journey home. They filled three wicker baskets with dollars, halves, quarters and dimes. $200 on a rough count, a contributors' splurge that helped the needy budget of WIN, monthly journal of the New York Workshop in Nonviolence, who sponsored the readings. Ralph Cook, co-ordinator of St. Mark's manysided arts program, said of the readings: "They are of a piece with the holy Eucharist, a feast of lines that is the bread and wine of life."

1966

In and Out

"Why is the crowd standing around? Behind police barriers, yet?"

"They are here to see the 'in' game. The Electric Circus is the latest."

"Mobs like that are the 'ins'? The tail is clear around the block."

"You don't understand. The 'ins' are inside, frugging away. To the 'now' rock group. It's up there on the marquee: 'The You Name Thems.' And they are digging the light show. The electric pornography."

"But what happens to the 'ins' when the mob pays its way in, and joins the 'ins'? Look at them, as tight as the subway!"

"Well, the 'ins' who are already in, are the true 'ins.' No waiting behind barriers for them! And you don't need a scorecard. They are wearing Norell's, or Quant's, or Pucci's latest. Beaded minis, gold lamé bell-bottoms, and like that."

"Yeah, but look at the non-'in' mob. They are wearing beaded minis, and gold lamé bell-bottoms, too. May be only copies, but it messes up the scorecard."

"No problem. First, when the mob gets in (fifteen-hundred strong, from the looks of it) and mixes with the 'ins'; it's a one-time trip, you see. For then the 'ins' have got to get out, and find a new 'in' place. Otherwise their 'in-ness' will get lost in the mob."

"But what about the clothes?"

"Same with the clothes. The 'ins' get out of their kicky bell-bottoms, and get into new 'in' outfits; from the Norell's, et al, once the mob shows up in the copies."

"Wouldn't it be simpler for the 'ins' to stay out, or away? Feather their own 'in'-nests, so to speak?"

"But then, nobody would know who is 'in.' The mob by its presence here, is the certifier. It acts the part of a kosher *stamp, sort of. Which separates the* trafe *(themselves!), from the* kosher, *the 'ins.' "*

"Sounds more like a columnist's, flack's or Barnum's *megillah* to me."

"Or 'in'-stant social merry-go-rounding."

"I see . . ."

"By the way, one scorecard that works is transportation. You can see it over there. The ones getting into the hired limousines, are the 'ins.' The others whistle for cabs."

"Thanks for the tip."
"*You're welcome. 'In'-deed.*"

1967

The Long Brave Line

It was the kind of rally (about 20 thousand at peak, seated and standing in a half-moon, spread out wide from Central Park mall's bandstand) that would have made juice in a passing politician. One imagines a Bobby Kennedy or Javits (yes, even a Nixon, when the political wind turns) dropping onto the scene from helicopter, eyes popping with the instant thought: "What are they *saying*? Whatever it is, I'd like to get up there and tell 'em: *'That's exactly what I say!'* " It was the rally, steadily gaining by hundreds, and then, by thousands, that succeeded the Fifth Avenue March For Peace in Vietnam — a rally of strong unanimity, youth in pigtails, vets and draftees, mothers lugging infants, the widest spectrum of New Yorkers, some of whose shouted *miras* and *Look at this man*!, were the exclamation points to that unanimity, of hope and reality: *Stop the war in Vietnam now*!

It was the kind of rally (under a distant sun that never quite surfaced from behind low leaden skies) that had everyone blowing into cold palms with breaths warmed by that hope. It was the kind of rally that sang — in echo to the twangy baritone of Tom Paxton, a minstrel whose droll biting songs teased pleasure and laughter out of many — a rally that sang, too, in the sober sorrow tone of big-voiced Barbara Dane's rendering of a soldierly lament. It was the kind of rally that cheered, lustily, when a real live Green Beret by the name of Donald Duncan exclaimed, "Don't blame the G.I.'s; they are only the vehicle. Blame the drivers of the vehicle, in Washington." It was the kind of rally that moved one speaker to say, "We in Latin America, and people the world over, know that there is another America, one that does not believe guns, bombs and napalm are solutions to serious international problems . . . And that America is *here, today*." It was the kind of rally that gave little work to New York's constabulary — the earlier sniping and egg throwing, from the terrier packs who tried to ride down hard on the march itself, was drowned in the seas of disciplined protest.

Before the rally there was the march along elegant Fifth Avenue, kicked off at early afternoon by a group of 300 or more veterans — most of them circa World War Two, and proud in step for having credentials out of a real, nonbullying, congressionally declared war. Even so, it was the kind of march that expected (and received) catcalls and worse — and sent it all back with the firmness, laughter and un-self-conciousness of the unafraid. The roving young toughs, trying to find a handle for riot and disruption, scurried here and there along the line. Sniping, barking, hissing, spitting. But they always backpedaled — back to the cobblestoned walk on the park side of Fifth, clutching misspelled signs and dime store flags to their chests, hoarse shouts getting pretty well used-up in dry throats. And then forward to the line again — furious and rednecked, as long contingents of Puerto Rican and Negro labor hove into view. And the shouts . . . *Send 'em back . . . traitors . . . commie finks.* Back and forward — this time, to confront the 500 or so from Greenwich Village — mothers with pink-cheeked kids in tow, lawyers and artists and shopkeepers. And always the shouts, the curious reality-lag behind the shouts . . . *Give 'em soap . . . Haircuts for beatniks.* So it went, back and forth. The roving and leathery young toughs, were not so much rabidly rightist, as near-lockjawed for want of positive slogans.

The march saw a hookup of the toughs and their putative opposites — the tiny knot of flagwaving Vietcong 100-percenters who carried the orange, blue and gold of the NLF with all the charisma of homegrown revolutionaries doing a left-left happening on Millionaire Street. Predictably, the toughs here got in their only real licks of the day, as they scaled the wooden horses and charged the VC's at one or two points. That the police moved in rapidly, and more, that they collared and arrested three of the chargers, might have indicated a turn — at least for the moment — in the political weathervane. Several hours later, at the tailend of the long rally, there was a noise of paparazzi-like activity, at the rear of the bandstand. Cameramen and reporters, the latter with pencils racing across folded copypaper, were holding an open interview with *the* existential novelist — novelist decked out in bulging, epauletted, James Bond storm coat, his words racing faster than the newsmen's pencils, his stance studiedly pugilistic. It went on for thirty minutes or more, in full view of nearly all, with total disregard to the business out front. One wanted to call out, " Hey Mailer, the meeting is *out there!*" (Typically, when CBS ran their clips later that evening, novelist was given a hog's share of the doings.) Small sandy irritants, in the pearl of protest brought forth that day.

1966

Abbasso Lincoln Center

Will the sixth New York Film Festival (Philharmonic Hall, September 17-28) be the last? Two posters at the New Yorker Bookshop underscored this question. One — the official poster — was a kind of Op Art congeries of lines and announcement of dates and place. It went for $5.50. The second — got out by the Up Against the Wall angries — showed a baleful theatrical death's mask, and bore the message: *Stop the Lincoln Center Film Festival.* The latter reflected the sentiments of a small but determined group of film underground called the Newsreel. Their goal was disruption, and they ran sharply worded polemics in the *East Village Other,* the *New York Free Press,* and the *Village Voice* for weeks before the opening. Basically the charge was that Lincoln Center was a cultural imperialism and that the festival underwrote a kind of elitism of film aesthetics that ignored real life issues such as Vietnam and Mayor Daley's Chicago.

The disruption never came off. It appeared that a split developed in the angries' ranks. Congruent with and perhaps feeding that split was the feeling among others that the elitism charge was not a closed book, and that the festival, in any case, was able to claim films by Godard and Bertolucci and several Czech directors whose content was closer to life than to elitism. Still the disruption threat worked to the extent that it put a pall of uneasy conscience and polemical rumbling over the festival. On the surface, the festival moved along easily, the public part checking out with a record number of fifteen SRO's. Close to thirty full-length films were shown. But the pall of uneasiness was never wholly absent.

One example was the phalanx of thirty or forty cops from the 20th Precinct who had been called in on opening night in case the Up Against the Wallers opted at the last moment to do their thing. The city could have saved itself the overtime. A handful of film revolutionaries did show up and neatly outflanked the cops to the rim of the plaza fountain, where they poured several boxes of detergent that activated the jetting fountain into pretty cascades of bubbles. When the opening night crowd made their exit, by which time the bubble showers had been spent, many stood around and wondered aloud where the action was. The mood among them was in a way capricious — not inappropriate as a coda to Czech director Jiri Menzel's *Capricious Summer,* which opened the festival. It was as if the festival directors — who for the first time canceled an opening night gala and thus removed what some called a "provocation" — had deprived the audience of that small bonus of confrontation, and maybe even of police overreaction, that a gala might have produced.

Things went smoothly almost to the wire, with a two-a-day succession for press and public of new films and a trio of retrospectives. (Ophuls' 1955 *Lola Montez* took honors among the latter.) The general level of response, in both press and public screenings, was more drift than high-tide excitement. Jean-Luc Godard caused the biggest tide. His 1967 film, *Weekend,* which is an apocalypse of blood and gore, in color, cartoony and mimetic, as devastating a score against bourgeois — in this case, Parisian — life as you are going to find, brought on a clamor of cheers and boos, the cheers having it in a ratio of about five to one. *Weekend* was shown one day before the close, and may well have served as an incubator, or at least as an irritant, for the one flurry of violence that surfaced. The setting for the violence was — how else to put it? — a sneak gala that was quietly and well-nigh surreptitiously planned.

The time was around midnight, Saturday, after the showing of the closing film; the place, Philharmonic Hall's glass-enclosed promenade, to the rear of the orchestra. Private cops and plainclothesmen had stopped up all of the several possible infiltration routes. After the public audience was ushered out, the gala invitees had to go through two checkpoints to get to the promenade. Small red-colored invitations had been issued, and it was a safe bet that no potential stink-bomb thrower could get past the cops short of levitating. The affair itself was pretty austere. There were trays of cocktail wedges, quick refills of New York State champagne, a Latin-American combo for dancing. Plus an aura of in-ness, that aura of rubbing shoulders with directors, stars from the films, and assorted members of the culturati.

Aside from some words about the security, coming from foreign guests mainly, things moved along in a kind of plastic calm. But the mood changed rather suddenly. Two of Andy Warhol's factory people — actor Alan Midgette and superstar Viva — were dancing away to a *bossa nova* crescendo, and to their own banshee cries. Midgette started to strip off his clothes, and Viva was unloosing her already very loose garment. Soon the crowd moved in around the couple, shedding a layer or two of their own plastic as they watched. Enter three of the cops. They laid rough hands on the couple, and dragged them inside the orchestra's glass enclosure. But Midgette and Viva would have none of it, and they resisted with karate fury all the way, to loud cheers from many of the guests. One young man, a short husky Italian filmmaker, who was dressed in immaculate semi-formal blue, started to beat a tattoo on the glass enclosure. He was yelling over and over, "Abbasso the pigs. . . ." The incident came and went

47

in a short span, with no arrests, two thrown out, no serious injury, and a sense of outrage. (A passing outrage.) The security circuit had been shorted by an over-load of cops.

1968

Hall of Issues

Greenwich Village's Judson Memorial Church, with its Venetian-style high tower looking out boldly on Washington Square Park, is an architectural fixture in a fast changing scene. Nor is it paradoxical that Judson contributes more to that changing scene — intellectually — than any other single Village institution. Its outer shell has a dark patina of age, but, inside its walls, Judson is a place where the avant-garde get a hearing. New drama, poetry readings, paintings, forums, political debates are all welcome. Indeed, the very pulpit of Judson's rector, Reverend Howard Moody, has often been a rallying point for issues that prayer alone could not hope to solve.

Latest among the Village innovations is the Judson-sponsored "Hall of Issues," a weekly forum and showcase for ideas. Ranging from profound to crankish, these ideas take the form of controversial displays, collages, pictorial essays, political and social comment, poetry manuscripts and assemblages. A hidden motif behind it all might well be that, as long as the participants keep on showing and talking, there's hope that our sorry planet will keep on rolling. Be that as it may, the talk and the issues have been at a flood tide since "The Hall's" opening, last December.

Located around the corner from Judson's Washington Square South entrance, "The Hall" is a sixty by twenty foot rectangular room. By gallery standards, it is bare and even cramped. The lighting is no more than adequate. Filled to capacity, (and, so far, the groups have been *all* capacity), there are sixty seated and about sixty standing.

The modus operandi is simple. Each Sunday afternoon, from two to six p.m., the public is invited to hang their issues on the four walls. Actually, the walls are newly-installed Celotex panels. They are high, and brightly whitewashed. A fee of 25 cents is the only tariff. Following each Sunday's hangings, the room is open for public viewing on Sunday, Monday, Tuesday, and Wednesday, from 6 to 10 p.m.

Summitry, or the talkout phase, takes place on Wednesday evenings. Each displayer is invited to take the floor. He (or she) may defend his work, elaborate on it, or joke about it. He may punish his audience. He may inspire them. He may waste their, and his, time. Depending

48

on the list of speakers, a strict time limit is kept — or, at any rate, attempted. Time is called for each speaker by each week's new moderator, who then invites the audience to give their views. Although there is a coffee break at 10 p.m., rarely does this cause any recess in the proceedings. If anything, it warms them. Coffee costs are absorbed by Judson.

So far, The Bomb has the dubious honor of being the most persistent theme. No one is for it — to put it mildly. Village artists, like Stanley Fisher, have contributed whole walls of angry, roiling collage attacks that take leave of the frequently offered academic approaches to the subject. Whether they are art with a capital A or not is a moot point. In fact, Fisher has had to defend his work strenuously. But he has done so not in formal terms, but rather in his own fervently stated terms, such as: "To pay obeisance to Uptown gallery standards in a collapsing world is to compound the collapse."

Easily the most popular Bomb indictment was a poster display by another Villager, Miss Judy Wilson. Over a large color cutout of the Con Edison symbol she had printed the message, "IN CASE OF NUCLEAR ATTACK We Will Continue To Send Our Bills On The First."

Some issues are presented in the form of photographic editorials. One such presentation was by a talented lensman named Harvey Zucker, whose keen eye and busy camera were much in evidence in each of fourteen photos describing last summer's hassles between the police and folksingers, in Washington Square. Since the photos were, indeed, vivid enough, Zucker's caption for them was soft sell. It read, "TAKE ACTION NOW TO PREVENT 1961's unnecessary unpleasantness." More often than not, understatement has been the mode.

By no means do all displays meet with applause. One which did not was a two-page copy of a letter to President Kennedy from Broadway actress Carol Lynley expressing her views ". . . against all forms of Federal Aid to the Arts." Miss Lynley's main concern was with actors. Of them she had written, "They're not in it for the wages. They're in it because it is their 'kick'." Included was a calendar cutout of a youth wielding a birchrod fishing pole over a pond and Miss Lynley's added caption, "I Want Federal Subsidy Too!"

Now and then, there is the cry of "bad taste." An example was the assemblage submitted by Beatnik poet Ted Joans, whose issue appeared to be "the population explosion". Joans had put together a mad scramble of empty contraceptive boxes, a pair of panties, and cancelled airline and steamship tickets from around the globe. He had included a brief "program" in the form of twenty lines or so of free verse. Joans' solution: a global handout of free contraceptives.

Issues often come from right out of the headlines. The best sources are the New York tabloids (*News, Post, Mirror*) and mass weeklies (*Life, Look, Saturday Evening Post*). A striking example was the page-one photo cutout of Astronaut John H. Glenn, from the *Sunday News*. It showed Glenn in full-face as he emerged from his space suit, seconds after his cancelled flight. (This was a week, or two, prior to Glenn's successful orbit.) The photo was indescribably tense. It appeared as if Glenn had been drained to the bone of all but a numbing frustration. Above the photo was the headline, "AN-OTHER DAY." A masterpiece of blitheness, under the circumstances, or so it must have struck the contributor. His title for the display read: "THERE WILL ALWAYS BE AN ENGLAND . . . and Headline Writers."

Issues come in over the transom, too. There were two from the same person in London; a sheaf of twelve poems from Marlboro, Massachusetts, redolent of Walt Whitman and written on fine onionskin; a new Spanish language quarterly from Mexico City, edited and published, for the most part, by U.S. writers and artists; and a new political literary quarterly from North Carolina called, "Reflections from Chapel Hill."

The range is nothing if not eclectic. Subjects discussed on a recent Wednesday evening were: World Peace-Labor Congress, How Many Dooms Are There, Religious Icon, Who Made Hell, Art for A Bomb Shelter and Love For Sale.

These Wednesday talkouts have given rise, and not unexpectedly, to two sharply differing groups. Any attempt to describe them entails risk, for labels are odious at "The Hall." At any rate the first group might fairly be called "foxes," and the second "hedgehogs." Or more mundanely, "outer worlders" and "inner worlders."

Among the first are members of Sane, and of various pacifist and Quaker organizations, active in the Village. Their main focus is to mount action against "Nuclearitis," in the words of one "fox." They focus, too, on such fringe issues (in comparison with The Bomb) as segregation, civil rights and fallout shelters.

As for the "hedgehogs," who in a real sense are a non-group, they insist on a "one to one relationship in all matters." The guideline is artist Stanley Fisher's. Easily the most engaged among the "hedgehogs," Fisher, on another occasion, had called for "a personal reformation first of all." Someone else has put it for the "hedgehogs" thusly: "We are here, *or should* be, to get at the root of things. Not the facade."

50

It should be noted that only once have "Official" views been aired at the "The Hall." The issue, then, was the McCarran Act and, as an attendant issue, the Attorney General's order against the Communist Party. Invited down were spokesmen for the C. P. and Justice Department. Only the former showed up, a Miss Betty Gannett, who spoke for thirty minutes, not altogether uninterrupted, and then answered questions. A protest petition was made available, for those who wanted to sign.

The spirit of thumb would seem to be: petitioning — yes, official speeches — no.

Far from indicating any signs of rupture between groups, the dialogues appear to have a broader and deeper effect with each passing week. Primary credit for the growth must go to Miss Phyllis Yampolsky, an attractive 29-year-old artist and housewife, who conceived the idea for "The Hall of Issues", last June. Miss Yampolsky, her husband, artist Peter Forakis, and their two-year-old daughter, Gia, live in one of the loft-type apartments in the West Village that came under attack by building authorities last summer. At that time, too, the Police Department was riding hard on folksingers in Washington Square Park. Mere rumbling was not enough, she felt:

"Though I'd been thinking about it for a long time, the forum idea seemed to jell just about then. I was on the phone for days. I visited people. I received encouragement and assistance from sculptor David Weinrib, and writer Meg Randall, among others.

"In one of our conversations David, who rejects any smell of political or social involvement, as do most artists, had nevertheless told me of a plaza outside Rome where artists with something to say, paint and post their banners, or whatever . . .

"Everything began to fall into place. It was clear to me that 'The Hall' would be for *all* issues. It would be run from below. A vocal underground, if you will . . ."

Miss Yampolsky worked out a statement of principles, which she called, "AGAINST THE INEVITABLE DECLINE OF A GREAT NATION". It is an unusual document; terse, passionate, infinitely engaged. Here are some opening lines: "Necessity creates an idea/ the idea makes sparks/and a man moves . . . and a man moves other men/and a Nation is born . . ./and if the idea remains/necessary/ and men remain dedicated/to it/a Nation rises . . ./But what necessity is going to/make us realize that we are/now our prime enemy?/ . . . that it is our own success/we must challenge and/transcend . . ."

The statement and an outline for "The Hall" format were mailed to several people last August. Among them were President Kennedy and Reverend Howard Moody. Moody's response was both immediate and hopeful. But it came from the West Coast, where he had been on a delayed leave. On his return, several weeks later, he and Miss Yampolsky worked out some ground rules for "The Hall of Issues". Reverend Moody gave over the use of the room. And the project was under way.

Two weeks before the December 3rd opening, a mailing of 2500 flyers was made to newspapers, TV and radio stations, political leaders and others. Though there has been some press coverage since, mostly of a local nature, Miss Yampolsky feels: "We are only at the beginning stages".

She believes that the idea is eminently exportable. She would like to see "Halls of Issues" everywhere in America. And around the globe, for that matter. She has been in contact with interested parties in Philadelphia (her home town), Washington, D.C., and Dallas. And she has received word from Meg Randall, in Mexico City, where a "Hall of Issues" on a capsule scale has been started.

During July and August, there was a six-week show of 25 of the best issues at Judson's Memorial Gallery. Eventually, she hopes to work out exchanges with other "Halls". All of which, she feels, will help create a climate "against the inevitable decline".

1963

Bloody Brick Among the Flowers

Man it's a cab from now on; I don't walk these streets at night . . .

The words came from an East Village actor-bookseller, who was checking out the register of a St. Mark's Place bookstore, where he did a four-to-midnight trick. It was a Friday night, several days after the slaying of the young hippie couple, found in a grimy cellar on East Tenth Street, their heads bashed in by a brick. Thus panic — "paranoia," most feared word in the hippie lexicon — had replaced fun and games in the East Village.

The miasma of paranoia, of cold comedown from the usual euphoria of St. Mark's, could be seen in the presence of more police on the street. Their stance reflected the change. They were in twos, eyes cold to the passing parade, non-communicative all down the line, where before they were good for a bantering exchange with hippies. And the hippies most of all reflected the change, their voices in a near dirge as they stood around in small knots outside the Dom, the Electric Circus, and the egg-cream watering spot, the corner Gem's Spa.

What happened put a searchlight on the whole hippie milieu. A lurking violence has always been part of LSD tripping in the East Village — and this time it broke through *from the inside*. Hence the couple can be looked on as sacrificial victims. The flower children — and none were more typical than the slain couple — have squatted in an area of tension, joblessness and fast-buck trafficking in pot and LSD. They attract, and they repel. The first because of a cloud-7 program of love, flowers and mantra singing. The second because the very program is out of kilter with the world outside — a world that seems to buy the hippie mode on Saturday night, and lurches off the rest of the week to its own thing of non-love, anti-flowers and something less than mantra singing.

The killings were brutal, and one prays the kids were in a deep high (police say they were on speed) when they were attacked. Of course brutality is the name of our game these days — witness Speck in the Chicago nurses' dorm, and Whitman in the Texas university tower. And witness the fruits of napalm, for that matter. Still, there's an extra twinge in the thought: here were two who were trapped in their own special bag of "love," with no defenses vis a vis the surge of violence in their own camp. Flower children playing with dynamite — when you talked to the knowing among them, you found too a pattern of infiltrating violence that included petty thievery, muggings, sexual assault, and death itself.

Meantime, an aura of myth wafts in around the couple. The New York Times covered the crime like no local story in years, zeroing in mostly on the girl, whose golden-upper-class background struck deep chords in the city room. The accent was: How wide the rift from Greenwich, Connecticut (the girl's home) to Greenwich Village East! And the girl — Linda Fitzpatrick, 18, shy and yet malleable, at least among the hippie set. Linda, one part "good breeding," the other drop-out — and head-prone. On her the purple drape of myth may well fit — is in fact already being fitted. Try on this one, for speculation: A reverse of Dreiser's *An American Tragedy*: Linda a latterday Clyde, finding death in a run to, not away from, poverty. (And maybe that's too facile, but time gives its own gloss to such material.)

And "Groovy" — James L. Hutchinson, 21, the hippie's hippie. Harmonica-playing, sharer as well as seller of pot and LSD. Linda's terminal entrance into the flower life . . . and then death for both. "Groovy." And the two men charged with the murders, both in their mid-20's, both black and from the East Village, drifters on the LSD scene. Try speculation two: In part a tandem species of Bigger Thomas — Richard Wright's Bigger who killed the white girl of his torment. And Linda and "Groovy" were as white as they could be. In-the-buff white as they lay on the cellar cot and received the mortal blows.

1967

The Peace Auction

Peace is not only desirable, it can be a cultural boon as well. Witness the two-part auction to raise money for the Fifth Avenue Vietnam Peace Parade Committee, an amalgam of two-dozen or more New York peace groups who sponsored the giant parade and peace-in at Sheep Meadow in Central Park this spring. First, a literary auction was held at the Ethical Culture Society auditorium, and $7,500 was raised for some 250 items of manuscripts, letters, first editions, and autographed memorabilia from — or relating to — dozens of noted authors. An additional $1,500 was contributed by writers, editors, and the public. Two nights later, an auction at the Universalist Church of New York City, Central Park West and 76th Street, resulted in an added windfall of close to $10,000.

The lit'ry sale drew 200 people, but most of the bidding came from professionals: Gotham Book Mart, Phoenix Books, House of Books, Literary Horizons, and individuals in the field like William Targ and Ted Wilentz. The auction was conducted by Stanley Waldman, a short young man with crisp delivery who confessed, after some mispronunciation of authors' names in his calls, that "literary items are not my usual thing." What was usual for Waldman — judging from his metronomic style and quick eye for bids — was an ability to squeeze the last possible buck out of his audience. Mostly the bids were modest, with Waldman intoning, "I have two-fifty more, are you all done . . ."

The average sale was about $20, but some items came pretty close to skyrockets. An example was a John F. Kennedy letter praising a new publishing venture. Waldman had escalated his calls on the Kennedy letter to $25 per round, and the buyers didn't seem to be hurting when the letter was finally knocked down for $400. It was the evening's highest bid. A Hemmingway letter went for $160, and a Leon Trotsky letter sold for $180. Some Einstein items went for $180 the lot. As for contemporary interest: a Norman Mailer ink caricature of Senator Everett Dirksen drew $32.50; some material relating to Allen Ginsberg's *Kaddish and Other Poems* sold for $22.50; and a banned issue of Ralph Ginzburg's *Eros* magazine garnered $25.

Up for grabs at the second auction were 150 pieces of art — oils, watercolors, sculpture, posters, and drawings. The money came coolly, but a couple of incidents turned out to be sticky. First a cherry bomb was exploded inside the church's entrance; later a bomb-scare call was made to the police. They arrived and found nothing. "Crank call," said one. "Peace-parade auction — it figures," said his partner sagely. The auction itself went smoothly, with 500 or so in attendance, and with many more individual buyers than were at the literary auction. Auctioneer was O. Rundel Gilbert, a fast-paced man with color in his cheeks, color almost the match of the red carnation he wore in his lapel. Rundel's high bid for the night was for a Calder gouache, which sold for $800. Other items that caused spirited bidding were a David Levine ink caricature of Tennessee Williams, $200; a set of three Roy Lichtenstein color poster prints, $225; a Robert Motherwell print, $100; and a Leonard Baskin woodcut on Japanese paper called "Man of Peace" which checked out at $400.

The two auctions raised close to twenty thousand dollars. Most went to the Parade Committee, which incurred a deficit of $30,000 in bringing out the Sheep Meadow gathering. (Over 100,000 people squeezed into the Meadow listening to speakers under leaden skies and the annoying obbligato of Mayor Lindsay's whirlybirds.) Prime mover of the auctions was Ron Wolin, a bearded, thirtyish fund-raiser, who came up with the idea last September and had to stay with it almost around the clock ever since. Wolin got the expert help of Arthur Cohen, Editor in Chief at Dutton, for the literary auction and of Dore Ashton for the art auction. Wolin praised their voluntary labors. And he was quick to add praise for the hundreds of authors, poets, artists and collectors who contributed their works and material. And finally, to the staff of young people who helped in the arrangements and who rode shotgun on each and every sale at the auctions.

Peace, literature, art, money. The mesh was a good deal more popular than, say, domino theories. More fun too.

1968

Short American Hiptionary

Hippie. The hippie concept has mixed beginnings, as with jazz. It can be traced in the kind of geographic hopscotch that goes: " And then the New Orleans beat traveled up the Mississippi to Mobile, Alabama. From Mobile it moved to . . ." One might say that in a strict anatomy sense, what is required is a rapid swiveling of the hip-pelvic area of the body. In short you must move fast, to get where the action is. As for the hippie, he (or she) is a person with a well-exercised pair of hips.

Where the action is. This hyperactive phrase, with its suggestion of an increased pulse rate, as in running to a five-alarm fire, comes on like a magic wand to the turned-on generation. *Finding* the action is less a matter of holding up a wet finger than of following the track of the crowds. They are usually tourists in any urban area who (by an osmosis born of boredom) are able to zero to the hot center — of mantra singing, daffodil throwing, bongo thumping. When there's enough steam generated between up-tight natives and/or police, on one side, and Hare-Krishna-singing hippies on the other, the result is a free swinging melee. Then the word goes out: "That's where the action is." Or to use the short form: "That's where it's at."

Turn on, tune in, drop out. To turn on is to ingest a loaded sugar cube, the result of which is an extended allcolor show — or private Cinerama — localized in the brain region of the participant. To tune in is to be off on a vibration trip, during which hobgoblins — again, allcolor — rear up and become the participant's mother-in-law, demons out of his childhood nightmares, or other such phantom pleasures. To drop out is to see a crowd coming out of the subway, after a hard day's work downtown, and to declare: "That's not my bag." The trinity is Tim Leary's answer to the Diet of Worms. Has done for napalm America what Martin Luther did for 16th Century Germany under the Pope.

Hare Krishna. An all-purpose spiritual chant invented by a bearded East Side poet, adopted en masse by thousands of dropouts from the WASP way of life, and de rigueur at all powwows at Sheep Meadow, Haight-Ashbury, Tompkins Square Park and the like. Sung to the accompaniment of bells, cymbals or tambourine — except when nonhippie youth are around, at which time the accompaniment is more apt to be sticks, stones or firecrackers. Police in most cases take a neutral stance, when in earshot of the chant — except when the chant is parlayed with offerings of daffodils, a flower which police claim is a disguise in yellow for poison ivy. The chant is an invocation to the beatitudes, power of sartori, oneness with the universe. Still the Hare Krishna now and then gets buffeted by an ill-wind, the result of which is more like a beating than beatitude. Hare Krishna is not related, as is supposed by some, to Harry Carey, Harry Truman, Harry Bridges or Harry Hope.

Tell it like it is. A locution of black power activists that, nonetheless, has a sound of childlike wonder, as in the minutes before bedtime for junior when he'll open his eyes wide and intone: "Tell me a story.

Like it is." Daddy, of course, is hard put to tell a story, more so a story "like it is." He's had a tough day at the office, and later on, at home with his loving wife, he begins to feel the strain of having to tell them *like it ain't*. Domestic bliss aside, the expression best comes into its own, when employed by someone like Boll Weevil, famed White Citizens law-and-order chief. Boll, when questioned by reporters, put his case this way: "My nigras — to tell it to you all like it is — tickle all over with happiness from them cattle prods. As for the police doggies, my nigras know doggie is man's *best friend*. If doggie gets a little playful, and nips one of 'em, nigra just *knows* it's all in good fun." In Harlem, on the other hand, to tell it like it is, is to call a spade a spade. Meaning, a black man with a 300-year-old itch no white ointment will cure.

Soul. Most times used as an adjective — in conjunction with such activities as eating, politics, music or social exchanges. Hence "soul food," "soul politics," "soul music" and "soul brother." In the case of food, if it's favored by minorities, it automatically qualifies as soul. Pigs feet, then, is soul food; for as everyone knows, that is a black man's treat. Borscht, on the other hand, is more complicated. When Jews have it, that is soul. But when Russians have it — well, 200 million are not exactly a minority. Or take whale blubber, the Eskimo's delight. They don't come more soul than that! As for politics, when the N.A.A.C.P. joins the Anti Defamation League of the B'nai B'rith, in picketing an Irish landlord who won't rent to Orientals: that is very soul. In music, soul is any jazz piece, the playing of which inspires a comment like: "Dig the cats. They riff like they own the note factory." And a soul brother is a black man who moves an inch or two on the subway seat, to make room for a white old lady in tennis shoes: that too is very soul.

Burn baby burn. A black ghetto happening, sparked by what might be called an "incinerator complex." Prime time is the long-hot-summer nights. In place of old style, garden variety garbage, the ingredients for a burn are human flesh, tenement hovels and honkie emporiums. In the past a white man's patent — e.g., Red Coats putting the torch to Washington, Napoleon putting the torch to Moscow, General Sherman's march to the sea, cotton cloaked Bourbons in the old Southland, the British Raj in India and Pakistan, jackbooted brown shirts in Eastern Europe, Russian tank men in Hungary, USAF flyboys in Vietnam. Now endemic to practically all U.S. urban areas. Here the black man has ignited, with relish and firebomb both, not only his rickety environment, but the cool of local white officials. The latter often press the panic button — after which the riot boys, up to and including the federales, come up the ghetto pass to play the new shoot-'em-up: cowboys and nigras. Burn, according to some sociologists, is a kind of fertility rite in reverse; a three-step of loot, shoot and bomb that helps ease the population crunch. Free-market economists also applaud burn, for its role ("Let's clear them shelves!") in the conspicuous-consumption trend. And others point out that burn baby burn, is as peculiarly American on the home front, as search-and-destroy is on the foreign. The black man in the psychodrama, not to be upstaged by his Charley show business cousin, and the latter's rally cry of "Have costume, will travel," has come up with his own unique rally cry. It goes: "Have Molotov cocktail, will throw."

Be-In. A kind of instant hippie evangelism. Park grass, open skies and trees is the usual church architecture. First there is the sacrament of the high, during which a penalty-prone grass more exotic than the park's is used. Other ceremonial gambits are flagellation orgies, with long-stemmed daffodils the favored weapon; burning of joss-sticks to keep flies, mosquitoes and people at bay; and mass gifting of indigestible food stocks. The be-in has inspired a whole family of related events — the smoke-in, the love-in, the wed-in, the bike-in, the ferry-in, the what's-next-in. At a be-in dogs woo dogs at a trot, be-inners woo the constabulary no less swiftly. Most of the latter — call them squares in blue — respond with indifference, shading off to mild annoyance. Typical was the cop who was heard to complain, almost with a sigh, "Nothin' in the manual says I gotta be a flower lover." The be-in invariably attracts suit-shirt-and-tie people who always ask, "What is going on?" And if they have to ask, they are in the wrong part of the park.

Head shop. The head shop is the liquor store of the hippies. Most often it is a small airless place, with a locked-in scent not unlike that of burning tapioca. Carries a thousand items for the head-hippie fraternity, from Tarot cards to paper wrappers for tea. Folk rock music a must, turned up to tornado volume. In square neighborhoods, such as New York's upper West Side, the head shop's first customers are middle-class boys and girls. Later the middle-class parents come by, to see what the children *see* in the head shop. The parents soon make their first purchase, pink or black candles to lend romance to home dining. Later still they purchase a hooka, to keep up with the young ones. Before long momma is spending more time, and money, at the head shop than at the supermarket, super's loss leaders be damned. That is when head shop owner doubles *his* trips to the local bank, cash-wise.

Do your thing. The hippie state of grace — as in grooving the sun on the park green, with a modest stash of pot to help pass the time of day. Other examples of do your thing: cats prowling back alleys at night, Mantle poking a 450-foot home run at Yankee Stadium, Khrushchev pounded a shoe at the U.N., salmon swimming upstream to spawn, LBJ urging Ho to the conference table, Nixon mentally getting us all together, hookers on Eighth Avenue asking — "Want a good time, babe?" Whether all the latter are in a state of grace, only the guru can know for sure. And he's not talking.

Underground. There are many undergrounds, from Dostoyevsky's to New York's IRT. The hippie's is that crosshatched spot on the cultural map where one finds the advanced styles, moods and beliefs of the "trendsetter." The cartographers of the map — and the inventors of that word "trendsetter" — are of course all from the overground: feature writers from such journals as *Life, Time* and *Vogue* who, with spyglasses polished and at the ready, are quick to search out the newest in hippie dress, manners and forms of communication. What they discover — and then write-up in avalanches of chintsy photos and prose — soon becomes the latest cocktail talk in thousands of split-levels across the land. What happens after that might be called "reverse cultural acclimatization": the hippies read the notices, and then act out what the overground has said about them. At that point the colored lights flash up on the psychedelic scoreboard: *WHO IS PUTTING ON WHOM.*

Digger. The digger is the contemporary Robin Hood, with a difference. Where Robin robbed the rich, and gave to the poor, digger jobs all classes into giving with a smile. From soup to nuts, from pads to garb. The largesse is open to all — the digger motto is, "Free but please do not steal." Digging is a kind of Salvation Army approach, sans blue bonnet and red tape. The economics of digging is simplicity itself — e.g., the price is not only wrong, it is superfluous.

Hippie, the "death" of. That paragon of folk wisdom, *Life,* held a wake for the hippie, not too long ago. And so they killed off what in large measure was their own creation. The papier-mache hippie, good for circulation. And marketable for all as regards dress, manners and social-sexual behavior. All gleaned through a keyhole of middle-class voyeurism. But lo, don't look now. Hippie musicals like "Hair" and "Do Your Own Thing"; mixed-media celebrations like "An Eclectic Christmas "; a hippie parody of "Hamlet," produced by the New York Shakespeare Festival — these and more such formats are leafy evidence that roots are deeper than *Life's* (horti) culture experts see it. And as Mark Twain said of his own case, the report of the death of the hip is very much "an exaggeration."   1968

Marathon Sing-In

They held the Sing-In For Peace in two sections, eight-thirty and midnight. Scene of the Friday night double was staid Carnegie Hall. The earlybirds were in good form. From the spirited exchanges it was clear President Johnson, Robert McNamara and Dean Rusk — along with U.S. policy in Vietnam and the Elsewheres — would win no popularity contest this night. The styles were bearded-hip, and college campus staccato.

As for the performers, they were comparable to an annual all-star game. Every team in the folk league was represented. From sweet-singing balladeers like Joan Baez and Eric Andersen, to popsinging poet-needlers like Phil Ochs. In his single Ochs zeroed on the antic mood, which alternated through the long evening with the somber, when he announced: "I've just returned from a sing-in for our boys in Vietnam." And Pete Seeger was the Stan Musial — tall, bouncy and aging star with more honor, hours of playing time and broken records (but not broken discs) than any. And there was Theodore Bikel, who performed as a sort of Casey Stengel of the evening, sending his array of stars up to the mike in rapid order. And ordering them, no doubt, to belt out the long one. For himself and for the audience. The long one for disengagement with war, with Johnsonian style consensus.

Some high points were Joan Baez's haunting ballad on a family theme (a question here — there was such a wealth of material — from political barbs to spirituals to madrigals to even souped-up rock — that one can't be sure Joan's *was* a family theme); Eric Andersen's dirge on the South, sung in a fine tenor voice, by a young man whose immaculate facade would fool even an Ed Sullivan; and as a late-hour coda, Guy Carawan's soul-dipped version of "Overcome." The last was perhaps most moving of all. Many rose from seats in boxes, galleries and parquet floor. They joined hands in the Selma-Bogalusa-Washington mode (old-style but oddly effective), and sang along with Carawan in swaying sideways motion that brought a hush over the house.

At intermission in both shows, a kilted young man marched the aisles, saturating the hall with keening pipe tunes and bonnie live jigs. It was a case of Black Watch traditional meeting up with American Campus Folk.

There were oddball goings-on outside the hall, all through the long evening. One such was the hawker with rows of buttons stuck to his lapels, buttons that announced the cause of "POT" at 25c apiece. And others who seemed to represent none but themselves, quirky joes, who shouted to the crowds to buy the Militant, or Sparticist, or National Liberation Front buttons. Mostly they were bypassed by folkers and small contingent of cops, almost equally. In all-star terms, they were the boys from Triple-A and Class-B. Not enough support from the fans, so they had to play the ballpark fringe.

The marathon was concluded at 3 a.m., but it turned out to be only a 7th-inning stretch. Bikel boomed an announcement that the sing-in would continue — after a march of two or three miles, from Carnegie to the Village Gate, where free coffee-and would be served. Hundreds assembled outside and after a couple of false starts (all privates; no sergeants) they stepped off into a brisk breeze. Three prowl cars kept company with the marchers, all moving down the Seventh Avenue canyon slowly. At the hour of dawn, with the first color making a washday backdrop in the sky, the sing-in was not as yet sung out.

1965

The Sound of Eardrums Bursting

Fillmore East is rockhaven on the borscht. Hard by Ratner's and the all-night cheese blintz. And the St. Marks egg-cream refilling station, the Gems Spa. Where uptown slummer, Tompkins Square rent fighter, hippie alms merchant and Ninth Precinct cop brush shoulders in little street drama called "Is the Full Moon Out Tonight?" Fillmore has its own thing, weekend rock gigs where, if the wind is wrong, you might end up paying a visit to nearby New York Eye and Ear Infirmary, for an eardrum check.

The other night the wind kept hovering toward dangerous — with a group of post-adolescents whose outre name got lost in my unsettled mind, and who in any case might best remain un-named. They made a tornado of bad rock sound that swooped the wide orchestra and mile-high pit — and the Ear Infirmary might well have had its biggest night yet. But the kid group was only doing its job — playing the role of backstopping mediocrity for the highly touted Jimi Hendrix Experience.

What do you say about the Experience trio? Well, they wear velvet that belts the eye, Hendrix in slinky lavender sharp as a bullfighter, and the second guitar in a wine that would make Bordeaux look pale. Drummer I couldn't make out, but half his outfit is wasted anyway, what with his sitting behind drums. To complete the garb inventory, Hendrix goes for broke in D'Artagnan wide swishy hat and loose gleaming bolero. And he uses his body — he snakes it around his

61

guitar, sidewinds it around the mike, pumps it at the crowd. Shades of — well man, who isn't doing it.

About that hat. One fast verbal set-to between a kid in the orchestra and Hendrix, limned a sexual terrain wide and droopy as the hat's brim. The kid yelled at one point, "Take off the hat." Came Hendrix's reply, "I will if you'll take off your pants." That's where it appears to be at, sexwise. Ambisextrous, straight swishy, and even straight.

The Experience make music too. Kind of all-out plastic rock, as a friend with more mileage in the area than me put it, and he didn't mean it as a plus. The crowd on the other hand seemed to groove the trio — anyway the former came alive with shrieks and moans that came close to audience orgasm. All of which would seem to be worth the price of admission, except the question "So what else is new?" comes up again.

Maybe the eardrum problem is the key. I couldn't attend, but someone who was there described a recent freebie rock outing on Central Park's Mall, where the Jefferson Airplane and others played, as a clamor of indecipherable sound coming out of a forest of equipment. The decibel freakout again. And this in the big open-skies yardage that is the Mall. So too at the Fillmore. The equipment the other night, huge vatlike boxes full of electrical dodads, sat on the goddam stage like some launching pad to Venus. I tell you, the screaming-meemies became perilous at times.

And maybe the McLuhan thing, more so in rock than in other formats, has got us in a dilemma. The medium may be the message, but in the meantime, with the decibel level going punchier by the hour, the axiom may have to be changed. To something like — the medium is the message, and can make robots of us all. With the kids, as they say in lifeboat drill, first in line.

1968

The All-Time Be-In

The ground was wintry, the sky spring, at the Easter Sunday Be-in on Central Park's Sheep Meadow. The kites flying — one, a wide and tall beauty, thunderbird nipping the March air, like a cat rolling in catnip. The pipes tooting — celebrants romping on the mushy field, four linking arms and marching for the sheer yardage. Fifteen-thousand at the height, some arriving at the front four or five in the morning. Be-in of young hippies, West Siders with children, mantra chanters who gathered round and incantated their Hare Krishnas; heads, eggheads and Easter egg rollers; girls in big straw hats, eyes rimmed in dayglow tracings, psychedelic in design. And girls in minis, mini-minis, shifts or mumus; actors, poets, spades with bongoes; a new-mode beautiful people, not out of *Vogue*, but out of that New York tempo and tone that spells fun, neighborliness, love. L-O-V-E scripted in chalk, lipstick or finger-painted; on foreheads, back of buses, a lone scarlet pennant. They yelled it, strummed guitars and sang it, winked it in passing.

Tempo and tone — in the instant greetings, body-hugging, "diggings." The sharing of gifts, flowers, eggs, fruit, poppyseeds. They made, not just contact, but an ambiance of high. And they kept pouring in — no cars, bikes and people only, on this Sunday. They poured in and nosed the incense sticks, cheered the papier-mache yellow bananas, played tag with kids, thawed the ice of numbers with Be-in. With serpentine dancing — hands joined and weaving in and out, across the soggy Meadow, patterns right out of a Fellini movie, only bigger. Hanging in the bare trees, shouting hellos, shedding daffodil petals on the crowd. Two lone fuzz, on horse. One lone fuzz, on foot. With nothing to do but "fight off" waves of goodwill, palms down to all those profferings, gotham's finest had to maintain their cool. And, here and there, the curious. Strollers, coming north from Fifth Avenue's Easter Parade. From the annual rite, not of Be-in, but of squeeze-in on blacktop and cement. The self-admiring rite of clothes, dresses holy-watered by the best boutiques.

All *Vogue* beautifuls who came by, like as not, to peer at it from a distance, and ask, "What's it all about?" And if they had to ask, they definitely missed it. So off they went in patent leather shoes, a little up tight. But the rite went on and on, arabesque of people *finding* each other, mutants out of the "cold" body of New York. And toward dusk, they policed the hill, southeast on the Meadow, the promontory that got most of the play. All day it was a hill of song, of waving and greetings. And now, as the park darkened, as the lights came on, in a thousand windows on Fifth and Central Park West, they gathered the refuse. Kids, collegians, couples, heads. And they lit small fires, in the wire trash cans. And the fires, the billowing smoke, made signals of farewell. And voices rose in song. First, a bearded young cat, hefting a guitar. He began with, "Good Night Irene." Soon they joined in. And linked arms. One-hundred, two-hundred, strong. And they eased from "Irene," into the civil-rights chant. Near-hushed, soul felt, "Overcome." Chorus after chorus; of peace, rights. After which, they moved off the hill, and made for the walks. Wound their way out of Sheep Meadow, for home.

2   Of Crows, Toads & Crocodiles

The Rascal Ticket

At a Wednesday midnight fund-raiser at the Village Gate rathskeller, Norman Mailer was shooting down a variety of political pigeons in his run for Mayor of New York.

He was armed with a whiskey glass, the contents of which he sloshed around menacingly, as he stood before the mike on the small stage, waiting his turn to savage the audience. A whiskey glass, in place of the usual sheaf of dull position papers. He was running the show, not with a Pepsodent TV smile, the kind that makes politicians merchandisers, but with tight-jawed anger, which caused more intimidation than admiration. He was laying bare his doubts, instead of playing the crowd for children, who had to be fed the usual doses of political pablum. Unorthodox, and scaldingly so.

Before Mailer came on, there was a gang-up of TV cameras, reporters and friends, all clustered around the reserve tables at which he, running-mate Jimmy Breslin, campaign brain Jack Newfield, manager Joe Flaherty and other followers sat. As to the audience, it was mostly a freak, and a worriment, a large part of it conducting themselves in that gratuitous "there's no tomorrow" mood that seems to have seized some of the left. Among them was the breed of Mailer follower, or sycophant, whose "Hello" is always loud, politics stylish, clothes right off the mod rack, message buttons giant-size, conduct less than couth. He (or she) will usually booze up, when in the same room with Mailer, as if the grape was the very fuel of revolution. Add to which a second boozer type, maybe less "political" than the first, but moving around as if on a home-brewed wave of the future, when all they'll need — to usher in the new day — is an image of themselves of being "in." That left about a third who showed up for business, people from the arts, campuses and professions who, in getting behind the Mailer-Breslin rascal ticket, might find some way to put a sharp-nailed finger to the crotch of New York City's moribund politics.

As they entered the long room, shoved into corners, shoe-horned into tight little tables, about 400 in all at the 1 a.m. peak, they were washed down by the rock sound coming from the New York Rock and Roll Ensemble, a youthful and musically vibrant quintet, who were dressed in yards of ruffles, 18th Century salon style. The thought hit you: "What are five nice Julliard boys doing in a place like the Village Gate." They played a 30-minute set, including some takes from Procol Harum, a turn or two from the Beatles canon, and some period things from their own Baroque-rock bag. Flapping their limbs to the music, on the tiny dance apron, was an assortment of couples, jet-setters all come hell, high-water or limited space.

Flaherty was first speaker, offering little more than a welcomer, after which he introduced Jack Newfield, who sounded a note that soon became one of the evening's battle-cries: a note on the paucity, and porcine tone, of local press coverage. Dorothy Schiff and her *New York Post* got the most cutting shafts, Newfield describing her as a kind of duenna of the editorial page, and of the city room as well, which was rather mild next to Breslin's, and then Mailer's, fill-ins on La Schiff's treatment of the ticket. Newfield then brought on Breslin, a short heavy-set man with a deceptive aura of calm, or street cherub with a tart tongue, but a political novice who called to mind Dorothy Parker's "A to B" remark, in sizing up the acting range of a Hollywood actress who couldn't, so limited was candidate (for Council President) Breslin's political range. Still, he handled his glass, off and on stage, as if it was an Irish scepter, and that lost no votes. It became clear that in this campaign, the booze is to the rascal ticket, what holy water is to the "meathead" candidates.

Norman Mailer was last speaker on the program. But it wasn't to be, not quite yet. For out of the cauldron-like miasma of smoke, din of more than a few pockets of bad vibes, catcalls of some who felt shut out (and shut off), there rose an almost spectral figure. The form was of a tall, thin young woman, black and smooth-skinned with neat, modified Afro hairdo, who slipped on stage, and over to the mike, she began to talk: a witness to what? Her words were a short-circuit, half-formed challenges, little darting gropes for *meaning.* "How many here are black," she wanted to know; and in truth there were few. Not waiting, she went on to say she'd been fired, for activity in her union. (Hospital workers? Service union? It wasn't clear.) And then stretches, almost, of a catatonic silence. And from the floor, hostile rejoinders. From a black man: *"Sheet,* sister; get your ass off that stage."

But she stood her ground — tall, abstracted, immobile. Enter Mailer, burning to the very gut. He climbed the short

68

ramp, came up on stage, gently put his hand on the woman's shoulder. The crowd — some of them — revved up their hostile shouts. Mailer cut them with a growl: "Let her talk." But it was to no avail, she could only fumble and stare. He finally urged the mike from out of her hands, telling her softly: "You're okay, dear. But this is my evening, after all." The woman faded back, to hoarse cheers from the crowd. And the incident loomed up as a paradigm of uptightness, or a mirror-image of the confused left.

The last part was a near-shambles, with Norman Mailer making a roast of the crowd, boiling them in vitriol, like no candidate on record. He held his half-filled drink tautly, cutting the air with his free hand, as he spoke, as if delivering Karate chops to their jugular, the curly mass of graying locks going wild as the David Levine caricature, as he bobbed and weaved with each crack of doom. First, he spoke to the black girl's taunt on the audience's skin. "You want to know how many blacks are here, and the answer is *none*, and I'll tell you why. They're waiting to see what Adam Powell's gonna do, and maybe I don't blame them." He then levelled at the crowd, saying they were "full of shit" in their expression of loyalty; that most of them were playing a game, rather than accept the fact it was a war they were going into; that he wanted none of their ego trips, and "If you want to help me, check your ego at the door, or stay the hell out"; and when a cheer rose from the floor, or an inarticulate word-grunt from a boozer, he shot them down equally with a rapid "Fuck you, I'm talking." The four-letter word was like a display piece in Tiffany's window.

Soon enough, the crowd was listening. And Mailer was able to develop, in a fast tattoo of anecdote, salty harangue, doomsday prophecy, the main line of his campaign. Neighborhood control: "If they want to worship on Sunday, ain't *nothing* gonna stop them"; "If the east side wants free love, better believe it, they're gonna be allowed to." Traffic/Pollution: "No automobiles in midtown, not a motherfucking one"; "We need clean streets and air, else we'll go down under a blanket of poison." Statehood: "New York City wants out, we're going to be the fifty-first state." He spoke to these points with passion, limning the theme that the city had greater talent, imagination, group identity, gutsiness, than any in the world, and warning that the meathead approach was destroying it all, and indeed, was turning group identity into group warfare. Change it would be, or the city would go down.

Oddly, the anger had left his voice, and Mailer's tone — at the end — was almost soft, and a little burry, all of which gave his words a near-religious ambiance. As to making converts, it looked like a hard road, on that night anyway.

1969

White House Comics School

It was the first get-together of the new class — the class of '72 whose curriculum included Stand-Up Comedy as a major, and Politics as a minor. Class was being held in the basement of the White House.

"The last shall be first," said the Chief, for openers.

"Does that replace 'Forward together'?" the youngish Press Secretary wanted to know.

All the Cabinet members, and lesser ranked people, responded to the Press Secretary's mot with light smiles. (He was oh so eager.) But the Chief ignored it, remembering the Palace Theater rule that you never let the straight man top the Top Banana.

Instead the Chief looked around, and said, his hands flat out: "We are not interested in confirmation for confirmation's sake." The lone Jewish class member glowed a little, as he thought back to his *bar mitzvah.*

There was a pause, after which the man from Interior, who was slow in getting his bearings — he preferred the openness of Alaska to the more circular ways of the Capitol — spoke up carefully: "Is that a paraphrase of my 'I am not interested in conservation for conservation's sake'?"

The answer was of course self-evident, and the Chief arched his brow, not in displeasure.

Sensing approval, the man from Interior thought he'd try one more. He said: "A tree looking at a tree really doesn't do anything." The response was hearty, all down the line. And the Chief himself offered one of his quick, monitored smiles.

A slight pause, and then an aide said: "As he moves closer to the Presidency, he is getting more Presidential."

The entire class beamed at this reprise of an earlier reference to the Chief (the aide made it sound so nicely nostalgic of the Pierre Hotel days). Still, there was a knot of tension. After all, was not modesty, unlike in the case of his predecessor, the touchstone of the Chief's new image? They all waited — and then the Chief, after coloring slightly, came through with a soft nod.

With the gate thus opened a little, the Director of Communications spoke up: "He has reassured the American people by his air of calmness and confidence." He went on: "A lot of gimmicks is not what the American people want, and besides that doesn't fit into (the Chief's) style."

Another aide spoke up, adding to the cornucopia of praise. He said of the Chief: "He is a quick study and an underliner; he has a fantastic ability to tuck things away."

The one-liners were coming faster. And the Chief smiled broadly. His think tank was really splashy. The man from Health, Education and Welfare, crisply: "I'm inclined to get into it (desegration in the South) case by case . . . Every community has its own chemistry."

At the word "chemistry," the Science adviser sat up, but then he realized the man from Health was only using metaphor.

And the man from Housing and Urban Development, jut-jawing his words with mock clownishness: "I was told by my high school teacher that two heads are better than one, even if one was a cabbage head."

Class hardly had time to savor that one, when the man from Defense spoke up: "I favor missile superiority for the United States, but I am perfectly willing to describe this as nuclear 'sufficiency'."

All turned next to the Vice-Chief, as he spoke for the first time. With the charisma of a man destined for the record books, he said: "If you've seen one slum, you've seen them all."

The Chief did a double-take (as if in memory of an old pain). After forcing an I-forgive-you smile, he said: "I guess I can live with that one, Vice-Chief, even if it did cost me some votes in the ghetto precincts."

Soon they were coming in a chorus, brisk variations on Interior's "A tree looking at a tree . . ." and the Vice-Chief's "If you've seen one slum . . ."

And more.

Class was coming to an end, and the Chief offered a summing-up. His tone was sober-straight, as he said: "Not bad, for starters. Try to look at it this way. We're playing a

Catskill fun place. Only difference is, in our case we're playing to 200 million, wall to wall. It's going to be tough keeping them laughing. So until our next class, I suggest you bone up on your foot-in-mouth manuel. The ad-lib is all."

Signalling the end of the first class, the Press Secretary gave his "Thank you, Mr. Chief."

1969

Boob Box Conventions

Glomming the presidential conventions from the boob box. The GOP's was plastic in soul, mahogany in flesh from the Miami sun. People like Reagan, George Murphy and Johnnie Wayne did their turns at the mikes with unflinching Hollywood aplomb. Mr. Deeds is always on his way to the White House. The three were witness to the proposition that America, in the eye of the great Central Casting judge that is its leader, can be reduced to a series of tooth-capped smiles, smiles that wipe away all the problems that lurk at us from around the TV pass. If one cottons to the TV smile long enough, one gets sucked into the miasma of *nothingness.* Vietnams and black ghettos are no more than blips across the screen. They will clear up if we just stay in there, stay tuned and watch for the toothcapped smiles that do away with distortion. The plastic and jowlly Nixon smile was the nothingness smile of all. Until he found an Agnew, more nothing than even himself, neuter wedded to neuter. As for Rocky, the winning candidate would not go down, the very name of Nixon getting boggled in the New York Governor's throat, as the TV screen showed. But the smile surfaced once again, at the fadeout, this time with a choice cat-eat-the-canary nuance. Nixon was turning on high-candlewatts of confidence from his hotel suite.

Plastic as the lesser part of the Democratic show. Tear gas, billy clubs, the fascist draw in the West — these were the greater part. Daley, the man with the "clout," produced the first real-life pilot of American style totalitarianism. He came on the box early, drummed home the law and order theme, honored his cops and firemen. His face was the face of an impenetrable porkiness. He introduced his Governor — he handed the man over like a side of beef — and Samuel Shapiro droned on and on, inducing a kind of statistical euphoria. By the time "Gov" was finished, we got a vision of the ultimate bookkeeper in the sky. Later came Carl Albert, permanent chairman, brought on with the usual hoopla, and with the cachet: "The Little Giant From Little Dixie." It was one of the better calls. A dwarfish man, with a big head, a rasping voice, and muscular talent in wielding the gavel. *Boom boom boom.* The toll of democracy, at its highest convocation.

A new resistance movement joined up with an old one. Inside the convention hall anti-Vietnam delegates found themselves playing the role of guerrilla to Daley's army of occupiers. The weapon was Robert's Rules. Members of the New York, Wisconsin and California delegations were the most active. The over-30s quickly identified with the resistance in the streets, using every parliamentary trick to get past the chair's "Good Lyndon" silence. It seemed a lost cause — but then came the unexpected. Senator Ribicoff's mini bomb of scorn. He planted it neatly, a one-line insert in an otherwise calm testimonial to McGovern. ". . . Gestapo tactics in the streets of Chicago". The bomb gutted Daley, his stonefaced guards, his delegation. They rose as one, like a Cicero mob shot out of a Cagney movie, and they spat out verbal bullets. Lip-reading the box is of course an inexact science, but we thought we got from one of them this gem: "Go back to Connecticut, you heeb bastard." (*Con-nek-ticut*, more likely.) Ribicoff's steady poise, his "The truth does hurt" rejoinder, index finger targetted at Daley's craw, had the jolt of a Tet. The iron silence around the podium was broken.

TV cameos. Or how to come up smelling like roses, in the Chi abattoir. Julian Bond turning down a Veep nomination, wryly telling the convention he was too young by law for the office. It was modesty speaking to power, and it made you forget the bile of the antiques. The New Hampshire delegate describing how he sandbagged the security check — by slipping a Dartmouth College I.D. card into the admission machine and getting a green light on it. The 20-minute filibuster of song that had the chair holding its breath and gavel — never was the old "Glory Halleluiah" rouser sung with more poignance and sting than in this after-film tribute to RFK. Tapes showing dissenting Davids getting beat on by Goliath rabble in Checker-cab hats or crash helmets — courage was contagious, and a goad to bullies. Senator Ralph

Yarborough, hardly of a mind to play "After you, Gaston" for Governor Connally, bad-mouthing the Texas regulars from his gallery confinement. His words and tone, politically Mozartian in their reason and swift humor, was in happy contrast to the colicky bleats of the marcelled-gray Connally. All put you on the edge of your seat.

And the last act. Enter, LBJ's loyal backstopper. Triple-H in his acceptance called up a myriad of clichés that made runaway use of the big-daddy word: "American." He practically stole the Billy Graham patent when he parlayed America and God. All of which seemed to work on the assembly like a midnight pacifier on a baby. The delegate babes needed the assurance of that word, needed the *identity* of it. They needed it against the danger, the bad vibrations, of those wolves in the disguise of hippies with flowers who were tearing up the streets of Chicago. Triple-H gave it to them by the numbers, and sent them home to goosefeather beds with arpeggios of assurance. All but that ghost of the convention, who was down on his ranch watching the box, watching his name trickle out of history.

Suggestion for 1972. Let's vote a Huntley-Brinkley ticket, or a Cronkite-Sevareid ticket. Delegates only mess up the picture.

1968

The Presidential Papers

1/ IRISH FLYER

Up the Irish. I don't mean St. Patrick's Day Irish, either. Up the Vietnam Irish. Up the Free Soul Irish. The hippie Irish in us all. Up the clay-pipe-smoking Irish. The Black Panther Irish who want freedom, recognition of the uniqueness of *black.* Demand jobs, and the eradication of whitey bullshit. Up the Sean O'Casey green crow Irish. Up the MGM grass-roots Irish of McCarthy. Up the Che Irish, with its undying charisma. Up the existential Irish. The ballsy Bloomsday Irish of James Joyce. The Harvard Yard Irish of Jack Kennedy. Up the skid-row Irish of Bobby. Up the Bobby Kennedy and/ or Gene McCarthy Irish.

This is less a speech than a demand. A demand that we the people take a fresh look at 1968 reality. The grim-reaper

74

reality of a great nation that's been playing the whore's role in a charnel house. Run by a politician galoot with a *your-fly-is-open* humor. Who talks about not tucking in our tails, even as he'd cause us to lose our brains. This bumbling man who holds a hot LBJ brand in his aging fist——and wants to initial us all with the infamy of his six-shooter ego. Who talks of courage and austerity, while golden eggs are being hatched in the henhouse of the rich. Who walks the corridor of his own darkening fantasy——and tries to wheedle us into the obscene notion that he's nothing less than a latterday Abe Lincoln. Who shines up to univac Generals, and runs lickity-split from confrontation with a concerned people. Who has the reverse Midas touch: everybody *he* touches turns to shit. Who packages "peace" with "I won't run": a mea culpa that may be a time bomb.

He has made his Roman choice. Deliver up the flesh of the young, bring it to the altar of the great Texas you all! Skull and crossbones uber alles! Death and crocodile tears! His choice is made. Can we do less than rise, and overthrow him! With the votes of all whose nigger Irish souls yearn for a new day, a new beginning. It comes down to saying, in the words of that undoubting Thomas who mirrors what is best in us . . . *We won't burn the flag, we'll wash it.* Is there time enough? Do we have wisdom enough? I sing two men. The third is no music.

2/ SCHOOL DAYS

Now class——let's try to answer the question: "What is a nixon?"

1st Student: It is a kind of eager beaver in reverse. Let it loose at a dam and——with sharp teeth and spatula tail——it will bring the logs down.

2nd Student: It is more like a hyena. Sniffs for carrion and dead flesh. Loves to sink hungry jaws into an easy meal.

3rd Student: It reminds me of an armadillo; no stick can penetrate its thick hide.

4th Student: It looks like a toothless lion, with television dentures.

5th Student: Its hissing sound reminds me of a rattler——in business suit.

6th Student: It is God's mistake——a bird, like the dodo, that can't get off the ground.

Class, you've done very well. Now be careful, on your way home, that a j. edgar doesn't spring at you from the bush.

3/ HAPPINESS CANDIDATE

My name's Hubert Horatio Happiness, orator in residence at the White House. As everybody knows, I'm the best darn speaker in the land. I'm available for Chamber of Commerce luncheons, CIO labor klatches, ladies' tea gatherings, Brownie meetings of America's dearest commodity—our kids. (*Joke.* I can out-Brownie even Dick Nixon, and that's as tough a cookie to crumble as any.) I sing of red-white-&-blue vistas, of the virtues of our lollipop democracy. I go to the people with the proposition that—in our great land—a man may choose to ignore what's on the dark side of the moon, which naturally leaves him more time to contemplate the glory of sunlight. Call that Happiness Rule Number One. I promise I'll preach and uphold that Rule, right down to the remotest little drugstore on the farthest plain. And remember—lollipops are good for you. And I might add that good Americans are more and more discovering the superiority of red-white-&-blue lollipops over any other color—and that goes even for my esteemed opponent, Dick Nixon.

4/ THE ROCKY THING

He's finally running—in asbestos track shoes, to keep friction at a minimum, and in plastic gloves, to keep his hands from getting soiled, in the hand-shaking. He spent $5 million, and got nixed on the first ballot.

5/ FIVE YEARS OF PLAGUE

The obscenity was on the air again, prattling away on the subject of American violence. From the White House he was saying it was a sorry hour—the black ink announcement of the second Kennedy's death was barely dry on the newspapers —and he was saying what sounded like "*Ah* tried to get th' Con*griss* to pass an *eee*fective gun law. . . ." And he was talking mollycoddle, and chicken-liver, and demonology, and white Texas jive. And his style was all his own, a throaty rattle of bourbonisms, a patchwork of Jack Daniels' soaked homilies, a cactus laced string of preachments right out of the American nightmare. He was saying America's enemies have struck. And sitting at his big daddy desk, torso leaning a little into the mikes, he could count his days of power—from the gunning down of one Kennedy, to the gunning down of the second—like some Pharaoh who straddles a long period of plague. Five years of a plague of violence—locusts of napalm, locusts of fire—with big daddy Pharaoh riding his gunships, spurring his gun hordes, across ricepaddy deserts. Never pausing, never reasoning, that the gun that kills, may kill your own. And now he was on air—smokestacking the nation with the white ash of remorse. And when's the last time a Southern pol got gunned down for trying to help the people?

Go down Moses, go down RFK.

6/ GENUS REDNECKUS ALABAMUS

Ah'm the only candidate of the true redneck country of the U.S. of A. When a bantam redneck like me can come up to Yankee country like Providence, R.I., and get me a rally goin' of more than 7,500, then I say I got me an underground rail-way that pays back them New England yahoos for all the coons who made it North during the no-victory war between the States. And remember this! Any other candidate tryin' to gain yo' confidence and vote, by peddlin' an inferior brand of redneck politics, is a candidate who's violatin' the Interstate Redneck Politics Law.

7/ BLACK PANTHER vs. WHITE ELEPHANT
& GRAY DONKEY

Black has had his identity burned to a crisp, by years spent in jail. Has had to hassle around-the-clock with the creeping meatball of the WASP establishment. Has been denied his manhood by a people whose idea of music is the rhythm method in bed. Has been second-classed in buses, and second-classed out of the American dream. Has been Central-Cast in the nigger role of slavie, clown and ogre, in that epic Hollywood fable called "America the Beautiful." Black has known all of this, and yet rises to the heights of an Eldridge Cleaver.

1968

Caulfield Holden in the New Frontier

Peace Corpsman Caulfield Holden here.

I'm doing this tape on request of some TV fellows, who want my views on the New Frontier. A kind of annual score thing. Hits, runs and errors. Of course they have the wrong *game.* They ought to have said, "Touchdowns and number of fumbles." Get their games mixed and where the hell are they. *Lostsville* or somewhere.

They came on strong in that hyper*thyroid* way of theirs. I mean voices near cracking in sight of New Jerusalem. "Caulfield," they enthused, "it will be a goner. Exposurewise. We mean SATURATION." (Saturation crap. Are they *rainmakers* for god's sake.) "Forty-million or more listeners. Top that if you can."

I'm not of a mind to top it. It's their problem. They itch with *modesty,* is where the trouble is. That and Galluping arithmetic. I guess their glory road is to top out on the whole U.S. *census.* Eureka, and they can have it.

My ideas on COMMUNICATION are probably goddam close to being un-American. I mean, for me it's a victory to get across to a solitary *person.* One sorry traveler I can touch with a fresh thought. That's really the most central crime of our *times:* subverting one person with a fresh thought. Who knows, the thought may be that goddam *pregnant* as to give birth to a whole universe. And like that.

HOLDEN'S CONSPIRACY for god's sake.

Now about the New Frontier. If there's a *phase* of it that's been overlooked by top bananas on the mass *media* (and that word has got to go), I am not *aware* of it. They view with alarm, analyze with caution, report from reliable sources, study in depth. The Joe Alsop kind of crap. Journalistic Russian roulette for millions of *readers.*

That is *their* problem.

I see the Kennedy thing as a family-and-friends outing *cum* travel show *cum* wrangle *cum* Mephisto waltz. The immediate clan is a combination of Boston-Irish-Brahmin and hell for leather politicos. Jack rules the White House roost with two heads. One makes pearly speeches that sound vaguely New Dealish. For the goddam *moment.* The other minds its political manners so as not to *offend* the BIG EATERS around the

American table. Such as Southern Bourbons, Loyal Cold Warriors, Blue Chip Arms Fabricators, Foreign Defenders of Our Way of Life.

Members of the Good Soup and all.

*

Boy it *kills* me the way Brother Bobby handles that Attorney General's office football. He kind of plays under wraps on the Ole Miss home field, but he is death on segregation on the *telephone.* If Bobby does not score wildly on Teamsters Union turf, he makes up for *that* slump with some tricky running against the Communist Party team. (True the latter are goddam *scrubs,* but they can hurt you. Ask any lousy *Birch*ite.) And does Bobby ever *love* to throw the long one at the Crime Boys. Only thing is, the mobbers keep *bouncing* back.

About Dean Rusk and the State Department—*that* stuff bores me but a lot of people take it seriously. I will say Dean has a *prob*lem. I see it in the form of parody of Tin Pan Alley. Like, "Do We Love 'Em in Madrid, As We Love 'Em in Berlin." When Dean said Yes, he loved 'em in Madrid, many did not applaud. But look at it from his side. He presses all that *loot* on willing allies. So he must enclose greeting cards. Some crap like, "Pray with us against Nikita K and we will pay. Love U. S. A."

As I say, Dean has that *problem.*

Take egghead Adlai Stevenson and gadfly Artie Goldberg. Two makeout guys with different styles. For years Old Steve was our unplumed knight out of the Midwest. He roamed all the *learned* byways. Took on some Big Ones with his verbal lance. Such as What Is Honor in Politics. Along came Fidel (that man has *bristling* plumage for god's sake) and the Bay of Pigs thing. So Adlai denied all. And that lance sure got crazy bent. But leave it to Captain Jack to make amends. He has this secret "Fidel Kaput" quarantine play, it *has* to work fine, if the stadium doesn't crash in around our *ears.*

As for Artie, he *slays* me. The way he comes on strong with "Why bother about Questions. I have *Answers.*" He has them for Capital, Labor, Opera, Freedom, Slavery, High-Low Steel Prices, Low-High Steel Wages. Old Artie has Answers he can't use up in nine *lifetimes* of Questions. Which is equal to *one* lifetime of Questions on the Supreme Court bench, so Artie ought to wear very well up there on High.

We are not dragging on the Show Biz thing either, for

money we're not. After eight years of Old Homily & Company, we just had to get a new *cast*. At least there's a goddam improvement in *syntax*. (And don't go reading into that last word, we haven't come to that *yet*.) But there's a problem. I mean Who's Rubbing Of On Whom? Take Sinatra and his Rat Pack. How do you *house*break them into the new decorum, after the Las Vegas booze and broads scene. I'm *bothered* by that stuff.

And you take Old Pablo Casals and his 'cello, or good Old Carl Sandburg and his poetry. The way they stir up headlines when they visit the White House you would bet they're *mission*aries come to bring Higher Life to culture-starved barbarians.

I will close my report with a word about my favorite New Frontier *character*. She stands no higher than a *toad*stool and all. And she really kills me. Take the time she came waltzing into the President's office, in her mother's spiked shoes and fur *cape*. That *Caroline* has my vote for being the whackiest *find* since Old Phoebe.

Now I have to get my ass back to that phony *class*. My boss Sargent Shriver's giving this lecture on the topic, "Don't Be An Ugly American to the Natives. Be Yourself."

1962

JFK's Conquest of New York

Was there ever such a weekend? Will there ever be another like it?—President Kennedy's knockout tour of New York City in May. Assessing it at the calm remove of a couple of months, I feel sure it will go down as the weekend the revolution came to town. And let's not argue semantics. There are all kinds of revolution. New York's was the nice, bloodless, non-messy, the-price-is-right kind.

The only peeves were the handful of necessary Republicans who hung around the arras edges. They had to listen to popular cheers. They looked for all the world like they wanted to be elsewhere. Maybe watching the Mets at the Polo Grounds. Or at the Washington Baths out Coney Island way.

Jack made it look easy. For one thing he never pinched his wife in public, first important step for conducting a popular uprising. But see how much more he brought along on the historic weekend. He won the father vote in a smash, what with several visits to the East Side convalescent home where his dad was recovering from a cerebral attack.

In his hospital visits, Jack won the patient vote by acclaim. Of course, everybody loves patients at hospitals, but Jack did this better than say Senator Javits or Governor Rockefeller. He stopped to chat, he passed the time of day with them. And he dropped a word about Medicare to these ward-bound constituents. It involved calculated risk, and he must have lost some votes among hospital bigs.

Jack took the brother-in-law vote in a walk, what with his bunking into, or just missing, Peter Lawford. It happened at least three times. He captured the churchgoing vote hands down. (Or bibles open, more likely.) No detail was reported more closely than the number of visits he, or members of his immediate family, made to private worship.

These were only personal beginnings, an entre to the more public phase of the revolution. On Saturday afternoon Jack beat a path through the West Side cement bush to the Chelsea district, where 10,000 or more campesinos of the I.L.G.W.U. hailed the chief. He came to dedicate a cooperative housing project, said to be the biggest in the U.S.

On hand to greet him were such veteran guerrilla fighters as David Dubinsky and George Meany. Jack's invocation of FDR, public housing, Social Security, the American working class, was in the best tradition of populist upheaval. He romped home with all votes save one: Rocky's.

That evening the revolution swept the East Side, or the money side of town. Jack broke cake at the Four Seasons with 400 blue chip party followers, who fattened the revolutionary exchequer to the tune of $1000 per head. The movement was even more festive and relaxed later that evening, when upwards of 17,000 partisans sat in gritty Madison Square Garden and had a ball. Marilyn Monroe, younger, blonder and flashier version of "La Pasionaria," sang "Happy Birthday" to the chief. Jack was rolling in votes and popular esteem, in the manner of V. I. Lenin at the Winter Palace.

All was in dramatic readiness for the final coup on Sunday afternoon. Jack returned to the Garden, where more than 18,000 older folk had gathered for swift endorsement of the rebellion. Jack slashed the smoky air again and again, his arms raised and palms flat, in that typical gesture all reactionaries had come to fear. Once again the watchword was Medicare, a cry destined to go down in history alongside such deathless slogans as "Liberte, Egalite, Fraternite", "Peace, Land and Bread" and "No Pasaran."

He showed a good deal of charisma, as when he blasted United States Steel's Roger Blough, and gave the finger to the American Medical Association. But he was gallant in victory. Doctors personally were not at fault, he told his followers, it was the medical capitalists of the A.M.A. who were trying to block the uprising. The togetherness ploy swept every vote but the latter.

One observer compared JFK's and FDR's revolutions this way: "Unlike the Hudson Valley bloodletter, who had the bite of an asp behind a jolly facade, Jack threatens with a baseball bat, and makes do with an olive branch." Observer added cynically: "The monied class scorned Frank and they'll lose no love on Jack—either way."

Close circuit TV brought the revolution to hundreds of outlying areas, where more legions of the aged sat before big screens and cheered heartily. What moved them most was the speech of Zelman J. Lichenstein, executive director of the Golden Rule Council, one of the sponsoring organizations of the weekend rebellion. At one point he said:

"What we are doing here at Madison Square Garden and at similar rallies over the country is assembling the Golden Rule missile. . . . Our engineers are weathered and seasoned by age, are doing a job of precision. Our missile cannot fail. We are ready to load the missile with the Golden Age Bomb."

The revolution had found its Mayakovsky, its poet a la mode.

Last scene of the historic weekend was Gracie Mansion, where Jack socialized with several hundred mayors at a garden party. They were members of the Mayors' Committee for Health Care Through Social Security, which insiders called a euphemism for what in reality was an amalgamation of revolutionary cells. It was an open secret that host Mayor Robert F. Wagner, who looked deceptively prim as he directed the serving of iced tea and pink lemonade, was indeed ad hoc field general of the uprising.

One veteran call leader went so far as to compare Wagner with the early Leon Trotsky, but others said they would wait and see.

When it was disclosed that the mayors had come to New

York at their own expense, all lingering doubts of success were swept aside. One wit alluded to this strange fact as the *real* revolution.

The big puzzler was troubleshooter Arthur Goldberg's absence. Some said he was on secret mission to the A.M.A. camp. And that at any moment the flash would come that Arthur had gotten out of them a signed testimonial: "What's good for the Golden Rule Council, is good for the American Medical Association." They added that General Wagner (or "Biting Bob") had more or less sealed the rumor when he was heard to warn darkly: "It is *that* or exile to Lambarene. Old Albert Schweitzer will know how to fix their stethoscopes. *You bet he will.*"   1962

The Icarus Bit

From: Commander in Chief
To: General in Command, Pacific Test Area
Thru: Defense Secretary Robert S. McNamara

Note: The orientation tips outlined herein are to be treated as Middle Secret. This means, Bob, that the hard core facts of our tests, which you will receive under separate cover, are not to be leaked tao such busybodies as, say, Joe Alsop.* Whereas in the case of the below material, which relates to the sensitive area of natives—Armed Forces co-operation, it is advisable that full exposure be given, so that the best possible face may be obtained for our tests in the area of people-to-people considerations.

We can expect a good deal of hollering because of these tests, so let's try to put forth a decent image peoples-wise, and maybe to the degree we succeed here we'll have countered some of the Khrushy-inspired—and in my view, wholly negative—yammering.

*

The Christmas Island atoll is the largest in the Pacific. Population-wise it is perhaps the smallest, a mere 250 or so according to the latest figures we can gather. Coconuts and pandanus fruit are its main products.

Naturally, when your forces move in it will appear to these naive but lovable natives that they are being surrounded. Forced off the reservation, so to speak. The trick then is to establish quick but not pushy friendship.

I would go about it this way: Appeal to their sense of history. For example, the Christmas atoll was discovered by Captain James Cook in 1777, and while we can't claim that redoubtable seafarer as our own, we can invoke his spirit in another way. First thing you should do on arrival is to seek out the local chieftain and, with all good grace, offer him a modest quantity of commissary stores; such as soap, cigars and cigarettes, Cokes.

I would then announce to the chief, "We speak the language of the great Captain Cook." Like as not, he will be familiar with the current mother tongue of the West—he may even have been to Oxford as a youth. Hence an appropriate line or two from Will Shakespeare, or a couplet from Robert Frost, would help to set up a nice romantic and/or literary rapport from the start.

*

I am sure, dear General, I need not spell out further the various amenities you can employ to beef up the people-to-people thing. Play it loose and cool, but play it sincere, always sincere. One suggestion I would make: I believe it would be most beneficial if you and your staff boned up on the orientation packet got out by my brother-in-law, Sargent Shriver, which is standard for all Peace Corps units. We have been most successful with this line, from Ghana to Timbuktoo, and there's no reason to suppose it won't stand us in good stead on Christmas Island.

We come to the most sensitive point, which is to explain to the natives the why and wherefores of the tests. We have to assume that a scantily populated enclave like the Christmas Island, lying as it does in sleepy, Elysian innocence in the Pacific fastness, with a primitive economy of fruits and coconuts—I say we have to assume that these natives lack the sophistication to appraise favorably the cold logic of our tests. They don't read Edward Teller. They don't read *Life, National Review,* or even *The New York Times.* So how do we bridge the chasm; the cultural lag, as it were. Well—I think there's a way to do it. Appeal to their innocence, their primitive imagination. We are, after all, a nation of image making; of soft-, medium- and hard-sell planning.

A-OK—let's proceed from there, let's equate the image making with the tests. First, put it to the natives that nuclear testing in the atmosphere is not harmful per se. (Heavens to

Betsy, we in the West take on more radioactive waste in our bones with a mere X-ray in the dentist's chair, than all the *alleged* menace of our combined tests. Moreover, the natives have no such worries as X-rays (nor of dentists for that matter).

Of course, there's that picketing Nobel Prize chemist, that Linus Pauling fellow, who thinks negatively on this matter, but we *know* the natives don't read him. . . . So, as to the image making, I believe we can propel the tests into the area of fire-and-light allegory, we can tell the natives that far from being harmful, the tests take on all the grandeur of pagan sun worship; that they propitiate the dark enemy, rival the ancient legends of Icarus and Prometheus, do homage to the Egyptian sun god Ra.

You get the pitch, General, do you not? We have come to their island to explode great White Man's firebombs in homage to all those sun gods and legends—and in homage to, eh, Peace. And to A CERTAIN WAY OF LIFE. . . . Nor would I attempt to spell out the latter concepts to them— after all these concepts are not always and everywhere 100 per cent clear even to we in the West. Just repeat to the natives, as in a catechism, the two concepts.

Peace, and A CERTAIN WAY OF LIFE. I would offer them as a kind of obbligato to each exploding bomb: Peace, and A CERTAIN WAY OF LIFE.

*

One final word on procedure. I understand there are at least a handful of practicing Christians on that island. (No, the denomination is not important.) Now, even if we assume that these believers are more sophisticated than their pagan fellows, we must also assume that the needs of *realpolitik* are somewhat lost on them. Deference must be paid. I therefore order that in no case are you to explode a bomb on a Sunday, the Lord's day of prayer. If your logistics gets tangled because of this try to double your payload on the following Monday. Any way you do it, I'm sure it will all even out in the megatons by the time of your final test.

My warm personal greetings, General, good shooting to you and your men.

*Aside to Bob. Please do not mistake my reference to Joe as an outright knock. Fact is, most times he's as good a cold war bell-weather for us as can be found in the entire press corps. Just look at the way he got his feet wet in the Vietnam rice paddies, and the way he came up with those homey dispatches about our doughty little allies, how they fight the good fight under severe odds, etc., etc. And I'm sure, Bob, that you took notice of the good word he gave your spanking new helicopter-infantry units.

Still and all, that Alsop fellow has a positive genius for laying the large egg now and again. I'm thinking of course of that strictly confidential line I gave him, the one about us being ready to shoot off some atomic hardware at Moscow, if we thought we had to, in our assessment, etc., etc. And doesn't he sure enough clunk it all over the pages of a national weekly, with the result that old K practically comes up choking in his vodka glass. And that's Joe for you, bless his Stop-Press soul.

1962

A Letter to a Russian Friend

Dear Stanislav K.:

Some kind of impulse, no doubt quixotic, prompts me to write to you at this moment of danger to peace in the world —specifically, the danger that began only a fortnight ago, with the Middle East explosion. You will remember that we chanced to meet about a month ago, outside the West 72nd Street Automat, and that you and the gentleman with you— you introduced him as the correspondent from *Pravda*—joined me for a quick cup of coffee (in that very middle class, apolitical and generally seedy cafeteria). As has been our habit over the years we've been running into each other—and the time before was at that marvelously alive poetry recital in the East Village, when your Voznesensky and the several East Side poets teamed in a passionate and beautiful evening of readings against the Vietnam war—we exchanged "notes" on the various New York scenes, happenings and events and —again as a matter of old habit, no doubt, we then discussed the latest black headlines. In substance I had asked—or maybe the word should be "needled," and for that my belated apology—whether your government was really aware of the risks, of the possibility of miscalculation, in giving Nasser carte blanche to pursue his dream—or nightmare?— of *jihad* or holy war against the Israelis; and I asked further, had not

86

the U.S.S.R. policy of detente, of trying to douse fires of war, become in Nasser's case a reversal; and further, was not your government's policy of feeding Nasser, in arms, rubles and the egocentricity of military posturing—was not this a poor "handle" for getting back at us—at the U.S.—for the abysmal war we are involved in, in the Far East.

You bristled at my words, as well you might have, except that I brought all of this around to my main point, which was: Just as the U.S. had been making of Vietnam a bloody shambles born out of cold war stupidity, just so was the U.S.S.R. now engaged in stoking up a bloody shambles in the Near East, out of the same stupid impulse. My final word was: Far from being a Zionist, with all Zionism connotes to Arabs and your government both, I viewed Israel (however imperfectly) as a beacon for small third-world nations trying to live independently of *both* giants; and further, of Israel over the years practicing a form of third-world assistance, in medicine, education, agriculture and industry, in places like Ghana, Ethiopia and India. Programs born of an ideal as ancient as the bible: "Love thy neighbor as thyself." And your very tight answer to all of this—as we sipped our coffee, smoked our cigarettes, and *teased* the words from each other—your answer was a very curt if musical: "Sidney, you are being too *simple.*" And while the *Pravda* gentleman, in an excellent show of listenership and courtesy to a stranger, appeared through all of this to be noncommital, your own increasingly shadowed response (and I use "shadowed" literally, for it appeared to me that your fine serious eyes, your very chin hairs, were taking on a darker pallor as we spoke) had left me a little sadder as to the hugeness of the problem: We must all become *simpler simpler simpler.*

Now, as I write this a month or so later, the war in all its ingloriousness for some, and no small glory for others, has burst full course and ended. The fat and lean of it, is that the United States was seized with oil-anxiety tremors; Russia in its own way, was likewise seized; Nasser and company turned out to be paper camels, and straw revolutionaries; Israel broke out of a numbers vise, and fought a battle for its very life. She (Israel), and she alone, came up smelling like roses. But the fury of the Sinai sun remains, to haunt and make near-crazed the stragglers. And the bitterness remains—is indeed carried from all ports into the U.N. Assembly. I in my selfflagellant way with news, was up until five a.m. reading *The Times's* transcripts of the two main U.N. speeches (opening rounds) of the day. Those of your honorable Premier Kosygin, and of the honorable Israeli Foreign Minister, Abba Eban. I search myself and concede prior sympathy for the latter spokesman in this case—and I still find I am amazed at the lengths the former went to fuel distorted griefs and reverse the roles of "agressor" and "victim." (The Premier stopped short of accusing Israel herself of closing the Strait of Tiran, but of little else.) It was as if your spokesman had fed a card with punch-holes that spelled "Hate Israel" into the Russian equivalent of an IBM univac—and out came that long and unrelenting indictment that Premier Kosygin read to the world. In contrast was Abba Eban's speech—on which I'll say no more except that you, and I, and history itself will tote up the two in calmer moments, and the buoyancy of truth will do the rest: The two speeches will rise or sink in accordance with their hold on reality; and not in accordance with their response to a transient realpolitik and cold war inflexibility. (How strange the politician would not be aware—or is he?— of the words of his country's two fine poets: Yevtushenko in his "Babi Yar" poem, and Voznesensky in his recent poem called "The Call of the Lake." How then reconcile the Premier's rage, with its musky odor of a revanchist pan-Arabism, and the two poets' lyric leaps to the heart of one of our era's chief tragedies: genocide of Europe's Jews. How strange that politician and poet do battle on such separate— such *very separate*—fields of truth.)

There was a third speech in the same issue of *The Times* (and you can see now why the candlewatt was on until five in the morning in my room that night). It was President Johnson's in which he danced the expected dance of a man who is dressed nattily up front (his words of conciliation on the Middle East), and whose rear is kept awkwardly hidden because of a rip down the seat of his pants (his tired reiteration of the business that "Thus far there has been no serious response from the other side"—by which the President meant North Vietnam, surprise to the world!) And may I say here, my good friend, that although we who disagree with our government on this lousy war are—and remain—all too gloomily a minority: we do so nonetheless out of a kind of second nature, or call to conscience, in a society that is still open to dissent.

In this regard brave things are happening in your country as well—so that our mutuality of interest where conscience is concerned, becomes for both an open-ended pursuit.

Best wishes,
Sidney Bernard
1967

Uncle is Listening

I have a friend, a labor organizer and writer, who's sure his phone is bugged. He believes he is being FBIed, CIAed, HUACed any one of 'em, maybe all. He lives on Long Island. He is talkative, and talks sense. He is full of enthusiasms, he is combative. A good production of Sartre or Shakespeare; a rousing afternoon for Y. A. Tittle against, say, the Chicago Bears—are equally grist for his curiosity mill. As for politics, he is a cross between "maverick demo" (his phrase) and bread-and-butter hip.

It is said of Ernest Hemingway that his verbal style was torrential as it was persuasive. If that is true then my friend, in the manner of his telephone gambits, is very first cousin to Papa. (But I doubt the government appreciates this.)

Why, it can be asked, is Uncle curious? The answer could be that my friend has been researching, writing and lecturing up a storm on the subject (my title): *Old Nazis Among Us and Their New Career Opportunities Under the Present Dispensation.* I wonder, knowing his stream of consciousness style, how the listening box can keep up with him. And what it can do, dumb brute fashion, with what it *does* get.

He talks through a bleep shower, often worse. When he calls me, like as not there is a series of tinny obbligatos that weasel into the conversation. Besides the bleeps, there are screeches, crunches and groans—all bugging to be heard. In combination they are like lunatic sounds from a precision tool shop suddenly gone berserk.

Does he mind? Yes and no. As a man schooled in the detection of anything wasteful or inefficient, he goes livid now and then at the gross amateurism of it all. He feels that a nation that can produce Telstar or anti-anti-missiles is a nation that ought to be able to produce silent-flow eavesdropping units. Another example (he says) of planned obsolescence—as in our automobiles, refrigerators, washing machines, split levels.

As for the morality of the thing, or lack, he is rather cool. They have theirs, he has his. But he does own up to one concern; for the spy clerk whose job is to evaluate—if that's the word—my friend's monthly tape. Being union all the way, my friend rues the man's working conditions. Clearly they are the conditions of a slavey who can't opt for the picket line. There is the attendant problem of the IBM gorgon that does the collating. Presumably the machine, after it is fed the month's conversational swatches, weighs the meaning of each swatch and renders a decision.

Call it the Audio Litmus Test (ALT).

We can only guess the spectrum of choices open to clerk and machine. First on the parade, and probably one that sets alarm bells ringing, may well be a slot called Ideology Breach. Was my friend "softnosed" during the Cuban crisis? Come to think of it, he did say over the phone that he would join the peace marchers outside the U.N., adding in a riled voice, "The hot-rod gorillas better negotiate this one!" Surely he qualified for a "Breach" demerit with *that* remark. The fact that negotiations did take place, on the very brink, was no doubt just as surely lost on that IBM gorgon.

It would seem useless to pursue other possible slots; there must be dozens of them. (Such as, Insults to the Chief (Bobby or J. Edgar); Anti-Bomb Syndrome; Knocks on Our Way of Life; Integration-And-Jobs Belligerency; No Win Yellow Policy; Khrushchev Ain't Bad Jokes; New Frontier at Poolside Stories; Irish Mafia Puns; Peace Corps Come Home We Can Use You Here Suggestions; and so on.) Poor spy clerk and IBM, they must be as insult prone as the oceans are salty.

Does old mongoose Archie Moore have the answer—a self-inflicted "lip-buttoner" punch? You remember, this was the punch with which Archie was going to up-end that impossibly talky Cassius Clay—but Archie not only did not lip-button Clay, he himself succumbed to the 10-second birdie call.

But I have to leave off now, my phone is ringing.

1963

Run 'em Up the Flagpoles

There is a dropout movement in Quebec; been raising hell in recent months, up to and including the tossing of plastiques, mainly in the streets of Montreal. The image is of a North American Gaullist gadfly, buzzing away at the empire lovers at Ottawa. They want to go French—back to the glory of Champlain—hang the descendants of Burgoyne—vin rose on every La Belle Province table, in place of muddy Guinness's stout.

Well, the empire backers are getting the message. And they are making offers. Nothing big, of course. No chopping up the heartland—a piece for you Francophiles—the rest kept safe for Rudyard Kipling readers—and glory to ever-visiting Queen Elizabeth, the Canadian mounted are sitting their horses proudly.

In place of walls around separate provinces, the Ottawans are making plans for a new national flag. Symbol-wise, this is no small concession. Anyone who has gleaned the star-sapphire in the eyes of empire subjects at the passing of the Union Jack, can attest to this. (Maybe the whole world is English, in this emotion-touched area.) At any rate, there's been talk of a new ensign that will highlight three Maple Leafs and/or Fleurs de Lis.

We, in the U.S., should be watching the results with interest. Last winter's Panama crunch, wherein pimply young colons got us into a blood-red, white and blue hassle, by raising Old Glory *higher* than the Panama flag, at a Panama City high school, might have been avoided if we had promised a variation on the Ottawa plan. Maybe this: A ripe—but not over-ripe—golden yellow banana, adrift on a blue field in the right-hand corner of Our Flag.

That is only a starter. The Ottawa plan, by extension, can help raise the ego meter of all those groups, minority-wise, who have of late had a mad on for their Uncle Sam. Examples: Negroes, White Citizens Councils, Homosexuals, George Lincoln Rockwell Nazis, Goldwater Neo-Whigs, Avant Garde Film Makers, Madison Avenue, and so on. In an effort to achieve greater unity in diversity, we here offer various re-design suggestions for Old Glory. But first: Let it be understood that the left half, with its stripes and bright white bank of 50 stars, is to remain unchanged. That, at least, should half appease the D.A.R.

And now let's run 'em up the flagpoles.

Negro Old Glory. The right half, a rich velvet black field. On it a collage consisting of a bale of cotton, a floating saxophone, a pair of dice that comes up eleven (Sammy Davis—Las Vegas), a pair of boxing gloves, a drugstore counter (sit-ins), a large scimitar (Muslims), a bible (Rev. Martin Luther King pray-in). To be checked out by a committee of Ralph Bunche, Bayard Rustin, James Baldwin, Sugar Ray Robinson, Le Roi Jones.

White Citizens Old Glory. The right upper half, a replica of the Dixie flag. Right lower half, a very *very* white field. On it a collage consisting of a cattle prod, a police dog with bared teeth, a tall glass of mint julep, a moonshine still, a rifle with telescopic sight, a gold embossed "Horses For Courses: Keep Nigras On Slow Tracks" emblem. To be checked out by a committee of Gov. George Wallace, Byron De La Beckwith, Bull Connor, Senator John Tower.

Homosexuals Old Glory. The right half, a screaming pink field. On it a collage consisting of a Horn of Plenty (Aesopian phallus symbol), a powder puff, a Parisian street pissoir, a gold embossed line from Jean Genet or John Rechy. To be checked out by a committee of volunteers, headed by Randolphe Wicker.

George Lincoln Rockwell Old Glory. The entire right half, a replica of Hitler's Third Reich flag. Embellishments, if any, to be added by a committee of one: George Lincoln Rockwell.

Goldwater Neo-Whigs Old Glory. The right half, a very royal purple (for, "Born to the . . ."). On it a collage consisting of an Arizona cactus plant, a George Washington figure on white charger, a Continental fife, drum and musket, an upside down page from the Federalist Papers, an upside down replica of the Declaration, a gold embossed "Death And Taxes Are *Not* Sure Things" emblem. To be checked out by a committee of William Buckley, William Rusher and H. L. Hunt.

Madison Avenue Old Glory. The entire right half, a cool lemon yellow field. (The Doctor Schutzkoph motivational team in a recent study on retina-subliminal reactions, touted lemon yellow very highly. Said the doc, "We find lemon yellow more implosive-explosive, image-wise, than any other color scheme in the book. By far.") On this lemon yellow field, a collage consisting of a floating 'tache case, a Schutzkoph punch card, an upside down page out of Roget's Thesaurus, a cancelled New York Central monthly ticket, a Martini shaker, a gold embossed "Advertising Is To Business, What Hieroglyphs Were To The Pharaohs" slogan. To be checked out by a committee of Marion Harper and Joseph Kaselow; who in turn will name a committee from among present Ad Hoc committees; who will check out its findings and report back, in its turn, to the committee that named the findings committee.

Avant-Garde Film Makers Old Glory. The entire right half, a blazing red-black abstract expressionist motif, in the style of Franz Kline or Willem De Kooning. On it a collage consisting of a floating hand camera, a hypodermic needle and syringe (Shirley Clarke's "The Connection"), a free-form mammary and genital motif ("Flaming Creatures," "Scorpio Rising"), a plugged film can with warning sticker: "For Hip Audiences Only." To be checked out by a committee of Jonas Mekas, Allen Ginsberg, Diane Di Prima.

If there are other "mad on their Uncle Sam" groups we've missed, and we're sure we have, let them speak up for *their* redesigned Old Glory. The U.S. should have, under one roof, at least as many flags as the U.N. (Well over a hundred, at last count.)

Let's move with the Ottawa plan! 1965

The Authenticity of FDR's Secret Testament

Dear Mr. Bernard:
I'm sorry to have to say no, but we'd need stronger documentation before we'd consider this. . . .

Cordially,
Jack Kessie,
Managing Editor,
Playboy

When the secret document was discovered, in a deeply recessed pigeonhole of Franklin D. Roosevelt's old rolltop, there was a good deal of worry among the immediate family. The implications were a threat, to put it mildly, to Democratic Party unity on the highest level. Talk is that Elliot Roosevelt, closest to being the maverick his father was, opted for exposure of the document.

On the other hand, FDR Jr., because of his cabinet level post in the present Administration, strongly favored a no-talk line. And very soon, after some hushed counsel among old politicos of the FDR stripe, an inevitable schism developed: for full and immediate disclosure; for equally decisive suppression of the mysterious document.

Because of a testy parallel with Lenin's famous secret warning, the FDR paper began to be whispered about as the "FDR Secret Testament."

It will be remembered that Lenin, after seizures which left him partially paralyzed, had warned in his remarks to party comrades, and later in the disputed secret paper itself, that Joseph Stalin was not to be trusted. And further, that Stalin's inordinate will to rule-or-ruin was to be resisted with the greatest force.

We know that Lenin died not long after, thus removing the one political and moral barrier to Stalin's napoleonic rise.

As in Lenin's case, the FDR testament has never been officially acknowledged. And yet, the rumors will not go away. If anything, the march of history, since FDR's untimely death, tends toward a straightforward confirmation, if not outright prophesy, of the great New Deal leader's deepest fears.

And what were these fears? What were the prophetic words written down by FDR only weeks before his last illness? Words which now, 20 exciting and historic years later, seem to threaten party unity at the highest level? We know that the locus of the alleged FDR testament, its warning, points to the very White House chair itself. The chair and its present occupant, Lyndon Baines Johnson.

But first it would be useful to sketch in some history, however brief the record, of the Roosevelt-Johnson relationship at the time of the New Deal. It will be recalled that in FDR's campaign for a second term, word had come up from Texas that a young, ambitious politico (L. B. Johnson) was doing Herculean work for the New Deal ticket.

Friends of Johnson, at the time, had quoted him as saying, "The train of American destiny is on a straight line, from Hyde Park to Washington, and I figur' I'm going to stay on that train."

Soon after, while Roosevelt was whistle-stopping in Texas, young Johnson secured a meeting with FDR. From all appearances it was a cordial meeting of two outgoing political pros, with the younger man doing most of the listening. And yet there was something about Johnson's behavior that prompted one witness to remark, off the record, that "Lyndon has the itch of ambition, without the conviction of talent, that could enable him to shove his way to the White House."

(The nuance of the word "shove" is important. As is the source of this and other quotes of the period, both of which in a moment.)

More significant than that wry quote, was FDR's own guarded impression of the young Texan. The New Deal chief was heard to say to a confidant, "That cow rassler needs watching. He has lots of Texas charm, but then Texas is an inflated state of mind, at best."

All of this (and subsequent quotes) can be found in that very useful personal memoir of the period, Professor Paul J. J. Kissenden's *Travels With FDR.* The author of this thin volume, now out of print, was one of the early Roosevelt braintrusters.

Kissenden recalls that the FDR-LBJ meetings were infrequent, and hardly of any consequence, in the years following the first one. Clearly FDR had little time to spend pondering over the career of one Lyndon Johnson, what with the mammoth tasks of World War II facing him.

And yet there were occasions when Johnson's activities, as a rising politico whose influence in party affairs was growing, came in for at least mild censure from Roosevelt.

Again, referring to the Kissenden memoir, it was the Professor's recollection that FDR, on one such occasion, capsuled his attitude toward the Texan with the uncharitable remark, "Johnson remains a cow rassler, despite the so-called civilizing influence of that great emporium of debate, the House of Representatives."

The president went on to say, according to Kissenden, that "He (LBJ) may be quick in the art of war-war, but he's crabfoot slow in the higher art of diplomatic jaw-jaw." The significance of the remark, though cryptic when taken out of context, can be seen from the fact that FDR at the time was busy planning his grand design of postwar coexistence.

As Professor Kissenden recalls, "FDR was having his troubles with assorted hawks in his Administration, those who imagined that only a *Pax Americana*, beefed up and enforced by a growing military might, would be a guarantor of U.S. victory. The secret code name," Kissenden goes on, "for this group, which was led by Vice-President Truman and Representative Johnson, was *Pax Old Glory.*"

That FDR was more than a minor prophet, can be gleaned from Truman's precipitous use of the bomb against Japan, after FDR's death.

One close FDR advisor, according to Kissenden's memoir, summed up the troubled conscience in high Administration circles with the remark, upon the destruction of Hiroshima and Nagasaki, that "While Harry Truman inherited, with all due constitutional trimmings, FDR's high office, never let it be said that he inherited an FDR go-ahead for that act of wartime vandalism."

Of course, reports Kissenden, Lyndon Johnson was presumed to be in hearty agreement with Truman on the bomb.

Here, then, is the background of the FDR Secret Testament. And what of the contents? The answer, as of now, is one of bits and pieces. A political jigsaw puzzle, at best. And yet the effort at a solution, at finding the spine of FDR's secret thought, must be made.

Taking rumor, allegation and unofficial detective work all together, what the testament boils down to is that FDR foresaw the day when Lyndon Johnson, if and when he "shoved" his way to the White House, could by a rash use of armed interventions, and precipitous military adventurism, loose a flood of anti-American fear and hatred around the world.

The spine of the testament was FDR's belief that Johnson would have no scruples about bypassing Congress, or indeed public opinion, in his weakness for military solutions. It is further alleged, by insiders who insist the testament is real, that FDR spelled out his fears in the document thusly:

"Where careful diplomacy is called for, you can depend on Lyndon to opt for careless militarism." ("Horse-trading is the word FDR used in the testament, says one of the insiders, rather than "diplomacy.")

And it is useful here to recall, from the Kissenden memoir, a wartime statement attributed to LBJ—what has since become known in Capitol Hill circles as the "Shoot From the Hipster, Texas Style Syndrone." LBJ's remark went, "I would never let legalisms stand in the way of military action, 'specially when we' all are winning."

Interest in the testament waned during the Eisenhower

years on Capitol Hill. It took the great Democratic Party rivalry of Senators Johnson and Kennedy, for the top spot in the 1960 campaign, to quicken the pace of speculation.

Time and again it was said that JFK was aware of the testament. And, most significant, that he fully shared Roosevelt's fears. But he preferred, the theory goes, not to use the document in his campaign against Johnson. His reason: the party image would suffer a mortal blow.

On recollection, from a member of the so-called Kennedy Mafia, would seem to confirm this. The member had said (to a *Washington Post* staffer, who has never confirmed or denied the quote) that "Jack Kennedy had his work cut out for him, all but sitting on Bobby like a hobby horse, for fear brother Bobby would leak word about the document."

For that moment, the member went on, "Jack had convinced Bobby that quietus was the better part of valor, if victory was to be assured." (And if the grammar was a bit off here, it should be noted that the strategy, most definitely, was quite on target.)

One touchy, side-note, as well, is very revealing of Bobby's fury as a campaigner. It seemed, according to the Mafia members, that Bobby's animus toward LBJ was flamed by a Johnson remark, made to a party neutral, that "I [LBJ] always had my suspicions, even in the Roosevelt days, of Harvard brain trusts, and all things academic out of the effete Eastern Seaboard."

The Mafia man recalled the incident this way: "The booze was flowing free when Johnson let loose with his Harvard gem. Even so, Bobby would not sit still for *that* kind of gratuitous jibe, aimed so crudely at his brother's superior scholarship."

The member summed up the incident: "Bobby was ready to blow the whistle on the secret paper right then and there. As it turned out, JFK was so convinced of his impending victory, both as party candidate and President-elect, that he was able to convince Bobby not to rock the boat."

It was revealed, in this context, that Kennedy felt the one sure way of handling his (JFK's) fears re Johnson, as well as the implications of the testament, was to have Johnson in the second spot.

"I'll keep Lyndon in the quiet pasture of the Vice-Presidency," Kennedy was heard to say to Bobby, on one tense occasion. "That way he'll have lots of time to dream of cows and bulls and green grass. He'll run the country, mentally, from the Pedernales; I'll run it for real, from the White House *and* Harvard."

Of course the terrible irony, of a depth matching Greek tragedy, was the Johnson succession by the equally ancient route of political assassination.

Which bring us to the present, a time of intense speculation over the FDR Secret Testament.

One Capitol insider, who himself refuses to go on record re the FDR paper, offers nevertheless some sharp evidence of the mood of disquiet over it. "No after-hours party," he declared, "no casual meeting of politicos, no private confab, in all Washington, is free of talk on that paper." What feeds the fires, added the insider, is President Johnson's "cold turkey intercepts in Vietnam and Dominican Republic."

Significantly, it is these very actions that prompted one observer to state, again off the record, that "Johnson's shooting from the hip is a case of pure prophecy on FDR's part; he knew his onion long ago, and that onion is stenching up the international scene beyond even Roosevelt's very effective sense of smell."

Additional undercoating for the Secret Testament, other insiders say, was Senator Robert F. Kennedy's strong attacks on Johnsonian policy in the Caribbean and Vietnam.

It was pointed out, by a pro-testament man close to the Kennedy entourage, that Bobby Kennedy "was using a kind of Aesopian approach in his attacks. If you read him closely, and *between the lines* [emphasis is the Kennedy man's], you begin to realize he is hewing very close to the contents of that FDR document. Which may indicate, and this is *my* hope, that Bobby is ready to spring the truth on that paper any time now."

And, there is further evidence of what can be called a "tell it as it is—right now!" line.

The theory goes that the avalanche of critical commentary on Johnson's military policy from large sections of the independent press, such as Walter Lippman, the *New Republic's* TRB, The *Times'* James Reston and Russel Baker, et al, came about from a conviction, if not an outright "I saw it myself" belief, that the Roosevelt Testament was bona fide.

One troubleshooting UPI reporter on the Washington scene

went so far as to claim that Senator Robert Kennedy has already leaked, to all of these newsmen, and to Murray Kempton as well, the fact of the FDR testament.

He gave as evidence of his claim, the peculiar coincidence of all of these commentators filing—on the same day!—a series of uniformly damaging columns relating to Johnson's policies in Vietnam and the Caribbean.

TRB in the *New Republic:* "Lyndon Johnson has to look out when Senator Eastland, the *Chicago Tribune*, Joe Alsop and, by inference, Barry Goldwater shower praises on his policy in the Dominican Republic and Vietnam. That isn't consensus, it's captivity. The appetite for intervention grows by what it feeds on. . . ."

Again, from the *New Republic:* "President Johnson has turned a civil war in South Vietnam into an American war in all of Vietnam."

James Reston: "He [LBJ] is not yet at home with foreign policy. It is not the sort of thing he can grab by the lapels. It requires great precision of speech, a sense of history . . . and these have never been his strong points. . . ."

And, again from Reston: "He is at the controls, like Walter Mitty, of every bomber over Vietnam. He lands in the Dominican Republic with every marine. . . ."

The UPI newsman, who pointed out the coincidence of these same-day comments, offered as evidence of the leak of the FDR document, by Senator Robert Kennedy, the following cogent incident.

"Senator Kennedy, the afternoon before these columns hit (other than the *New Republic's*, which were filed at the same time, but appeared on a later weekly schedule), had phoned Murray Kempton, from his suite at the Carlyle, and invited Kempton up for some drinks.

"Kennedy, during the soiree, had told Kempton he was on the verge of an open break with President Johnson; that Johnson's penchant for bully boy tactics, where cool brains were called for, was something that not only he [RFK] was ashamed of, but that President Kennedy in days gone by had this attitude, too.

"As a clincher," the UPI man continued, "Senator Kennedy admitted that the FDR Secret Testament was, in fact, a reality and was, substantially, a warning of just the road Johnson was taking in Vietnam, etc.

"The revelation of the testament's existence by Senator Kennedy was not for direct attribution. If, on the other hand, *Kempton* wanted to pass the truth of it along to other journalists, he, Senator Kennedy, would not veto the action."

(It should be noted that the RFK leak, as the UPI man revealed it, has Kempton getting the tip *first.* And that in fact Kempton was the "fence," whereupon it was handed down to the others by him. The apparent contradiction of sequence is understandable, given the explosive nature of the incident.)

Murray Kempton, the UPI informant went on, "wasted no time. He put in calls to Washington and New York, to Reston and the others. He discussed the document with them. All were in agreement that it was real; and that the implications were damaging in the extreme, to President Johnson and U.S. foreign policy both.

"The big rub," continued the UPI man, "was whether to break the story then and there. After much soul-searching, the consensus was against breaking the story—at least without prior authorization from the family."

All these newsmen, the UPI man added, "have long felt it was not in their province to break the story; that the testament was, in a true sense, a family document. And that FDR Jr., who is believed to have possession, alone had the option to run with it or suppress it—as he apparently chooses to do."

As a postscript to the RFK-Kempton leak, the UPI man gave it as his belief that Senator Kennedy, who in the past came very close to "springing the story" more than once, "had this time around a damn good motive for his act: a Johnsonian remark that he, Kennedy, clearly interpreted as a craven jibe at the memory of his beloved brother, the late President Kennedy."

The Johnson remark alluded to by the UPI man, as reported in the *New Republic,* went ". . . he [LBJ] rather tactlessly said he wasn't going to sit in a 'rocking chair' and let a Latin country go Communist. . . ."

Senator Kennedy, the UPI man concluded, "vowed he'd take care of the insult 'with a bonus offering.' The leak to Kempton, shortly after, was the bonus. And it is a beauty for President Johnson!"

Not surprisingly, the rocking-chair crack, which one Capitol Hill wit quickly labelled, "LBJ's rock," prompted others besides Senator Kennedy to speedy anger. One loyal JFK man, who was with the late President at Leyte Gulf, declared with unconcealed scorn that "Lyndon Johnson, unlike the late President Kennedy, has a need, bordering on compulsion, to play military heroics from the safe shores of the Potomac."

And as more undercoating, there was sharp rumor of a Drew Pearson column that never saw print, a column that described a meeting held in the Cabinet Room with President Johnson, the combined Chiefs of Staff, and four top-level civilian members of the Administration—Rusk, Bundy, Humphrey, Katzenbach—in attendance.

The meeting was called, according to Pearson's column, to discuss the severity of protest—especially on campuses—over the Vietnam bombings and Marine landings in the Caribbean.

President Johnson, the column went on, was determined to firm up Rusk, and Bundy, and even the Vice President in what he believed was a weakening of resolve, on their part, in face of those protests.

The core of the column, as described by one wire-service newsman (who had seen the column on the wires, before the "kill" was issued), was a dressing-down handed to Rusk-and-company by the senior military man at the meeting, a four-star General. Pearson reported it thus:

General: "Gentlemen, it's either talk with these commie bastards, and run; or button up and give 'em the sharp end of our bayonets, Vietcongs or Dominican Castros or Who-evers." At which point, the President looked down on his aides and said, "Now, let us go out and tell these professors and students to stick to their books, and leave the hot kitchen work to the military. . . ."

Here, again, the peculiar coincidence of all these damaging comments surfacing on the same day, deserve attention. The UPI man's theory, that the timing and ferocity of the comments relate to Senator Kennedy's leak, appears unassailable.

"It is clear," the UPI man put it, "that Pearson and the others were emboldened, in their attacks on Johnson, by the contents of the testament itself, by FDR's fears, as written down over 20 years ago, of a Johnsonian era of confusion, and runaway militarism. Bobby Kennedy's disclosure to

Kempton, at long last, was the handle they were looking for."

The bits and pieces fit together tightly; and the existence of FDR's Secret Testament, as a topic of conversation and item of worry, is fast becoming number one in Washington and the nation.

Nor will the testament be wished away by levity alone—the kind of levity offered by Abe Fortas, close as any to the Johnsonian ear, when he told a newsman recently: "Secret testaments come and go—from Ptolemy to J. Edgar—but they don't rate much more than a two-dollar losing racetrack ticket—usually."

1966

Tiger, Tiger Burning Right

The lobby crowd at Carnegie Hall was not the usual musical one. Certainly not for a Richter recital, say, where proffered tickets would attract swarms like Automat crumbs to pigeons. Tickets were going begging, and several young men in Madison type dress stood alert for those who had none. They were ushers for the Moral Re-Armament organization, who were sponsoring a drama called "The Tiger."

The drama was supposedly a re-enactment of the 1960 midsummer Tokyo demonstrations that kept President Eisenhower on a watery hot seat, as he cruised from one Far Eastern port to another and finally decided against a Tokyo visit because of some extreme political turbulence in the air.

It was a Saturday matinee performance, last of five in the New York area. The big pasteboard sign outside had a tigerish look indeed. It showed an angry horde of students in the posture of what police would characterize as "riot formation." Actually they were in the throes of a sinuous snakedance that, terpsichore aside, might conceivably scare the kimona off every last adult in Japan. Even the Japanese lettering looked angry.

The audience was drifting in a bit wet. Two dozen police with little to do but stay dry in the light rain were posted in front of Carnegie and on the street. Passersby sought the shelter of Carnegie's iron canopy, and some, after reading the pasteboard, fell in line for the offers of free admission to "Tiger."

A sedate calm ruled inside the hall. With five minutes to

go before the 3 p.m. opening curtain, there were still large holes of empty seats. The papered house, a rarity for ticket-hungry Carnegie Hall, consisted of a strange amalgam of bland young New York couples, a sprinkling of Negroes in fezzes, several knots of English-speaking orientals, and older women and men of the kind that seem to levitate from one to another of West Fifty-seventh Street's very special world of mystical, theosophical and Christian Science meetings.

Two of these oldsters, sitting very prim and overstuffed in their heavy rainwear, obviously women of strong passions in a world that jarred them, were engaged in some preliminary words that— to *them*, at least—must have seemed very cogent to the business at hand. The nature and sum of their dialogue could be rounded in the parting shot of one of the women when she said, "People always bite the hand that feeds them."

The house lights began to dim and, perhaps due to the oncoming somnolence, or their own inertia, or both, the two ladies edged slowly back into their velour-lined seats and sighed audibly. A minute later they rose with the rest of the hall when the entire company of "Tiger" (about fifty and all from Japan) came on stage and sang "The Star Spangled Banner." One of the ladies murmured, "How nice that they sing it *our* way."

Anthem over, the cast faded behind the curtains. A man from Moral Re-Armament came forward and spoke into the microphone. Though his voice had less of passion than the two ladies were capable of, he gave his three or four minute talk on MRA's program with some crispness and conviction. Before leaving, he explained that "Tiger" had been touring leading cities around the world for the past half year, and, as evidence of its success, he referred to the reactions of former White House press secretary, James Hagerty, "which you all no doubt read in the papers."

(Hagerty, after seeing a performance of "Tiger" in a White Plains auditorium, responded with untypical noblesse oblige. As reported in the *New York Times*, he refused the cast's apologies for the Tokyo business, declaring that the play was all the apology he needed.)

The final pre-show speaker was a Japanese doctor, a short middle-aged man who'd been introduced with the words "His father was a chamberlain to the Emperor." Lunging into the microphone as he spoke, he gave a resume of the play and explained that "every incident and line you will see happened in the streets of Tokyo."

For the next ninety minutes or so, the audience took in the nine-scene tableau, which was acted in Japanese with superimposed English interpretation coming over the loud speakers, with interest and polite applause. "Tiger" was more documentary than play, one scene following the next with a staccato beat, what could be called a right of center agit-prop account of the Zengakuren demonstrations, and here called over and over again "riots."

It opened with a sure political prop, given the anxiety-directed audience MRA seems to tailor to.

A white spot picked out an ominous figure in Chinese Red Army uniform who barked commands from a high podium. His words were to unseen legions of Japanese youth, egging them to carry the day against imperialists. Nothing missed in the makeup, the man was a carbon copy of Chou En-lai.

Next came two or three scenes which showed Zengakuren leaders baiting a trap for a huge rally outside the Diet. The youths' methods, as depicted on stage, were nothing if not workaday. Surely, an early Lenin handbook had been pored over.

Then a sudsy scene of a youth leader in the uneasy bosom of his wealthy family. Five anguished minutes. A river of tears. He bolts from home for the Diet rally.

The two ladies and others responded to all this as to Revelations being read by someone with the shudders. Came the big Diet scene, and they were really in a box.

Carnegie's ample stage was in semidarkness. Roaming spots picked out an angry cortege that snaked to and fro to the shrill bleatings of a whistle. On command, the hydra-headed human-animal shouted Zengakuren's watchwords: "Storm the Diet. Down with the government."

At play's end the hero, mildly bloodied in the Diet set-to, renounced violence for family togetherness. A *deus ex machina* device was used here, its form a pristine family friend newly arrived from an MRA congress in Switzerland, who saturated all with his missionary rectitude.

"Tiger's" unstinting didactic flavor could be savored in some of the more tart lines that came over the loud-speakers. One example: "Listen, if someone gets killed tonight, we've

won. . . . The people will be won over, the Diet will fall."
This by a Zengakuren leader, wild-eyed, firm, zealous, with
more sulphur than sense in his politics, obviously.

The MRA line was soaringly adumbrated:

"There's a way to fight for social justice without violence."

"Japan's destiny is to be the lighthouse of Asia."

"I can see now that the students are being used. . . .
And that the country is being used."

"I was being run by ambition to be a student leader. . . .
Then I cleaned out my own life."

There was even an echo of the Biff and Willy Loman confrontation scene in "Death of a Salesman." Father, an influ-
ential and liberal-oriented business man, and son, who turns
from Zengakuren to MRA, wistfully talk over the past. Son
says: "Later, when I found out you had a mistress—and I
hated you—I turned to radical political action."

After the show the MRA man appeared and, with interpreter
in tow, introduced several of the cast. One prime member
turned out to be "Mr. Mitsui of the great Mitsui industrial
complex." A man of around fifty, diffident and non-Method in
style, Mr. Mitsui said "My brother drifted, my sister turned
to Communism. It remained for me to look after the 30,000
workers in our plants. MRA helped me realize my obligations."

Others spoke the MRA catechism with equal fervor. To a
man and woman, they would henceforth renounce radical
politics, selfishness, unseemly ambition.

The two ladies clucked approval during the mass confes-
sional. A soft, wrinkled beatitude lit their faces. When the
collection baskets were passed, they eagerly gave some coins.
Others in the hall did the same. It was nevertheless clear
that audience largesse could make up but a fraction of
"Tiger's" cost.

1961

"30" for the President

His last hours were sharp, full of vigor and cheers. At the
Texas airport, upon his arrival from Washington, big crowds
had formed. They pressed in close, trying to shake the hands
of the President, and his young wife. He was in the South
country, a country friendly above ground, a country seething
with rancor below.

Before going to a breakfast meeting at Fort Worth, he walked through a misty rain to a parking lot across the street from his hotel. He spoke there to more cheering partisans who could not get tickets for the breakfast. A thin barrier of wooden horses separated him and the crowd, to whom he apologized because his wife was not with him, explaining, "She is organizing herself — it takes longer."

At the breakfast gathering, he stood tall to his listeners. They handed him a fine cowpoke hat, sometime symbol of lonely cattle country, used now for the ceremonial magic of votes, and locality pride. He fingered the smooth felt, but declined to put the hat on, joking that he would wear it at the White House when he returned.

Never, it could be said, was he more himself. He had journeyed down to mend political fences, but it hardly meant he had to mend to the other fellow's custom. (Hats, anyway, always rubbed his head wrong.) And his sway was complete. He told the businessmen, oilmen, solid citizens that — to use the Northern vernacular — they never had it so good. He said it with crisp confidence, his "a's" and his smiles equally broad.

(He had it in mind to say later, in the speech he never made, that words alone could never suffice for deeds — leastways, words that had little or no bearing on dangers and challenges that faced us all.)

The next leg was a short hop to Dallas by plane. Waiting at the airport were more cheering crowds. As the President's wife emerged from the plane, they shouted "Hi, Jackie" and squeezed forward for a closer look. She carried a bouquet of red roses, but she managed to shake hands with several greeters. It was her first real junket with the President, and it was clear she was having a fine time of it.

After that, came the 11-mile motorcade through the city of Dallas. The President's party rode in open cars. Bubbletops, he often said, were not for him. Like the wearing of hats, they too rubbed him wrong. Here, again, he was being very much himself. He loved contact at all points. The contact of political leader and voter, the contact of ideas that sprang out of debate and dialogue, the contact of man and his environment . . . And the contact, finally, that was perhaps deepest of all — between man, himself, and his own trapped conscience.

As the motorcade moved along, moved inexorably to its

final station of the cross, the President was wreathed in a pattern of smiles. They were a mirror, those smiles of his, of the above ground welcome that was being showered on him. "And you thought the crowd would not turn out to greet you," said the Texas Governor's wife, happily.

They were just about the last words he ever heard.

1963

Of Crows, Toads and Crocodiles

Dear Sidney Bernard:

I'm sorry to have to return the enclosed to you, but . . . the piece about the assassination is too corrosive and bitter for us.

Cordially
Jack Kessie
Managing Editor,
Playboy.

The television networks say they lost 24 mil' in advertising spots, on that November 22-25 weekend of our lost President. Big, generous, public spirited — just look at the figures. CBS alone in 1962 had a 500 mil' gross — and a 50 mil' net. So how can we do less than feel for them, feel for that last-quarter-'63 loss of 24 mil'.

They had to stop the commercials! *That's Marlboro Country!* had to stop, so that Chet and David could explain the *significance* of it all. Brand Name soap had to flake off for the weekend . . . So that anchorman Walter could travel around the punditry horn and — with all his subaltern Walters in tow — could tie-up for us *The Meaning Of This Act For Our Future* — in thousands of miles of verbal confetti.

We lost our President, but don't let it be said we lost any opportunity for selfpraise, for merchandising, for exercising the tear ducts. Some eight or ten weeks after, NBC led the parade of handclappers with full-page newspaper ads. Clasping its own verbal bouquets to its own generous bosom, they allowed as how the National Broadcasting Company felt proud of the men and women of all networks. . . . For their dedication to duty, their display of tact, on that long and trying weekend. And, the head man at ABC, that big-city tabloid of the Nets, owned as how the medium had earned — by its good works on that weekend — exploration rights into "more serious" (*sic*) areas of national life.

Not a word on the voyeurism of their cameras. Nor on the magnetic lure of their cyclops machines — for such as Dallas police, a District Attorney in cowpoke hat, a Stripsville citizen with bursts of love for Texas Home Country God. . . . (If old Roger Maris can stand up to that camera — hero on spikes — and waggle away at the ump — for all America to see — man you can't deny Stripsville his moment — he had a picture date with history.)

We lost our President, but didn't the publishers do a job of it! The picture book explosion. Special memorial editions. On every newsstand in the Fifty. We lost him, and they found him. All those velvet negatives! Caroline, John-John and Jack. Jackie and Jack. Kennedys in the bosom of the Kennedys. Noisy in spots, but sincere. (Right?) Quick buck commercial, but a piece off the top for charity. (Right?) Volume after volume. In every bookshop in the Fifty.

There was the sequins-shot neighborhood lady, still a bit wet out of the beauty parlor, pink hair escalated in a cotton candy beehive, curlicued poodle dog lapping at her ankles . . . She flounces into an upper Broadway candy store, her green-shadow eyes do a rapid crossfire on the mag racks, she simulates pity and sighs: "Such a *beautiful* man. . . . Such a *beautiful* family. Any new books? Magazines? I've seen *all* you have — can't get enough. It's so sad. . . . Such a *beautiful* man." And that poodle — lapping lapping lapping.

And the shellac boys, the disc fabricators. They wafted his voice back to us, from the hot kilns of their boiler rooms. One platter was called, "Four Days That Shocked The World." The liner read, "Not an album of speeches. You are there . . . events become history." Nearly forty "events" all told, juiciest being an "On-the-spot report from the basement of Dallas jail at the moment Oswald is shot by Jack Ruby — Exclusive coverage — Ika Pappas, WNEW news." The disc concluded with, "Taps, etc." Righter than rain, once again. Toads, too, can croak at the funerals of Kings — or a President.

There was the mimic par excellence, who had cut a gold disc out of the parlor image (strictly his own) of the President, in the happy *only yesterday* times: He vowed sadly there would be no more of *that*. Presumably the story of his life will henceforth be, "The Day My Chatter Stopped."

And the newspapers — hail to our free press. The New York *Journal American* frontpaged a four-part syndicated article by

Jack Ruby called, "Why I Killed Lee Oswald." The city room parlay of them all! Trial by newspaper — circulation by sensationalism. And for home movie buffs this item: An 8 *mm* cinema treat from *Castle* — highlights in the career of JFK — 200 feet in the can — at $5.95. *("Turn off the Television, Mabel and let's show 'em the Jack Kennedy thing.")*

Others, not to be denied a quick buck, were reducing his image to a kind of "God Bless Our Home" gimcrackery. Plummer McCutcheon who, for all anyone knows, is on the same high plateur as Hammacher Schlemmer, was offering the John F. Kennedy Commemorative Plaque By Wedgewood" — at $6.50 the piece. *Wedgewood Smedgewood,* this was a glazed, saccharine, terra cotta bit of fluff.

More notable still, gimcrackery-wise, was the JFK salt-and-pepper set — pepper in the form of a rocking chair, and salt a china figure of the President, with three holes (*sic sic sic*) in its back for pouring. 97c.

Among latecomers in the memorial sweeps, there was a reproduction job of a JFK portrait by (who else?) Norman Rockwell. This high-varnish, mass-produced item from the Rockwell industries carried the warranty: "True rich colors are transferred to artist's canvass by an amazing process. . . ." And more: "The distinctive texture of the canvas becomes part of the picture. . . ." And still more: "Each canvas is hand mounted on artist's stretchers for lasting beauty . . . Price complete now only $9.95."

(Strange how the lingo comes up straight Midway snake-oil, no matter what the product is. Which may or may not prove that in the land of Barnum, there is an ever-normal granary of yokels.)

Another latecomer—a coin of the realm item. "The *John F. Kennedy Half Dollar Sterling Silver Key Chain* and Money Clip, $5.98 each." The ad read in part: "An honored memento of our late beloved President. The recently issued Kennedy half dollar made into a distinctive key chain or money clip (not illustrated) . . ." Very touching, sentiment-wise. And very modest, that phrase "recently issued." Fact is, the enterprise on this one was nothing if not bakery swift. A matter of days only before those coins were out of the US mint, and on the various workbenches being tooled for market . . . Diner's Club, American Express or Uni-Card accounts honored (the ad stated).

3 Literary Decathlon

William S. Burroughs: Surfacing

It was a crushing crowd, for so small a theater. Bill Burroughs had come to give a reading. Bill Burroughs — William Burroughs — William S. Burroughs. Any name they called him, he was there among them in the flesh, on this chilly Sunday afternoon. The man from way-out and deep, from the hashish dens of Tangiers, had surfaced on the East Village. A literary Lazarus rising? And droves of the "in" literati, poets in beards, girls wind-blown off the campuses (and Bronx and Manhattan middle class pads), close-shouldered into the tiny, 129-seat East Fourth Street Theater to see and hear him. At a two-dollar tab.

They sat in tight, buzzing intimacy — waiting for his entrance. The narrow aisles looked like encampment day. Lank-haired chicks, many wearing boots and leather, leafed through copies of *Nova Express* and *Naked Lunch*. Now and then they would exchange a literary *bon mot*, with their cooler appearing and equally lank-haired male companions. Everybody seemed anxious to display some credentials, some word-of-mouth or first-hand evidence of his knowingness in this very special scene. And outside in the lobby and on the street, the unlucky ones who hadn't made it, had to satisfy themselves with *just being there*. The ambiance of a really hip scene was a kind of "presence" all its own.

Pretty soon Burroughs almost shuffled on stage. Tall and bony, wearing business suit and vest, he came through the yards of furled red curtains silent as a cloud. He removed his topcoat and soft felt hat, placing them carefully on top of a white chair. In front of him was another chair, more like a baby stool, on which was placed a mike with its thin neck jutting out toward him. He carried a large, highly polished leather briefcase; placing this down in front of him, he eased himself (like a diver fighting the bends) into a high backed leather chair. Only then, for the first time, did he offer a tentative look at his audience. It was a pale look, but it galvanized his viewers to instant attention.

He spoke his first words, a kind of ramble which he swallowed, a preliminary ellipsis to the business of the reading. His voice was sandpapery but pleasant. In the near hush of the tiny theater, the accent was of a sharp midwestern twang. The orange house lights went down, two spots each from the stage wings went up. The whole stage area was bathed in this orange-red coated light, and Burroughs' first lines, upon drawing some books and manuscripts from his briefcase, his upper torso almost jackknifed into the mike, had the strange and compelling remoteness of a seance.

He read from *Nova*, the voice now barking, but low and pleasantly. Pretty soon it was evident that many of those lines, no matter how recondite or special or indecipherable one may have found them to be on the printed page, came across live as lines with a special blend of way-out humor. The mode of his reading, quick barks of staccato narrative, pushed this tone of levity across the apron with a, literally, near stunning effect. And the response was a targeted one, sharp bursts of laughter that gave the house a vaudevillean excitement.

After 20 minutes or so of reading from books and manuscripts, Burroughs unlimbered out of the chair and shambled back behind the curtains. He came forward again, almost on the instant, to announce that next would be a tape. "I do all the voices," he said. It was off-hand and cryptic, as far as he'd go, in terms of stage directions, and it brought forth a thick ripple of laughter. He disappeared instantly, and the crowd sat back and waited.

The tape turned out to be a collage. And, once again, much of it was wildly funny. Burroughs had snipped together, as it were, four newsy motifs. These consisted of a plane crash over Jones Beach, a densely officialese dispatch from the American forces in Vietnam, the last hours of Dutch Schultz' gangsterish *gotterdammerung* in a Newark hospital, and, a midwestern "man-with-the tin" vs. outlaw caper.

The taped Burroughs recited these snippets in alternating bursts, and tone colors, appropriate to each subject. His voice, for the plane crash, had the dumbshow flatness of all radio doomsday announcing; for Vietnam, it went muscular, laced with empty military bravado; for Dutch Schultz the style was high-pitched gangland rococo; and finally, for the sheriff-outlaw vignette, he employed what probably came easiest — a nasal shorthand toughness that evoked a frontier saloon milieu.

The audience took all this first as a challenge: would they dig the collage style, coming from a high priest of the school? And dig they surely did, judging from the sustained free laughter, some of it in boffo volume, that bounced off the small house's box shaped walls. There was good cheer enough, at the tape's finish; and when Burroughs once again slinked back on stage, he broke down to the extent of allowing a small crescent smile to appear on his otherwise tightly controlled features.

He resumed his jackknifed position, barking into the mike in a low, oddly pleasant key, for ten more minutes of reading. Bits and pieces from *Nova*, such as "Crab Nebula," a planetary cum sci-fi cum cybernetic jargon passage. This he offered in what could be called, mockingly, impassioned-science-sterility style. One other piece — a bizarrely funny "chase" sequence, cops and a clutch of homosexuals in a Chicago park — had the audience doing a slow bellyroll of laughter, from deep in their seats. (Burroughs, in his reading, kept on shifting his sources. Now he'd dip into one book, now into another. It was hard to tell which piece belonged where. This gave the illusion, odd and effective, of collages within collages. Or, literary Chinese boxes within boxes. Or even "fold-ins" within fold-ins, as Burroughs has called them.)

After an hour or so, Burroughs abruptly turned himself off. He gathered together his books, briefcase and clothing and, even though the audience applauded him warmly, succeeded in hiding any response, any of the charismatic pleasure that is a performer's right on the completion of a good gig. Without further ado, he slid behind the thick red curtains and was gone.

Outside in the lobby and street, there was much speculation as to a second performance. *Would he?* Burroughs could have done a double-header, with another SRO, no doubt of it. But when it was put to Alan S. Marlowe, the lanky young man who produced the reading for the American Theater for Poets, Inc., Marlowe looked piqued, even mildly pained. "He's not about to repeat . . . *He's* gone."

1966

John Simon: Gouging

To the Editors: John Simon, more scold than critic, debuts in *Commonweal* with an attack on Joe Papp's free Shakespeare that, far from being a model of fairness, is rather an example of critical obstinacy ripping at the seams to score points — points that in several instances are either gross, overstated or downright misinformed. (He is petty as well, as when he faults Papp for dropping the "u" in "Love's Labour's Lost.")

Complaint: "I see few things to recall with genuine pleasure. Perhaps no more than three . . ." Two of his pleasures relate to acting — Phillip Bosco's Angelo and Penny Fuller's Celia. He ignored Paul Stevens — a perceptive actor who, this season alone, performed beautifully in back-to-back roles — as Hector in "Troilus," and the dotty Don in "Love's Labor's Lost." (I stick with the program, on that spelling.) And, Roscoe Lee Browne — an exciting young actor who, despite his being a Negro (than which, according to Simon, nothing can be worse, for mounting a Shakespeare play), made of Ulysses, in "Troilus and Cressida," a character of subtle, probing and ironic commentary.

He butchers, elswhere, James Earl Jones (a Negro, after all) —

whereas others, unlike Simon, saw in Jones's Othello an actor of capability and power. There's his reference to Julie Harris's "baby-talking Ophelia" — to which one can only add, as a reminder to Simon, that "If Ophelia is your game, best you stay away from *most* 'Hamlets'." He speaks of Betty Henritze, "who has only to appear on stage for the aesthetic eye to boggle . . ." What is an "aesthetic" eye? Apparently, it is a Simon eye, more eye than the rest of us poor mortal playgoers are equipped with. Hence he, Simon, is capable of the boon (or is it hypercritical disease?) of overlook (as in overkill).

Complaint: "But the sad fact is that, through no fault of their own, Negro actors often lack even the rudiments of Standard American speech . . ." Ipso facto, they are death on Shakespeare's lines. A canard in face of the rise — albeit a slow rise, and few in number at present — of a new pool of capable Negro actors. Simon, as if to bite the tail of his Negro-actor bugaboo, goes on to endorse a judgment of painter Larry Rivers (and see how he, to score a point, invokes a kind of extraterritoriality in the arts — Rivers the painter, into Rivers the Shakespeare expert) who averred "I don't think putting Negro actors in white parts is possible — I don't see how you can keep life out of the stage."

The bilge of this is a double bilge. First, how many whiteys have played Othello? Second, and more significant, is Simon's clotted provinciality. (I speak not of Rivers, let him go back to his studio popping.) Simon is ethnic-blind on the Bard. The Habbima, no English speakers, do Shakespeare and stir an audience. Germans do him, the Russians do him. And he can be sure Kenya bushmen-turned-actors will do him when they are ready. Shakespeare is poetry cum life; hence his plays have, beyond the small critical umpiring of a Simon that would deny this, a kind of world patent that allows all people to — yes — fumble around in if it comes to that.

And there's this Simon complaint: "Thus a black Henry V runs counter to the lifelikeness of the play . . ." The critic here can infer nothing, because he knows nothing, of color as a living metaphor. Thus *he* cannot see that a black Henry, in our time and place, can be eminently right. And that the usually birdbrain *Cue,* in the instance of Simon's quoting it, can also be right when it invokes Bogalusa or Selma (re the crowd scenes in "Coriolanus"). *Lifelikeness,* the critic says. Well, let him take a taste of this slice, as told to me by a veteran actor who was witness to it. When black Robert Hooks as Henry made his "For England and Saint George" rally cry, at a Papp traveling Shakespeare performance in the Hell's Kitchen neighborhood, a bunch of local kids of spectrum colors came off their seats and joined

Henry's actor-horde across stage and into "battle." It was done with a kind of flair, my informant said, that had both audience and actors rocking with excitement. And that, my actor witness told me, was as pleasurable a piece of business as he'd seen in some years of both acting and playgoing.

Finally this Simon complaint, one which brings his physical, if not his aestheetic eye, into question: "With Mrs. Vaughan's Roman citizenry about four-fifths Negro, Rome became, clearly, the capital of Abyssinia . . ." My eye saw, at the outside, a one-for-one casting of Roman citizenry, black and white. Period. (And of course when Orson Welles did "Julius Caesar" in blackshirt costume, Rome became, clearly, the capital of Mussolini's fascist empire, not imperial Rome.)

There is need for prodding, constant need. Joseph Papp, for one thing, lavishes too much attention — and gelt that can be used to better advantage — on artifacts of production and trivia. The result is often Potemkin villages of Shakespeare. But anyone who has been at the Delacorte, felt the enormous pull that place hard by Belvedere castle has, knows to the heartbeat that New York is richer for this *mise en scene*. As for John Simon, his talent for the rip is surer than his talent for the sew.

1965

Yevgeny Yevtushenko: Dancing

Russian poetry has taken to the road in a theatrical sense — and has stirred an extraordinary audience response in the case of the United States, in "stick" towns like New York, Chicago, Pittsburgh and San Francisco. The two leading exemplars — Yevtushenko and Voznesensky — of the Russian school of poetry-as-recital did, in a way, no more than what comes naturally on home grounds. The forte — especially since Mayakovsky — of declamation, of "styling" poetry as an acted-out experience, was what gave the road shows their vibrancy. By and large, the American experience has been different — at least insofar as acted-out poetry goes. The closest example was of course Dylan Thomas — and he was an on-loan quantity at most. Earlier, and indeed, milder, examples were — Vachel Lindsay and Carl Sandburg. But the guitar, more than voice and theatrical effects, was the adjunct to the lines. The general rule could be put: whereas Russian poets, at least in recital, get in front of the poetry, American poets get behind it; even in the Read-Ins against the war in Vietnam, this basic style does not change. In any case, Yevtushenko and Voznesensky stirred U.S. poetry juices, as did, too,

Pablo Neruda, who in his own way is an exemplar, within the Spanish-speaking poetry tradition, of the same style of declamative verse. The contrast, finally, was dramatically on view when Voznesensky gave his New York recital; here the Russian and several American poets (who read translations) appeared together and the two styles got full, back-to-back display.

For Yevgeny Yevtushenko's reading last fall, the calls for tickets were coming into the 92nd Street YM/YWHA at a flood tide — not simply from regulars but from poetry lovers like *Time, Life* and *Newsweek*. Less than 700 seats, and just about all of Manhattan suddenly wanted in. Nor did it help much if you had a friend at the Russian Embassy, or knew so-and-so at the poet's New York publishing house, or had to be there to *cover* the reading. Best you could get, finally, was a ticket to closed-circuit in the art gallery, adjacent to the auditorium. After which you, and most others in the gallery, managed to slip through unguarded doors, ending up hugging the auditorium's dark mahogany walls for the reading.

After a half hour's delay, the reading was opened by Robert Lowell. A long table at stage right bristled with three microphones — before two of which sat a short, bearded interpreter, Edward L. Keenan, and the poet's English reader, Barry Boys, a handsome young actor. Lowell, tall, a little stooped, came to the stand-up microphone at stage center, and waited several seconds for the crowd to quiet down. Hesitant, and with an air of almost painful diffidence, he then began his remarks by alluding to Yevtushenko as a "world-wide cultural and political figure." One who had, Lowell continued, stood up for a number of causes, among them the right of poets to talk about politics. Lowell, now crossing his legs in splayed position, now drawing back from the microphone to score a point, referred in passing to his own political confrontation, offering in a fillip of irony the thought that "if you're Jane Austen, you can ignore Napoleonic wars if you want to."

The undercurrent of Lowell's brief introduction seemed more than just hands-across-the-border protocol. There was an edge to his words, as of hanging lightning; and the diffidence of delivery, the way he clasped and unclasped his hands, the steps he took (as if in pain) away and toward the microphone, all added to a taut portrait in motion of a middle-aged poet doing battle with himself — and in a way for the audience looking on — to find that means by which art and conscience merge and must stand. He made a small joke of what Yevtushenko had told him, that we must find a way "to get rid of the two black cats that stand in our paths." And he ended his remarks with what seemed an invocation: "I have a sense of a classical moment, of someone Greek standing in the wing, preferably a lady, telling us that the hour is one of danger. . . ." He hesitated again, pursed his mouth, put away the few scratch notes he held, notes that he referred to only once or twice. Robert Lowell then said the words, "I give you Yevgeny Yevtushenko," and he was off behind the curtains even before the Russian poet came forward.

That sense of foreboding, grave but gritty, gave way to a lighter mood, as Yevtushenko looked out at the crowd. He is tall — aged 33 — and carries himself with almost a bamboo give. He was wearing a gray polo shirt, which fell in a neat line below the waist of his gray-and-white striped trousers. For several seconds his eyes, which under the lights had a blue-gray brightness, did a darting dance to all sections of the hall.

Yevtushenko's sharp bony face was a polygraph — and remained so all evening long — of a whole range of inner tunes, and the one that registered first, as the crowd applauded and cheered him (some from their seats and many who were standing) was of a man happy for the greeting but impatient for the poetry. His first words were "Spasibo . . . thanks for coming," given in Russian, and then repeated by the translator, who had joined him at the microphone. When the crowd finally eased back in their seats, the poet reminded them that they might have had enough of speeches, during the last days of an election, and that in any case he was there for the poetry. Yevtushenko nodded to his reader who came forward from the table, while the poet and translator returned to it, and the evening was opened with Boys reading "Babi Yar" from manuscript.

No monument stands over Babi Yar
— the opening line, read by Boys in motionless calm, brought a soft ripple of recognition from the audience. Boys soon gained momentum, now weaving the lines, now drumming them across in a tone of anger. At the table, the poet cast a sharp eye through the hall. He shifted in his seat, or cupped his cheek tightly with his hand. And his angular face, lips pale and expressive, hair a finespun brown and cut short, was never quiescent. When Boys rang out the three jagged lines, "Hounded,/ spat on,/ slandered," a cold anger flickered across Yevtushenko's features. And when he came to the Anne Frank passage:

I seem to be
           Anne Frank
     transparent
               as a branch in April.

119

And I love.

> *And have no need of phrases.*

Yevtushenko's face lit up in innocence. At the end of the piece, the poet rose from his seat and exchanged places with Boys. He waited for the applause to fade and then recited "Babi Yar" in his own tongue, from memory. He employed a sharp, evenly paced declamative style, with stiff or sweeping gestures of the hands, the hands now and then molded into fists; and his lean body full of sway, as if to dance the muse. And the voice, pitched a little high and silvery, a voice of near-inexhaustible drive.

"Babi" was followed by "Sleep My Beloved," a lyric charged with soft lamentation, which Boys and the poet recited in near-hushed tones, drawing audible sighs here and there. Next came "Portrait of Childhood," which delineated a moment of violence, as well as of shame and disgust, out of the poet's youth (the violence of a gang of toughs beating up a stranger) — Yevtushenko giving the lines a passion that fell on the ears like blows. A lighter and broadly satiric mood came next, a sort of filmic Baedeker of international James Bonds called "Impressions of the Western Cinema." Here the poet drew rounds of laughs and some mock hissing as he ticked off a veritable rogues' gallery of spies (including ". . . the Chinese agent, the gaunt Li Chu"). Also "The City of Yes, the City of No," which described the poet's metaphorical journeying between the No city ("Each object there/sullenly scowls") and the Yes city (where "Any star in the sky/ just begs to fall into your hands") — the long and bitter "Colosseum," a monograph on man's cruelty from the sacrificial days of Rome to the more impersonal killing of the nuclear age ("Hallooers,/ hounders,/ from your safe seats/ you squeal/ at us to be fearless") — and the two ending poems, "Why Did You Do That?" and "Hail in Kharkov," the latter a joyous, Dylanesque evocation of falling sheets of hail, on one level, and a political rally cry (anti-Stalinist) on another. (The poem's theme: people who run from a storm — and people, the young in heart, who revel in it.) The English translations were those of George Reavey and Geoffrey Dutton, about half and half.

It was a two-hour set, with no intermission. And with a question period to come, announced by Yevtushenko with a broad grin, which could have been read as glee *plus* a small anxiety. What came out, and soon enough, was something in between the two — i.e., a waspish show of temper on Yevtushenko's part that was a surprise to some and worth laughs to others. The Q. and A. went this way: *Man* (from far back): "What did you think of Senator Robert Kennedy?"

120

(The poet met Kennedy, the day before, at the Senator's New York apartment.) *Poet* (crisply): "An interesting man. . . ." *Lady* (with cultivated voice): "What is your *phee*losophy of poetry?" (Question arrives as if by fourth-class mail.) *Poet* (blinking): "I write poetry — that is my *philosophy*." *Man* (cautiously): "What do you think of the poetry of Mao Tse-Tung?" (Audience laughs.) *Poet*: "Well — I hadn't thought. . . . Maybe the same as he thinks of mine." *Man*: "Would you read some more — Mandelstam, Pushkin . . . (this or that) poem of yours?" *Poet* (tartly): "I don't believe in dictation. Not from audiences, or elsewhere." *Man*: "What is your relationship with John Steinbeck?" *Poet*: "My relationship with him is — *private*." *Man*: "Is your pretty wife Galina, with you? We'd like to meet her.' *Poet* (quickly): "Maybe she wouldn't like to meet *you*." And more questions, some perhaps not so "loaded."

The crowd was a broad mix of New York's cultural *cognoscenti* — college youths of both the brushed and lank-haired variety, assistant English professor types, people from the stage and concert halls, several poets from above and below the 14th Street geographical line (i.e., the line that separates *avant* from establishment poets in terms of, say, style, if not necessarily politics) and a good number of older, and old-European types who in the main appeared to be getting the full drift of both the English and the Russian versions of the readings.

There was a sense all evening of the electricity of a happening, combined with the bravura (the latter a touch old-fashioned, and maybe even "square") of a one-man Chautauqua, Russian version. By contrast, our own readings, say from Richard Wilbur to Marianne Moore, are to Yevtushenko what a sleek GM car is to a troika. Soundless gear shifting, in one case; an earthy clobber of wheels on cobblestones, in the other. As to the poetry, the differences seem just as sharp. Where most established American poets are private, alienated and/or Ivy League-paced, Yevtushenko is open, didactic and full of immediacy. Put another way, our poets seem to "suffer" their art; Yevtushenko beards his and comes up with a song.

There is, of course, an affinity between the Russian poet and our own *avant*, those of the East Village explosion starting with Allen Ginsberg and Ferlinghetti. The *avant*, as is Yevtushenko, are attacking establishment mores, but pot rather than politics is the spur. (Vietnam excepted.) And only in Ferlinghetti, among the *avant*, do you get an approximation of Yevtushenko's lyricism, and then only fleetingly. As to the poems' lasting or literary qualities, this was almost beside the point. On one level alone, the performing one, he is a poet to see.   1967

Leroi Jones: Fire-Eating

The poet-exile of the ghettoed canyon, LeRoi Jones, returned to New York's East Village for a one-night stand. He returned as if catapulted out of a bottle with a skull-and-crossbones label that read: "Black Magic, Danger!" The scene was the 1930's style Village Theater, on Second Avenue and Sixth Street, a former Loew's palace that bombed on a steady diet of Hollywood flicks in recent years. Conversely, there has been a healthy box-office rise, with such live programs as folk rock evenings, fund-raising affairs for Diggers and hippie defense, and a while back a series of Tuesday evenings of Tim Leary-Trips style LSD celebrations.

For his Monday-night gig, Jones drew an only-fair crowd of about 500. But it was an alert and chancy audience for whom Jones's three-ply threat as a poet, playwright and Black Power polemicist had the distinctly loaded promise of "Telling it like it is." For openers there was a rambling introduction by a young man named Yousef Washington who sported a zebra-striped and hip-length shirt and a pancaked hat, both items contributing to a sense of the new African chic. A black silver-tipped cane which Yousef twirled now and then, like a vaudeville bit of old, was an added (and somehow jarringly off image) prop. He kept up a teasing, mock-friendly patter. His gleaming teeth were one part smile, one part menace, as he told the audience in a sing-song: "Of course, this is an *integrated* evening. And we'll *see* what this evening does to you — to your integrated stance." Yousef brought on a quintet of youngsters called The Jihad — who in piping voices did a mix of recitation and song, material by Jones, that had the effect of Black Power agit-prop. Grade school Division.

It was naive, touching and funny all in one. Not presumably what the impresario had intended — but you don't get Red Guard dynamics, let alone takeover, on any odd night.

After yet another of the evening's many delays, during which the stage would remain empty, causing loud chatter and stomping of feet by several, Jones finally made his gliding entrance. He was un-smiling, a short man of taut and spare build, who moved to the microphone a bit gingerly. Decked, as were most of the cast, in African shirt and hat, Jones was like an actor trying on two roles simultaneously. And basically warring ones. He was the youthful (age 32), serious poet, honing his lines with a chanting rhythm. And with the taste of them, if not always the sense, most sweet. He was too the smiter of Establishment idols. The platform politico, or executioner-prophet, announcing white decline, plague and death. The latter themes were expected ones, from poems that Jones said were "from 1964 to the present."

They spoke, many of them, of white man's rapacity, black man's midnight beauty ("We are the beautiful people with African imaginations"). One of his pieces, a scissoring diatribe against "the dead Jew . . . Jesus," seemed to gut the audience into a visceral silence. The tribal Jews — and by extension, the whole Western nexus — were charged with stealing their arithmetic from the Arabs, among other things. At which point a thought arose: Were the Jihad toddlers using, in their Newark classrooms, Arab or Western style "three R's"? The poet stuck additional pins into the mush, as he sees it, that is Whitey — in such lines as "He owes you everything, even his life" and "Smash their jelly white faces." On a more particular note, Jones lashed out at President Johnson (and various members of his family), Roy Wilkins as an archetype of tokenism, and black studs who bed down with white chicks.(Black gets consumed, body and soul, in the latter poems. Which may or may not be a symptom of Jones's private hangup — married for years to a white middle-class Jew, and now it's splitsville.) His delivery was measured and sure; and his tonal color — flatly angry, now dry and mocking, now sinuous-soft — evoked fire, ice and even glints of pathos.

The ice stirred the audience most — stirred them to loud if not always happy applause, but also random hissing and an occasional needling ("Why don't you sing it, 'Roi?") from pockets of discontent, here and there on the orchestra floor.

During the lengthy intermission, there was a choose-up of sides, sort of, taking place in the lobby. The crowd was made up of East Village hippies, avant garde poets and jazzmen, Uptown intellectuals, and black-men-white-gal couples. The remarks were mostly cool, but private feelings did get said, despite the exterior of cool. Polar moods were neatly capsuled by poet-jinn Allen Ginsberg ("You can strain out the hate, you still have a gifted writer") and poet-Fug, Tuli Kupferberg ("Anti-Semitism is a sick joke, and he wears it full"). Others took more time to decide — which made them in a way the grays of the evening.

The second half opened with four silken-voiced male singers, whose hymn-like offerings ("The chain gang hour," someone jibed) were at odds with Jones's earlier fire-and-brimstone. After this came the last, and probably most effective, set. Jones read several more short poems, the intermission lull bringing on, if anything, an increasing vigor. He then did a short new play called "Home on the Range," with Jones handling all the roles. The piece was Ionesco-like in its spareness, but had its own special flavor of black humor, in both senses of the phrase. Briefly, a spade tummler-spoiler packing a rod, pops in on a typical family scene — mother, father, daughter and son are watching television [genus Americanus TV-us]. The spade has robbery in mind, but first he wants to *communicate* with his victims. They of course are bombed, near catatonic in their pop-eyed thralldom to the box. All they can offer, to the spade's increasing bafflement ("You mothers, what kind of language is *that!*," he cries), is a zapped roundelay of vaguely Germanic gutturals — sheer bits and pieces of grunting, groaning non-talk. Jones, who was a German-language major at school, did the WASPish family in with a flair that could have been borrowed from Prof. Irwin Corey. But the final moments were of a piece with Jonses's own Mau-Maued thralldom: a gung-ho mob of blacks (arsonists? revolutionists?) break in on the family and bust the place wide open, as the robber announces doom to the audience. Presumably, an all-white audience.

"Home" was mordantly funny, until the deus ex machina of revenge was rolled in. And the audience responded in kind. For 20 minutes or so, the laughs and bellyrolls came like water from an open faucet, only to sputter down to bubbly half-chuckles of air, followed by a dry spout of all-silence — as Jones screamed out the last lines. It was a long evening, from 8:30 to near-midnight, curtain to curtain. And more than a routine one, even for Second Avenue. One noticed that the black-and-white couples — of which there were a dozen or more, held hands just as stoutly, on the way out, as when they arrived.

1966

Hart Crane: Bridge Vaulting

They came on a Saturday at midnight to pay tribute to Hart Crane and his bridge; about 75 all told who had to overcome barred entrances from the Manhattan side, and who walked the planked overpass to a spot approximately midway between those two gothic towers Crane sang of; they came for readings sponsored by a new quarterly called *Writer's Forum* whose young editors showed an inspired sense of what poetry's all about.

The barriers — call them reefs in an age of bombast, in a city constipated with private hangups and public problems — made the affair so much more targeted. Biggest one, of course, was the ceaseless rush of rubber below; of traffic scuttling both ways on the bridge Crane, and Tom Wolfe, and Maxwell Anderson sang in the past. That bridge with its spider webs of roped steel, with its twin towers of surpassing beauty at both ends; that bridge which has fought a losing battle of engulfment.

And yet, as the poetry lovers scaled the barriers, landing on the planked walk, and proceeded a half-mile or so to the middle of the bridge, all must have felt the rapture of those arches; walking through them in the lights of the kleigs as if through hanging portals of a great promise. The eternal Brooklyn Bridge, the engulfed Bridge. At 12:30 a.m., by the big Paramount clock tower on the Brooklyn side, the readings were begun with some opening words by a *Writer's Forum* editor. He said, "We're here to honor the memory of Hart Crane; born in 1899, died in 1932; poet and a suicide, off the stern of a cruise ship, in the Caribbean."

Short, bitter valedictory. But a nuance of proud challenge came across, in the way the young editor sang the phrase, "a suicide." The poet's battle for truth, for beauty, is enviable as it is sacrificial, in the final sense. And Crane's bridge lives beyond mortality, his own and ours. The editor introduced a stocky, sun-burnished (all those re-hearsals, in the park) member of Joseph Papp's traveling Shakespeare company, George Stauch, who had walked the bridge fresh from a performance in "Taming of the Shrew," at the Baruch Playground. Stauch, little daunted by the loud woosh of rubber from below, read in a sharp booming voice sections from Crane's "To Brooklyn Bridge" and "The Harbour Dawn ".

> "O harp and altar, of the fury fused,
> (How could mere toil align thy choiring strings!)
> Terrific threshold of the prophet's pledge,
> Prayer of pariah, and the lover's cry, —"

The silent, gliding journey of scows on the river; the wink of the warning light on the Woolworth Building's spire; the steady amber glow from Liberty's lofted torch, in the upper bay, lent a certain decor and orchestration to Crane's rolling, charged lines. They spoke of time, and the river, and the bridge, and the bind of souls — and Crane's lines rang brass, flowed fire — lived again for a new, mostly young audience — lived again over the obstinate woosh and echo of the rubber below. The eternal Brooklyn Bridge, the engulfed Brooklyn Bridge.

Later on others read from their own work; H. L. Bibbs, from a long city-funky piece, lines that sang with a jazzy beat; Will Inman who offered his own tribute to the bridge, and a second poem in

125

memory of Tom Wolfe; and Sylvia Berry who put spinach behind a normally soft delivery, in her reading of four short "city songs" (as she called her pieces). The crowd for the most part sat on the wood planks in a heaped, skedaddled mass; ears cocked firm, quick with laughter (for Bibbs's lines); a Saturday midnight encampment that Crane's ghost could, and no doubt did, relish.

One young man, somber and thick in beard, turned the readings into a private happening; he vaulted onto a narrow catwalk, walked 15 feet or so to the north edge; he stood there for some minutes, peered out far and wide, in a silent and shadowed contemplation of the river; of the sweep of buildings, the nighttime cityscape on Manhattan's east shoulder. He stood there, unnoticed by most, until one of the editors spied him. He was called back, and he came. You know, you'll be spotted for sure up there, the editor said; and the cops'll be down on us (*Writer's Forum's* editors didn't feel they had to ask for, and so they proceeded without, a permit.) Sure, sure; the bridge Alpinist agreed; but you really can't get Crane at his core, what with all that racket from below. And I had this air in me; I had to get up there, and *see it all* . . . you know.

The editor nodded; he promised that next time they'd ask the Mayor or Bridge Commissioner, or whomever for a 2-hour hiatus on all traffic; so that readings would be readings, and let the rubber go elsewhere for those 2 short hours. POETS AT WORK, the Alpinist suggested; PLEASE EXCUSE THE DETOUR. The two smiled and rejoined the group. Shortly after the readings came to an end, at 1:40 a.m. And back they all went, through those twin Roebling archways. Most towards Manhattan, the others to the Brooklyn shore.

1966

Norman Mailer: Shadow Boxing

I was present at your Carnegie Hall evening, one among what I'd guess was about 1000 people, a turnout that any poet in good standing would no doubt be very pleased with. Now, I was saddened, when I wasn't annoyed, at the persistent feeling that you were not measuring up to the poet; that your singing was not fresh, was indeed heavy with the weight of old things to say, edgy with the overuse of a private weapon against evils that touch us all. An example of the latter was your rehash of what is at once a startling and gauche inspiration — e.g., that President Kennedy prove his awareness, his concern, by moving his family to New York City at the moment when nuclear disaster threatens. Thus would the President, by implication, prove his awareness of the moral imperative of life over death; and, by extension, he would prove he had the courage to act out the fatality of death, if the national "will" called for it, even at the price of death for his own family.

Not only is this a reductio ad absurdum on a level with "my father is braver than your father"; it is a shabby and simplistic grab for the gimmickry of political dialog over the harder and more heroic and perhaps quieter need for honesty in that same dialog. The buffoonery of the proposal forces a straight if harsh answer: that all of us know, the President knows, and perhaps only Norman Mailer doesn't know, that the bomb that is meant for New York City is the bomb that is meant for Washington, too; and the only conclusion one can come to is that Mailer's need for private malediction over heroic and sometimes quiet honesty is a need he cannot resist.

The private wrangle, cloaked in a kind of Dr. Caligari shock topicality, is what disturbed me most. You have narrowed our politics, even our fears, into a safe corner of parochialism. Parochialism plus mysticism plus demonology. It is a three-way parlay that permits you the luxury of talking, of writing, on and on about cancer, about existentialism, about orgasm. This is your politics of the hour. When a lady in the audience asked you, in effect, "Well sir, what are your views on integration, on unions — what is there, if anything, that you stand for . . ." — you blinked once in a peeve, blinked a second time, and then, archly, and with an annoyed shrug, you said: "I have no view on integration, or unions . . ." And you went from there into the quick dive, the retreat, of your cancer, etc.

Moments earlier I had tried one of my own when I asked from the floor: "Had you read about the slaying of a young union leader in New Jersey, a man who was gunned down by a pair of hoods, a rub-out that was clearly tied to the victim's anti-Hoffa activities?" (And can you name anything, this side of Bobby's and the FBI's vendetta, more existential than said activities?) You refused to field that one, shrugging it off with a dull "I didn't read about that — I can't follow 'em all." And I, caught under the steamroller of your "30 seconds, and no speeches" dictum to your audience, had no chance to push the line of my question, which was: "Were you not just a little to the rear of events; a little bit enmeshed in the fantasy of involvement, over the reality of it?" It can be said that unlike Lenny Bruce, who eats of the very heart of the poisoned artichoke, you are being merely the gourmet who diddles the leaves and thinks

127

he's had the feast.

You ended your evening with your much-advertised "existential caper," which you dangled before the audience like a piece of forbidden fruit. Though I believe the coinage was more showbiz than existential, the caper did have its small point. Several were straggling toward the exits. You were waiting for them to clear out before doing your reading. It was at that moment that a tense, sweet-faced young miss, no more than in her mid-teens, who was standing boldly in the aisle about ten feet from me, took a sharp stance facing you, and called out: "But must you read it?" The miracle acoustics of this hall carried her voice to the farthest reaches, carried it with the nuances of caring and urgency she so clearly felt. You did hear her, and again when she repeated: "Must you read it — really?" And you read your piece, your poem, and it did have a certain air of scatology, and it made no difference. The young miss, by way of an intuitive caring, was correct.

1963

P.E.N. Congress: Disengaging

The cold war is dead. This appeared to be the main theme, although not the official one, of the 34th International P.E.N. Congress, which held forth at New York University's Loeb auditorium in a full week of panel discussions, floor talks and social exchanges from July 12-18. Among the more than 600 delegates and guests from all parts of the globe, the concern for what could only be called the *human condition* took precedence over any formal literary or political creed. And the tinkling ice in the drinks at the many after-panel affairs, melted no faster than the last thin layers of reserve the writers, poets, essayists and playwrights may have carried into the Loeb, in the first hours off the planes and ships that brought them here.

It was a powerful theme — one of prophecy and intuitive rightness, wherein the minds and hearts of many of the most creative and advanced were being bared in a kind of many-sided litmus of what mankind yearns for next. In a sense the theme was bared when Rosamond Lehmann of England's P.E.N. asked for a writers' dialogue of 20 minutes of silence, a silence that presumably would allow refuge from the discord and clogged special pleading of politics per se. It was bared in another way in Madame Victoria Ocampo's (of Argentina's P.E.N.) lament that illiteracy among the masses was a sad fact that must concern writers, an illiteracy in the case of Latin America and Spain that saw millions of peasants responding to the "passion of Garcia Lorca without being able to divine the literary meaning of his poetry."

It was bared in more direct ways from the floor — once, in a dramatic set-to between two delegates who were the most lionized of the Congress. These were the Chilean poet Pablo Neruda; and the Italian novelist, Ignazio Silone. The novelist had chided the poet for not aligning himself with P.E.N.'s protest over the arrest and jailing of the Russian writers, Andrei Sinyavsky and Yuli M. Daniel. The exchange was brief and unresolved. But here again the principle of the writer's commitment to the primacy of his art over any ideological imperative was affirmed on both sides. Silone's strong meshing of the theme clearly gave no comfort to the solitaries in both polar "camps"—such as the East German delegate who merely muttered from his seat, on the one hand, and the florid and linguistically flush South Vietnamese delegate who in a kind of supercharged French tried to bring the Loeb brick walls down with a speech on the "bloodbath of communism," on the other. In the case of the Marshal Ky partisan, what he succeeded in doing was to unite a hitherto undertow consensus into an open expression of what could only be described as disgust. One tense and white-faced lady from England strode the aisle at the finish of his speech, and with a look of killing impertinence at the back of the neck of the now seated Vietnamese, said to a colleague who had joined her, "That man is a freak and how he got into this hall to peddle such obscenities is a mystery and an insult." Once again, a baring of the theme, the kings of ideology are dead! And the cool or now and then angry repetition of it, from the floor or over clinking glasses of bubbly, was no more nor less than an open-ended affirmation of the writer's new-old rule of creativity and dissent in an environment of danger. The danger, as P.E.N. president Arthur Miller had warned at an earlier panel, of "nuclear smashup in our future."

It was bared in more poignant and private ways—as in the case of the large delegation of Writers in Exile, a group of 30 or so who no doubt wore their identity badges as ensigns of a brave protest, at first, only to find an increasingly thickening mist of indifference (where it wasn't one of outright unfriendliness) rising between them and the vast majority of the Congress members. Most of these writers, from such countries as Estonia, Latvia, Poland and Ukrainia, walked the Loeb auditorium and corridors like some permanent floating camp of a lost exodus, the passion and rationale of their cause (yesterday's anti-Stalinism, mostly) having long since been used up. "You can go back if you want to, that's the essence of it," one American writer said to a sad-faced Latvian of the W.I.E. delegation, at one of the last of the social gatherings. The affair (hosted by the Poetry Society of America) was the mildest of the weeklong series, and between bites of his biscuit and quaffs of his gin-laced punch, the exile could only offer a shoulder-shrugging pantomime of nays that loomed large as a 1960's version of Chekhovian sighs for lost cherry orchards.

The cold war carcass was again on enigmatic display, in the shaggy and heavy-footed person of Valeriy Tarsis, who took the floor to deliver himself of a rambling elegy on the subject of Tarsis; an elegy so shot through with gems of self-flagellation ("I am a corpse" "I am bored with life"), that few could find it in them to express anything more than an awkward pity. And the theme was bared in the P.E.N. "Writers-in-Prison Committee" report, a report that showed those joining lines of the cold war where politics becomes the jailer of the writer. Cases cited were repressive acts against authors by the Turkish, Ukrainian Soviet, Portuguese and Peking China governments, and the fines totaling $45,000 against Catalan writers centered in Barcelona. An American delegate, who privately voiced his uneasiness over what he termed "Our antiseptic posture at this Congress," took the floor to remind the committee of the arrest, trial and imminent jailing of writer-publisher Ralph Ginzburg.

The Congress social interludes were perhaps most potent of all, the cold war ghost being far more absent at these affairs than any Banquo at Macbeth's table. Nowhere was this felt more keenly than at the large United Nations reception. When the ghost did surface among the hundreds of shifting, densely gemutlich conversations, the drift away from it was sure to be swift and final. The delegates were busy imbibing long cool drinks, hopping from one hot tray of hors d'oeuvres to another, pursuing all the while the rushing hare of new dialogues, insights and friendships. One American observer found himself in a decathlon talk on U.S. politics, with two fast-drinking but clear-thinking P.E.N. members from Jamaica, as honing and stimulating a talk as he could remember. Oddly enough the American was mostly on the attack, vis-a-vis President Johnson's civil rights and Vietnam policies, one of the Jamaicans (who had interviewed the President for a home chain of newspapers, shortly after the 1965 inaugural) saying that Johnson had struck him as a "remarkably forceful man who wanted to do the right thing"; and that the U.S. "must come out of the civil rights battle a stronger nation, or the whole world is the loser"; and that Vietnam "was a mouse in the President's throat, one he'll eventually cough up, for he wants his place in history" — the American in rebuttal saying the "rights battles are more than negated by what we are doing in Vietnam"; and that "it is as if the American people, through the office of the Chief Executive, were laying down and playing dead before the military"; and that as to history, President Johnson "may well have lost his niche on Vietnam alone." To and fro it went, the ambrosia of the gins-and-tonics, the sharply refracted early-evening light (a kind of slate-orange) from the East River, and the background chorus of a hundred-fold other conversations, all contributing to that aura of power Shelley might have had in mind when he announced that "poets are the unacknowledged legislators of the world". And yet, at the bottom of the last drink before parting, there was the sense that "unacknowledged" was still the operative word (alas).

Of the four main topics in the weeklong Congress none roused the delegates more than the first: *The Writer in the Electronic Age.* There was a whiff that here too was a species of the cold war — one that involved writers, poets and novelists in a headon tilt with the new expertise of cybernetics, and with the movers and shakers of what *Time* has called the "Knowledge Industry." The chairman for this panel was Marshall McLuhan, an evanescently cool spinner of instant communications theories that presaged, among other rosy developments, the "end of the printing press." McLuhan, on his first wind alone, startled some foreign writers with his prediction that literature would be outmoded by the electronic revolution and "writers will increasingly move from the ivory tower to the control tower." Hungary's Ivan Boldizsar said he felt "Knocked out, stunned." "But then," he added, "I felt knocked out 30 years ago when I read Oswald Spengler's *Decline of the West*." Recovery was sure and by mid-afternoon there was a mounting barrage from the floor—a barrage that accented the creative role of the writer, no matter the *form* of the communications — and a barrage that had McLuhan listening hard ("Probably for the first time anywhere," jibed one American delegate) and, to put it in racetrack argot, even "iffing-off" some of his bets. Among those who drew applause was delegate Paul Tabori from England when he said, "Machines can be just as stupid as people." And there was the off-mike remark of an American news-paperman that seemed to say it all: "It's not so much 'The medium is the message,' as (in the case say of most of TV) 'The message is phony.'" All in all McLuhan's communications punch cards were being sent back to the dais with more than a few marks, folds, tears and staples — the P.E.N. delegates and others were that rough with them!

One's mental camera was always at the ready, and of the scores of vignettes that were snapped, some that stand out are: The tall, ramrod slim West German delegate, tightly put together in dinner attire and cummerbund, offering at the Museum of Modern Art's collation for P.E.N., a string of faintly gutteral Yankeeisms that charmed you, at the same time that it made you, almost, tick at the ears. The Indian lady, part of a large delegation, who from the floor extended a warm invitation to the Congress, saying that when it next convened in India, she was sure every delegate would appreciate the beauties of Mysore (and leaving unsaid any word of India's poverty). The marathon appearances of playwright Elmer Rice, who at age 76 was a study in health and sunny skin tone that defied all geriatric norms. The gentle, white-haired Irish poet, Austin Clark, who in the middle of some light strokes of reminiscences on Pound and Joyce, introduced his fiercely black-bearded son, Dardis, as "Dublin's answer to your beatniks." The 10-member Yugoslavia delegation, mixing as easily with Western writers as with Eastern, employing a two-way-stretch bon homie not so freely come by among other Easterners. And two of the Yugoslavs, late for a session at Loeb, tracking past the tired hedges of Washington Square Park — in a headlong rush — as if from out of a copse to meet up with Partisans at spot "X". The burly delegate from Iceland, Matthias Johannessen (editor of the largest newspaper), who after getting an opinion on "Your leading poets," sat up straight and said, "I'm glad you put Allen Ginsberg on your list" — a pause — "Do you think you can arrange an interview for me?" (A good journalese ploy, and one did give it a try. But poet Ginsberg was p-r Ginsberg at that moment, waiting around in Washington to testify before a Senate committee on narcotics.) The glee with which another Indian delegate dismissed "Annie Get Your Gun," which seemed to be the consensus among the 250 or more foreign delegates who accepted invitations. He said: "Many never came back for the second part, it was much too busy, noisy and brash." And the Loeb roomful of 75 or so poets — from all meridians of place and style — many reading from their work in brief turns — the room smokefilled and crowded — but the lines coming over in a variety of foreign-language music, at once captivating and rare.

And the U.S.'s own pair of V.I.W.'s (Very Important Writers), Arthur Miller and Saul Bellow, both age 51. Miller, lanky and open-shirted, moving around, or sitting on the dais, always in a cloud of cigarette-pipe-or-cigar-induced bluegray smoke. Tieless and tireless. Making his points, rejoinders and summations with the care, if not always the brevity, of a well-constructed play passage. And at a press session — responding to the query "Why is the avant-garde group, such as Ginsberg-and-Company, absent from this Congress?" with a flash look of bewilderment. And Saul Bellow, hair thinning and going to white. Giving his anti-literary-establishment speech, with its jabs at the flanks of some (un-named) fellow-delegates present, in a style of "This hurts me more than it does you." Jabs building to haymakers, as in: "The University therefore is producing quantities of literary intellectuals who teach, write or go into publishing houses. So far as I can see this new group, greatly influenced by the modern classics, by Joyce, Proust, Eliot, Lawrence, Gide, Valery, etc., have done little more than convert these classics into other forms of discourse, translating imagination into opinion, or art into cognitions. What they do is to put it all differently. They redescribe everything, usually making it less accessible. For feeling or response they substitute acts of comprehension. . . ." To some pained expressions, as in the wearing of a tight collar, in the audience.

Most of the 450 foreign writers, if not sated with the abundance of topicality and social amenity, were pretty much physically spent, by the time the last day rolled around. In concert they had been shuttled from and back to Loeb more than a dozen times, big gray buses with cool airflow and large tinted windows being their moving lookout on a Manhattan scene that constantly absorbed them. Also, they had spied out places on their own, places mentioned to them by American delegates, or by those among them who had made their own discoveries. Greenwich Village was the most visited, first, because of its closeness to Loeb, and second, because many of the foreign writers wanted to check out bookshops like the Eighth Street and Marboro's (and Scribner's, Brentano's and Gotham Book Mart further uptown) to see if American editions of their books were being stocked. When the answer was yes, a request for better display would usually follow, tempting one tart clerk at Eighth Street to observe, "They bugged us the same way local authors bug us." For icing on the social cake, there were several small dinner parties, strung out in a daily raffle, and hosted, among others, by Edward Albee, Barbara Tuchman, Lenore G. Marshall, Ken Giniger and Elizabeth Janeway. And for the *pink* icing, available to just about all the foreign delegates, there was the "day in the country" outings held on the Sunday before departure, on three Long Island estates. The plethora of goodies made one writer say, "Parties given by rich sponsors, nouveau or otherwise, who like to collect authors, I am always ready for. What gave me a shock, and a pleasant shock, was to be wined and dined by *authors* who are rich."

Not the least reason for the Congress's success was the almost 100% absence of J. Edgar Hoover and State Department shimmies in allowing unrestricted passage into the States of all and sundry delegates—the exception being writers from Cuba, Peking China, Albania, North Korea and North Vietnam, a ban no doubt matched by the latter governments' own. That the U.S.S.R. refused to field even their promised "six observers" was an absence they alone will have to measure.

1966

Langston Hughes: Strutting

Intermediate School 201 in East Harlem is a new plant with an excellent auditorium and stage — a kind of reduced version of New York University's Loeb building with curving brick walls and wide-open sight lines. Physical shape aside, the school has been involved in an administration hassle from the start, Board of Education and parents having sharp differences on how it should be run.

In a Saturday evening visit to the school, where the New Heritage Repertory Theater was offering an evening of Negro poetry *cum* dramatic readings, no whisper of the dispute was heard. (Prompting the thought: Art is where it's at; life trails behind.) Rather the opposite — for two hours the mood was strictly upbeat among the mixed audience of around 100, consisting of neighborhood parents and students, teachers from the school, and several Harlem actors, poets and dancers. The production had the umbrella title *Hip, Black and Angry,* and that too is where it's at.

Director Roger Furman, an energetic man who doubled in the lights booth, and who made a curtain plea for continued support of the Repertory's efforts, had arranged the readings in a series of quick-paced tableaux. The acting company of around a dozen made fast costume changes, from one piece to the next, and presented each poem with an eye (and ear) to its dramatic, or sardonic, or even political overtones. The result in sum was an evening of heightened theater impact, most of which gave added urgency to the poems. Now and then, and perhaps inevitably, a particular piece seemed to be put across too crisply — and speedily — with the result that the poet's private mood would suffer from the meditative level of the printed page, to the more open and "showy" level of the theatrical. That some of this can be improved goes without saying — the company after all is underexposed, what with but four performances under its belt. And that poetry-into-drama is an alchemy that doesn't always "work," even given the best conditions, goes too without saying.

The opener was a short piece by LeRoi Jones—a kind of chanting rally cry with the company snake dancing off-stage, and through the audience, and back on stage again. Later came a five-part recital of a poem from Africa — with a proud motif of negritude in the lines, "I am a Negro/black as the depths of Africa . . ." Emphasis was on the urban scene, and here the group did its best work, capturing in sharp focus the seesaw moods of the ghetto: love-despair-humor-anger. Most of the urban pieces were by Langston Hughes and Gwendolyn Brooks. Mr. Hughes's light, airy tone, and Miss Brooks's glints of poignancy and glossy wry commentary, were among the evening's chief pleasures.

Comic tour de force of the program was a piece called "Soul Food," a breezy jape on all the clichés of the black man's dietary weaknesses. The company recited the piece while doing a spoof of an 18th-century minuet — each of the three men and three women done up in elegant lacy frills and their movements as elegantly outrageous. "Thirty pounds of pigfeet,/*soul food*" one of them would mince; "Forty pounds of fatback,/*soul food*," the partner would answer.

All in all, upward of a dozen poets were represented. Music from a sound track, and several weaved-in choreographic turns, gave the program a variety fullness. The performers were Emily Banks, John Byrd, Barbara Carter, Danielle Haynes; and Yusef Inman, Charles Jenkins, Janet Leader, Henry Miller, Ethel Parks, Doris Washington and Joseph Washington, Jr. An insert in the program read: "This performance is dedicated to the memory of Langston Hughes."

In answer to our query, Mr. Furman gave the Repertory's goal as "very quiet LeRoi Jones." He explained that last year's Black Arts Repertory (directed by Jones), with its emphasis on "hate Whitey," had met with resistance in Harlem. Furman said, "Our audiences resent the mother-epithet thing on stage. They want art. The other they can hear on street corners."

1967

Sholom Aleichem: Laughing

The real long-hot-summer's insurrection is taking place in Central Park on almost any night and Sunday afternoons — starting north from Harlem Meer (Negro and Spanish dance evenings) to the middle reaches at Delacorte Theater (Joseph Papp's free Shakespeare evening and Jewish, Negro and Puerto Rican poetry-folk song programs on open-date Mondays) to the southerly open reaches of Sheep Meadow (for those massive *and* high-quality Philharmonic music-ins, and the Sunday be-ins, smoke-ins and what's-next-ins) to the still further south Wollman Skating Rink (where jazz and folk of the pantheon are heard at Rheingold beer prices) and doubling back over the whole park, athlete-wise (for week-end bike-ins with no vehicular presence more threatening than a baby pram or horse-drawn hansom). A marathon of alfresco pleasure, most all of it free.

On a recent Monday at the Delacorte the program was "An Evening of Yiddish Poetry and Folk Music" and one's feeling was: You don't have to be Jewish to enjoy — or, conversely, the whole world's Jewish in this area of the arts. The foibles and folk wisdom of a Sholom Aleichem, to cite one part of the program, translate with ease to all conditions and climes. The material partakes of an irreducible human capacity for self-jesting, basic pride and rapport among one's fellows that goes beyond national or ethnic barriers.

This mood of universality was put across trimly and professionally. And the setting — the magic backdrop of Belvedere pond, the high stony crag upon which the castle sits, the hazy orange three-quarter moon above, and the nestling intimacy of an S.R.O. crowd of 2,300 in the oatmeal bowl theater — was a par excellence treat. The evening opened with readings from several Yiddish poets — Yuri Suhl, Itzik Manger, Martin Birnbaum, Moishe Nadir and Itzik Feffer among them — read from sitting position on high stools by Suhl, Birnbaum, Michael Gorrin and Zelda Lerner — and translated by James Ray, in what turned out to be the only strictly Anglo-Saxon accent of the evening — albeit an accent that swayed like the bulrushes with a dip here for humor, a firming there for pride of being and a tensing in a third place for loss or suffering.

Covered were such topics as sweat-shops, the futility of war (specifically, the Czar's war), labor in its best and worst guises, the ghetto, and Jews as a timeless and wandering people. Most moving of the dozen or so poems, judging from the rapt involvement of the audience, was a traditional epic by Feffer called *Ich Bin a Yid*, which recounted in stately cadence Jewish woe through the ages — from Torquemada on through Hitler. The title line motif ("From under swords my sigh was heard,/ *I am a Jew. . . .*") became a capsule of triumph over adversity, as if no loss or calumny would ever erase inner identity. Moishe Nadir's *Mein Leben* or *My Life* was on the other hand a quizzical and humorous other side of the coin: "Give me your life," says the Czar. "It's not mine to give," comes the answer. "It is God's. War or no war, it depends on direct orders from Herr Jehovah."

The verse was followed by folk songs, performed by Martha Schlamme, and in Yiddish song, Miss Schlamme is *baleboste* (or "boss"). She was blonde-topped, and dressed in a near-mini fishnet orange gown, all of which made a blend with that misty orange moon, the moon peeking on intimately from a nine o'clock position to the stage. Assisted by Mordechai Sheinkman on piano, Miss Schlamme offered comic songs from the East European *shtetl*, songs of adolescent love and family set pieces that are steeped in tradition. Although hers is not a big voice, she nevertheless had a rousing effect on the audience, an effect not unlike a Melina Mercouri of Yiddish folk. Miss Schlamme was followed by a reading in English of Sholom Aleichem's "The Clock That Struck Thirteen," brought to life by Miss Lerner with clarity and high humor.

Last on the bill was a concert reading of "A Tale of Chelm," from *The World of Sholom Aleichem* by Arnold Perl. And here the evening was in full orbit — out in that serene and heady and improbable high ozone of the Yiddish author's comic-serious genius. "Why is the ocean salty?" asks Mendele the book peddler of Rabbi David. "You don't know?" The Rabbi responds, in a tone of chagrin. "No." "Because of the thousands of herring that swim there." And this joke from The Melamed, or village teacher: "If I were the czar I'd be richer than the czar. Why? I'd do a little teaching on the side."

The meaty part of "A Tale of Chelm" had to do with The Melamed going to town to buy a goat—"Not just any goat, but a *female* goat," his wife Rifkele warns — so that the couple could enjoy a gourmet treat of cheese blintzes. What happened on the way and back was a tour of folk humor ("Canterbury Tales East"?) that brought waves of laughter every step. Will Lee in the teacher role and Zelda Lerner as the wife were particularly good. James Ray as Mendele, Michael Gorrin as Rabbi David and Martha Schlamme as The Goatseller completed the cast.

The full program was directed by Bernard Gersten — who everywhere coaxed rather than pushed his material and principals. Itche Goldberg was literary adviser and the lighting — always a strong plus in Delacorte productions — was by Martin Aronstein.

1967

Street Hamlet: Jiving

The success of the New York Shakespeare Festival's open-air mod *Hamlet*, which is touring the neighborhoods these summer nights, can probably be measured in inverse ratio to the unhappiness of purists who watch it. The latter (and there were some at the performance I caught) can be spied out by that certain grimace or swiveling of the head, as if from pain, that occurs when, say, Claudius gets a cream pie in the face; or Hamlet pops gaily into bed with Gertrude — proving that in street theater, anyway, direct action on the Oedipus front is its own reward. There are lots more such high-jinks — Ophelia strutting the boards in mini-sequins dress and jet-set tic, two spadecat jivers playing the roles of "Rosencraft" and "Gilderstone," a platoon of GI-dressed, pistol-toting guards in a royal court that's like a penitentiary, and so on. Director Joseph Papp's conceit, overall, can be said to work well, much in the way good subway graffiti works.

Hamlet is played by a lithe and bouncing Cleavon Little, a young black actor who, far from worrying over that "pale cast of thought" that so hobbles the Dane, has at his role with an athletic celerity, an open-voiced bravado, that jolts the audience to the funny bone. From his first entrance — in boxing shorts and sneakers — Little is a walking, jumping and skipping farrago of passion eased by Olson-Johnson tomfoolery, poetry bearded by street-corner minstrelsy and high philosophy reined in by blasts of horse sense. When Hamlet-Little is asked what he reads, he looks out owlishly through horn rims with no glass, and replies after a delicious pause: "Ebony, baby." That moment is the witching moment, not of Hamlet's ominous ghost but of revved-up parody under an open sky, with a neighborhood crowd you can play on for all the comic stops.

The production is boiled down to about an hour and a half, with no intermission. I saw it in Washington Square Park, where it was snugly mounted between the austere arch and the waterless fountain. Bongo regulars, hippie boy and/or girl watchers, Village and New York University lit'ry folk, political pollsters and activists, mothers with kids, kids with mothers — all seemed to be responding to some piece of the action. Rock music (by Galt MacDermot) for the bongo boys; lots of jive "business" for the hippie; crisply delivered monologues for the lit'ry; bits of Black Power references for the activist; Pop wardrobe for the mothers; and balloons and toy pistols for the kids.

Sets, stage, lighting and sound open out from, or are fed by, four flatbed trucks. These pack up and move to new locations, directly after each performance. About 800 folding chairs are made available. (They were filled and there were about 1,000 standees. All free, of course.) Joseph Papp hopes to raise enough money to take the *Hamlet* to Philadelphia, Newark, Washington and Baltimore, on the completion of its New York run. It's a bubbling natural for that long-hot-summer's night.

1968

4 Four Arts

Film

Shorthairs from a Festival

*Film festivals, like mini nations at the United Nations, pro-
liferate around the world. An estimated 300, many at colleges
and town halls, unwound their merry way last year. New
York's Lincoln Center festival is — or at least, should be —
among the most prestigious. Still, a festival annual is no
guarantee, ipso facto, of good-art-in-the-can. Too often, the
shadow of an important event, with its mimicry of fashion and
expertise, is taken for the substance of good and original
cinema. Here's a report on a Lincoln Centre annual.*

You can get a bad case of film poisoning with no effort at
all, at an eleven-day run like the New York Film Festival. The
Fourth annual had 24 major screenings, and more than twice
that number of shorter film fare, at barnlike 2,800-seat
Philharmonic Hall. Nor was it a matter of good, mediocre
or bad. The press screenings brought together a hardcore of
30 or 40 working critics, and twice that number who were
vaguely "covering" the Festival, and twice again that number
who were there for the same reason the climber finds himself
at the Alpine foothills: *The films were there.* You had this mix
of bread-and-butter film specialists, busy and buzzing film
hangers-on, and the largest group of all — the compulsive
"Gotta show up" crowd for whom a film festival is a new
kind of cultural beehive with the drones of the hour far in the
majority.

At that, it took something in the nature of monastic vows
to have to come in out of the fine, dappled sunlight of Philharmonic Hall's glass-enclosed promenade, and blink away in
a dark void for three sets of films each day. And the comments after each film were like paternosters from the faithful.
— "X is not up to previous work, but he's still miles beyond
Y" . . . "Could be A's best yet, glory be his cinematic soul"
. . . "The camera is a holy instrument, when handled by a
cinematographer like Z." Examples in shorthand of the

mystique of the verbal, the intramural feedback of *words words words* that is endemic to these affairs. Each film was the mere skin of the art, to be peeled away strip by fine strip, finally to come to the very core of the thing — one's own showboating comments, which were more often than not prolix and fevered.

The irony of course is that an art form which stands or falls on the concretely visual, on the sweep and depth of image, storyline, acting and directing, gets taken out of its visual context and is made to wallow in a sea of verbiage. This was especially true in the after-film press interviews — with such as Agnes Varda, Pier Pasolini, Ivan Passer, Milos Forman and Alain Resnais. Invariably in these bullish sessions the film-makers would reach points of "No comment" or non-committal shrugs when faced with questions on style, comparisons with other directors, or similar formalistic hair-splittings — which of course was the only possible response (short of camping) for those whose "textual" frame of reference, of necessity, was the product of their labor: *the film itself*. As to storekeeper items like "How much—?" "Who financed — ?" and "How long did it take — ?", our flash thought was, "How much — ?" "Who financed — ?" and "How long did it take — ?" to make the jump over an ocean and have to face *such* questions.

The Festival directors tapped their own special area of escalation — the press kits were thicker than ever and the side-bar events (27 in all, mostly panels) were far more numerous than in the past. The events under the umbrella of "The Independent Film," were clearly a sop to an increasing coterie loosely called the film "Underground," whose mixed media, expanding cinema and film happenings — all of which critic John Gruen had chicly (and cheekily) labeled products of the "Combine Generation," which sounds like a cultural Mafia — are in one sense both anti-film and at loggerheads with the Festival's own esthetic guideline. More is more — not "Less is more" — was no doubt the guiding principle. This of course is the classic working out of one section of Hopkinson's Law — and the predictable route of the next festival will be that of a deepening maze in which the selected main-arena films can get lost.

Escalation on the social front saw the opening night gala moved, from Philharmonic Hall's narrow promenade, to the more roomy and elegant New York State Theater digs, across from the fountain. Black ties and Madison Avenue gowns were the rule — and from the plebian New York champagne served at the Third, there was a switch to bonded whiskies and steamy hors d'oeuvres. The midnight mood, after the well-received humor and professionalism of the Czech entry, Forman's "Loves Of a Blonde," was out of kilter — to the extent that the hyperthyroid din of rock 'n' roll deadened that earlier mood. The shuddering noise was the work of a five-piece combo, whose name might well have been, "The Nouvelle Rave." The combo had the film intelligentsia backing away, to State's out-of-doors promenade, where the latter could at least get off some rocks (of film comment) of their own, without being drowned in electronic sound. For most of the others, the big attraction was Andy Warhol's latest party bon bon, a severe-looking and stringy young blonde named Nico. Dressed — or undressed — in an all-out transparent lace mini, V-string of shocking turquoise, bra of tiny size and dark hue, Nico shook the night away to continuous sets of rock. It was a part-Warhol, part-jet-set bash, with all holds barred.

Andy, incidentally, was alert as ever for the main chance, using Festival week as a likely time-launch for his "8 hours of the new epic film by Andy Warhol." The epic was of course "The Chelsea Girls" (which has made bundles of loot around the country since), and was premiered at the 42nd Street Film-Makers' Cinematheque, the den-showcase of the underground located in the Wurlitzer Building basement. "Girls" is actually a four-hour job, which makes use of two parallel screens, i.e., two images are projected side by side — in a mix of color and black and white, usually. At one of the Festival panels (topic, Expanded Cinema), the very "in" Henry Geldzahler broke into his own moderating, to announce to the audience: "Last night I saw Andy Warhol's new film, which I urge all of you to see. Sitting in the small dark hall, I felt not like a moviegoer, but like an early Christian in the underground, watching the new marvel." And having ourselves seen 50 minutes of the epic, at which point a saturation had set in, we wanted to answer: "We felt like a Roman without a vote, verily."

The overall note was a happier one than at past Lincoln Center Festivals — at least for management, and at the box-office. There was a cluster of "Sold-Outs," most of them with no prior touting or damning from the press. And there was the lady critic from a weekly journal who, when asked her opinion of "Loves Of a Blonde," and a second Czech entry called "Intimate Lighting," replied tartly: "Oh yes, check and double-check!" Apparently the ticket-buyers out there had not heard.

Addenda. At the last or Fifth annual — September, 1967 — the film buffs' talkathon was thick as ever. Nor did much that was new surface. There was an emphasis on Vietnam — American, French and English film-makers shafting, for the most part, America's involvement. These off-the-headline films caused what little stir there was. The touch-and-go argument was that polemics, no matter the passion behind them, was not necessarily art. However the case, the festival directors should get points for chancing topicality, and chancing it far more than in the past. For the rest, there was a much-anticipated Rossellini entry, "The Private Life of Louis XIV," which turned out to be an original work for French TV (of all things), and "arty" as it was slow-moving; a highly-praised Swedish color film, Bo Widerberg's "Elvira Madigan," visually stunning but lightweight in impact; and Gillo Pontecorvo's brilliant "The Battle of Algiers," an Italian-made para-documentary (our label) that harkened back to the "Open City" realism of the 40s. There was scads more — 30 or so major films, and an equal number of shorts. It should be noted that less than a handful have been picked up for commercial showing — and if that's not the name of the festival game, what is? Or to put it another way — is the film festival trip necessary? Look in on the Sixth, next September, and polish up your specs, in the meantime.

1968

Cleopastrami

The Alex North overture to the costliest film ever made, *Cleopatra,* is a bombast of brass and drumrolls that near-deafens the ear. As the four-hour non-odyssey wends its mighty, weary, and empty way to a finis, that opening musical splurge is truly the handle for all that follows. To put it another way: If one is supposed to feel a flutter of excitement and anticipation, one had also best pay heed to the small voice within that warns of timidity — timidity before the authority of the $40 million that was lavished on the film, timidity before the grinding publicity that has attended the film, timidity before the not-so-private saga of its two main actors-principals.

Brass, then, is the dominant note. A brass that tries to drown out the aching meretriciousness of its parts; its brazen-poor screenplay; its wildly disjointed acting; its ABC of nursery room history capering. Deep in the second hour of *Cleo*, there is a confrontation between Antony (Richard Burton) and Brutus (Kenneth Haigh). The highly forgettable script makes recall of the dialog more than a chore. At any rate, the gist of the face-off is Antony's rude charge that Brutus possesses more head (honor, ideas, etc.) than heart (courage, battle-field glory, etc.). And Brutus, stung by Antony's goading, reminds the latter that no doubt he, Antony, would be first to sever that head.

This note too is suggestive of the way *Cleo* was made — the emphasis on lumpy and disjointed "actions," the clamor of cinematic showiness, in place of believable characterization and the flow and drive of history. In that four-hour captivity, there is little for the mind to do. As for the eye and ear, they grow increasingly weary, become increasingly opaque. The IBM that was needed to tote up the cost of this film — its juicy actors' fees, lavish decor, marching land armies, clashing sea armadas, blasting score, "there's no tomorrow" choreography — that IBM is again needed to tote up its astronomic mistakes.

The first, and cruelest, mistake is Elizabeth Taylor. She's the Liz T Doll — a stupidly expensive product, overblown as a gourd with old wine, parading a fake carnality that would barely (for all its fleshiness) pass muster in a middle-income bordello. She can neither act, nor even *camp* the role. And she's the fulcrum of legions of other mistakes. In the Caesar-Cleo half, she is witless (where Cleo must be teasing, guileful) and randy (where Cleo must be sex incarnate). This forces Rex Harrison (as Caesar) to play elegant standup comic — he is Englishman on holiday, out of his milieu, a toga-clad conqueror toying with an overaged Lolita. In the Antony-Cleo half, the descent is complete. Liz is the rakehell from Scarsdale, who *bickers* her journeyman into defeat. She might as well be telling noble Antony that the mortgagers have to be fought off, the TV-Rumpus room is not big enough, the Volks must be replaced with a Caddy, the Joneses have to be topped. And poor Burton, for all his charisma, is the 5:09-er who loses job, expense account, battle wardrobe — after which he kills himself in the toolshed with his trusty pruning shears. Not Antony and Cleopatra on the upper Nile, but Elizabeth and Richard in upper Scarsdale.

There's the narrator — an off-screen voice that tells no story, but parrots chunks of history, daddy-o in the nursery sorting those ABC blocks for all untutored moviegoers. And the four battle scenes — done in a kind of crawling pantomime — and in toto not more than a patch on Eisenstein's Battle on the Ice *(Nevsky)*, Olivier's Battle at Agincourt *(Henry V)*, Griffith's Civil War battle *(Birth of a Nation)*. There's the double mishmash of Joseph Mankiewicz's directing and screenplay. He's très predictable. His metronomic intercuttings — a parlous love scene here *(and don't spare the incense, boys!)*, a phantom battle there — are embarrassingly old hat.

Pluses there are — Roddy McDowall's epicene, jackal-and-fox Octavian; Kenneth Haigh's brief turns as Brutus; Hume Cronyn's sturdy, if a bit square, Sosigenes; the Forum plottings, which manage to echo, if only lightly, the director's earlier, black-and-white *Julius Caesar* (script by W. Shakespeare) — but hardly $40 million's worth. And spectacle — Cleo's golden barge; her entrance into Rome atop a four-story basalt Sphinx; Alexander's translucent tomb — what of *that?* Well that, dear fans, is 20th Century's contribution to our packaging revolution. (Never mind about content, *dig* that Todd-AO wraparound screen, and all that color.) Which you'll help write off — at $2.50-to-$5.50 per.

NY *Times'* Bosley Crowther, long resented by West Coast film bigs, on the iffy premise that he's tough on the home product, had the critical set all shook up with his molasses raves. The consensus: His obsessive notices were more like *mea culpas* than reviews.

1964

We're Doing It to the Russians

In my filmgoing salad days, when Eisenstein and the 42nd Street Stanley were the avant (and when directors Truffaut and Chabrol were presumably exchanging furtive looks at choice French postcard art in the *lycée* hallroom), the Russians had a stock character for satirizing Our Way of Life: the American crooner. The model for this, as I remember, was old Rudy Vallee. It was in retrospect a forced target.

Today, with the likes of such as *Taras Bulba*, we are doing it to them. But solemnly and unconsciously. In epic form and in Eastman color.

Taras Bulba is a Hollywood version of a Russian Eastern. Gogol's fine romantic tale (Sainte-Beuve called it a Cossack *Iliad*) reduced to junkyard situations of good guys vs. bad guys, not at the pass but on the steppe. Except for the quality of horsemanship, which if not 100 proof Cossack is at least 90 proof Hollywood, all the rest is about as true to its source as a George Lincoln Rockwell treatment of the Hebrews in the desert.

But that is a minor point, you don't look for history in a brothel. The casting, there's something you have to see to believe! When Tony Curtis (as Andrey, son of Taras, and a novitiate at the big Kiev seminary) is told by his father superior to "Remove your cassock and prostrate yourself," the Ebbets Field leer of boyish hurt Tony gives the holy man is enough to dim every candle in St. Basil's (hard by the Kremlin).

And when Tony makes love to a young Polish princess (she of an enemy clan, the Poles are occupiers) you have a transplant of Romeo-Juliet on the steppes with Tony-Romeo drooling such pearls as: "You are not of my peoples' enemies; you are of my kind; you are my love." Which lines, if not exactly designed to ease East-West tensions, is not going to do for Russo-Polish tensions either.

But the real thespian prize is Tony's jousting with papa Bulba, played by (who else?) Yul Brynner. Tony, his marcelled black hair and eyebrows showing on screen like neon velvet, calling out "Papa . . ." (in froggy voice, offkey as an untuned bull fiddle) "Papa . . ." and again "Papa," at a reunion outside the Bulba hutment. And then Bulba son and père wrasslin' each other to the ground, in one of about a half dozen (I lost count) "No *paaapa*, the seminary did not make me a softie" grapples.

And Yul, skulking round in orange parachute-silk drawers, drawers wide and billowy as the very steppes, skintight skull from which hangs a goodly yard of sausaged hair, handlebars that droop deep as a ravine; and Yul giving out with the "Zaporoshi-*eeee*" (the goods) war-cry against the Polish *hetman* (the bads); well, Yul is Yul; from the old Cossack *shtetl*. As vodka-drinkin', barbecued-meat-eatin', on-hossback-fightin' an hombre as ever came off the Eastern range. And there's Sam Wanamakerski, a sort of chicken-colonel Cossack fire-eater second only to Yul, with the wildest goosiest set of face whiskers this side of a Smith Bros. coughdrops box. Sam in drawers less billowy than Yul's, but with a war-cry that's wilder by at least a half dozen *"eee*'s." And to round out the blini-in-thick-cream (from Chasen's) cast, watch for the only true Russian *sabra* on the lot, Vladimir Sokoloff, who plays an elder statesman Cossack. Central casting or no, Vladimir beards the enemy with all the foxy bravura of old Klim Voroshilov sabering down General Kornilov and the Whites.

Of course it can be said, as a cop-out, that Hollywood has been too busy mining (and you can make that "ruining," and not lose the sense) the Bible (*King of K's, Barabbas, Sodom and Gomorrah*) to get into the mood of mining remoter areas of costume splash. The Russian scene is a particular toughie: you know how enigma-cloaked they are to us even today, for all that we boast as fine a corps of hot-stove Kremlinologists as exists west of the Wall.

True, they've been in the precinct before. There was a few seasons ago that hero-sandwich of a *The Brothers Karamazov*, where the kidney-pool scripters didn't so much do it to the Russians as to Dostoevsky. But what could they do with 'em, going way back to the 15th century, with all that Cossack plumbing on the outside?

All told, *Taras* is a two-hour bowl of cinema borscht that revenges us for the way the Russky filmmakers used to put down our singing son of Sigma Hiya.

Item: Gold Medal is out with a paperback, what they call an "original," taken from the Waldo Salt-Karl Tunberg movie treatment (for which Salt-Tunberg are supposed to have received 75 thou' each) of *Taras Bulba*. The literary fence is one Robert W. Krepps. The man has, as they say at Lindy's, plenty *chutzpah*. (He also did it to *El Cid*, from the movie of the same name, for Gold Medal.)

1963

Entertainment on Grub Street

New York's 42nd Street, with its jutting marquees and floating humanity, is the oldest established night-time debauch in the nation. The three main ingredients are sex, food on the fly, movies to cruise by. The sex — if that is the word — is usually of two kinds. There is the adolescent, ride-a-motorbike kind. There is the cruising, right-out-of-queendom kind. Food is quickie franks or hamburgers, wolfed down from the perpendicular, at the never-dark and ever-menacing Grant's. Flying pizza from the King of Pizza; and three or four other emporiums of the King's ilk. Instant spaghetti and meatballs, from Romeo's. Which leaves the movies, the street's main industry.

The crown among 42nd Street movies is the re-release cheapie. It comes in a never ending round. To qualify for a second, or third, or fourth (and more) go round, it seems that a re-release must be randy, violent or guttery (three-in-one is best), or it simply won't make it on this showcase street. The habitué who comes charging into the area is a man (and woman) who *knows*, for he possesses an antenna as sensitive as a roach's for those three-in-ones. Recently five of these 42nd Street type re-releases succeeded one another in the several palaces, succeeded one another like a poor drunk's runaway belch. Easily the randiest of the five was an opus called "Cape Fear." It is also the most voracious of the re-releases, having appeared on the 42nd Street midway at least a dozen times. And it will blink back on again, at any moment.

What is the special savor (like the broth of "Macbeth's" three witches!) of a 42nd Street re-release? Let us start with *Cue*, the glazed-paper weekly with capsule brain: "CAPE FEAR (105 m. Univ. '62) Gregory Peck, Robert Mitchum, Polly Bergen in melodrama of terror. Taut, tense, frightening as revengful ex-convict plans terrorization of lawyer's family, rape of his wife and daughter. Pretty harrowing; you can decide *(sic)* if this is entertainment. Well plotted, well acted."

151

I saw it, and I decided that Hollywood is a bankrupt non-art with but one road to travel. It can only go cheaper, more salacious, more violent, more mechanically slick. Move the IBM's and univacs into the studios wholesale. Feed the machine right amounts of gore, sleazy voyeurism, pseudo social comment, brass knuckles violence and presto!, out comes a film like "Cape Fear." The future is already here.

(A few seasons back the English, dear chaps, bombed "Fear" with one word. They called it, "Nasty." They asked for 161 cuts, an all-time high that must have creased the brow of its cheapie producer with *pride*, as well as worry. And while we abhor censorship, we read them clear on this one.)

There is a deadly monotony of sleaziness in "Cape Fear." The feeling all the way is that it's all happening in your own head during a bad siege of nightmares. A released convict comes to a lakeside town and swears vengeance on the man "who helped send me up." Robert Mitchum plays the con with golemlike relentlessness. His target is a local pillar, a small-town lawyer with an attractive wife and juicy-pubescent daughter. Gregory Peck is the lawyer, as white in virtue as Mitchum is black in villainy.

The gore sifts out of the movie can by the yard, like mixed concrete out of those platoons of trucks at Manhattan building sites. Our hero's model shaggy dog goes to a howling death in the moonlight. All signs point to strychnine poisoning. No proof of course that golem did the dastard act. Gotta keep the suspense moving! He next scores with the town's sex-drifter, in a pickup scene. After they exchange talents in a cheapjack hotel, Mitchum gives the girl a merciless beating. The scene is sicknik, bloody and gratuitous. Indeed, Krafft-Ebing is a Fig-Newtons-And-Tea party next to it.

Mitchum's main target is the daughter, and the voyeurism comes on strongest here. One scene will suffice. Lawyer, wife and girl are scrubbing down their Criss Craft at the lakeside dock. Remember, the three have sworn to remain inseparable in face of a stalking enemy. Hollywood motivation!; off go the parents, and curlykins is left to scrub away on her own. Our Little Miss is dressed in very tight playsuit. Her cupiddy rump and pubescent breasts are nothing if not sculptured.

Along comes golem out of the shadows. And it used to be, along comes Rin Tin Tin about here. But no; the two are on camera alone. Despite dozens of holidayers (Georgia back-woods division) tooling around in dozens of Criss Crafts . . . the two are *alone*. Golem leers hard at Miss Muffet. He leers for what seems like five minutes. And our little Miss Purina *agonizes* at her core, plays out her part of mental rape and trauma under a blazing sun. Hollywood style. Camera key-holed sharply. From his leer, to her tortured eyes. His leer, her rump. His leer, her breasts.

In the patois of the Rat Pack, a ring a ding of a scene. But only a sampler of the Nouvelle Obscene footage to come.

Nothing graces the IBM talent more than its lusting after the holy grail of social significance. "Cape Fear's" entire cast, good guys and blackguard alike, are walking Bill of Rights experts. The paragon is the town police chief. At one point he says: "I can't bag him (Mitchum) on a 'vag' charge, as long as he has some dough on him." And later: "He has his rights same as you and me, as long as he commits no open crime." To which he adds, archly: "No one wants to change that." (It all sounded fine, but a voice that quavers with exclamation, is a suspicious voice.)

So it went for those 105 minutes, a filmic stew of choice morsels right off the Hollywood & Vine compost heap. And the four others, to change metaphors, wore the same gory hairshirt. They were: "Psycho," "A Walk on the Wild Side," "Experiment in Terror," and "Sweet Bird of Youth." (Of the latter it need only be said that T. Williams, for a change, gets his dream factory comeuppance. They murdered not only his play, but his play's children, his poetry.)

Finally, how curious (or is it?) that both "Fear" and "Terror" are tuned in on exactly alike worlds of apelike sex cum free-form violence. In "Terror" a killer-man shadows two nubile sisters (one of whom could be skipping-rope companion to our earlier quarry) in a 115-minute epic. He's going for the double jugular, nothing less. And mostly by telephone, yet. The gimmick of gimmicks here is the killer's voice, an instrument of throaty wheezing that can only be described as baroque-hysterical. No telephone call can ever be the same after this film. Not even if you own one of those pink Princess jobs. *Movies Are Buggier Than Ever.*

1965

Diary

It didn't hurt, prestige-wise, to lead off with a European hailed Russian "Hamlet." Nor did it hurt, social-wise, that Fest directors Amos Vogel and Richard Roud," . . . suit(ing) the action to the word," had a nice midnight spread of champagne and fish-eye wedges waiting — the post-movie bit — for the culturati. The scene was box-shaped, handsome, neo-Italianate Philharmonic Hall — the event, the 2nd New York Flm Festival.

The opening night crowd, many in black-tie dress, entered from the broad flagstone concourse. Some tarried for a few moments, taking in the many-colored (though hardly many-splendored) fountain as it made middling jet streams and swooshing-wet noises on the balmy night air. The small fountain, to make a comparison, is to Chicago's Buckingham Memorial, what a mouse is to an elephant . . . And film fests are occasions for comparisons — everyone, but everyone, having their esthetic yardsticks at the ready.

Inside the gold, maroon and blue Hall there was a buzz of anticipation. The meat-end of the crowd consisted of USSR cultural forces, various Big Figures from the Lincoln Center, cultural and diplomatic supernumeraries, and platoons of well-heeled and just-plain filmniks. After the lights were doused, a small opening speech was given by Center President, William Schuman. Schuman, after some nice words for Russian Director, Grigori Kozintsev, of whom he said in substance, "He sure knows his Shakespeare," then introduced Kozintsev who in a rough seesaw English said he was most happy to be there — 400 years after, and in honor of, the Bard.

The single Russian entry proved to be a handsomely produced wide-screen, black and white — English titles, some distorted — big though not "Alexander Nevsky" — big score by Dimitri Shostakovich — that all in all had the audience happily receptive . . . Both to the film and the flowing champagne afterward. Actually the huge and plushly appointed Philharmonic Hall seemed a bit barnlike for the viewing of non-Hollywood flicks — but Kozintsev's came across by the sheer authority of its outdoorsy, bravura qualities.

Clearly he knows his Eisenstein; his sets were lavish, his decor rich in period flavor. Additionally, his use of massed forces, i.e., splurging 100 armed men where 10 would do; as well as the big sweep of his camera in those outdoors are further evidence of the Eisenstein (" Nevsky," "Peter the Great") stamp. And yet there were critical barbs — overheard during the grape and fish-eyes, and in the morning press. *Times* loved it; *Trib* didn't.

In sum the nos said it cut no new path in the "Hamlet" canon. Oliver's cropped up, offered as a titbit among the "knowing," and that — for us — was the evening's non sequitur, sequin styled. For — as we wanted to say, but didn't — what would "Larry" have done with the Peter role, if he were doing *that* film in English? Just so the Hamlet of Innokenti Smoktunovski — e.g., lacking a "native" handle, he stoically and a bit stolidly had climbed the endless ladder of the soliloquies — the confrontations — and reached, if not the Olivier valhalla, then a good lofty Slavic perch of his own.

In point of fact there were three or four scenes, at the least, that showed beyond cavil that Mr. Schuman's brief on Kozintsev was more than an opening-night rite. *Item.* Hamlet's verbal fencing over Polonius' remains, where the prince drew not only Claudius into his skein of mockery, but the entire court of ancients and hangers-on as well. The scene was broad, shafting — a brilliant set piece of youth (verity) putting down cranky age (corruption, dotage). *Item.* Laertes hot return to the fortress-palace, to avenge his father's death — a stealthy, shadowy, wordless tour de force of insurrectionary take-over. *Item.* The Ophelia mad, and death scenes — where the expected, and choked up, mood of obsequy-sorrow was, in this case, turned into a richly peopled, handsomely cadenced film choreography.

On the second night the Fest directors chose what they no doubt felt was the high for a U.S. film: The Columbia produced, Sidney Lumet directed "Fail Safe." There was no grape on this occasion, though Amos Vogel gave a small prefilm curtain talk which, in effect, was an endorsement of the film's "serious" purpose. But what came through to us was serious doubt, in terms of both editorial content and filmic drama. Lumet, in hot pursuit of a Big Statement on the menace of nuclear war by accident, only succeeded in deepening the mystique of inevitability. Over and over again there was a pattern of dead-sober and characterless speechmaking . . . "Those failed machines can destroy us all" etc. This gauzy curtain of platform hyperbole tended to numb the senses to what is, in a most profound way, a human and not a machine problem. Stanley Kubrick, who is to Lumet what a wasp is to a fly, knew the distinction well — and thus gave us in "Strangelove" a black comedy that allowed for no cop-out on the part of the panic pushers.

Clearly the big bug is in the format itself — that new rash of films adapted from such fictions as Burdick-Wheeler's "Fail Safe," Fletcher Knebel's "Seven Days in May," Richard Condon's "Manchurian Candidate" and others. All of these qualify as sci fi pol (science fiction politics) soporifics at best. And as muddy, best-selling, doomsday-touting tracts at worst. The flaw of course is that they fail to see people, for the forest of univac symbols they work in. The mainstreams of life, for the digital swamps they reside in. Lumet's treatment — with its crypto-stagey closeups, its TV-like domestic vignettes(while the world itself teeters), its simplistic manos a manos, President to Premier hot-line exchanges — compounded the fiction all the way. And most disturbing of all — for us — was the second-night audience's doom-mood, as juxtaposed with the opening night's brightness and vivacity.

Spirits lifted later in the week, with Jean-Luc Godard's "Band of Angels." Not a major film next to say his "Breathless," it nevertheless confirmed Godard's high standing in the (by now) receding Nouvelle Vague. His method abjures realism, for the more poetic, and shifting, film impressionism that somehow calls up Debussy's tone poems. At its best "Band" captivated. The touching "images," the quick changes of mood — from youthful highjinks, to sudden inklings of loss — all gave additional proof of a film stylist at his nearpeak. Of course the mannerisms still intrude — those little coltish bits that have no relation to, and in fact diddle at the heart of the script. Like a hophead and his needle. Godard apparently can't shake himself loose from this coy and cloying habit. But the fault is minor, and he's clearly an original.

The Hollywood jinx continued with "Lilith," shown on the first Saturday eve of the Fest. This one was directed by Robert Rossen, from his own screenplay based on the J. R. Salamanca novel. The program note read, " 'Lillith' is set on the shifting frontier between sanity and madness. Lilith is a girl with an uncontrollable hunger for love . . ." And so on. Now, what actually took place on screen was a tortuous and torpor-inducing 112 minuttes of uncontrollable hunger—on Rossen's part — to make an artsy film. He succeeded — what with upside-down camera shots, wooded glens saturated in mist, pseudo "Hiroshima Mon Amour" sex clinches. As to the story — Lilith's so-called hunger, and how she traps a young sanitorium orderly, who is her later undoing — all in the plush setting of an expensive Maryland booby hatch — this was in practice a movie bomb made out of equal parts of TV shock "drama," documentary style freudianisms, and fruity non-acting bits that went almost as far back as the John Gilbert long-silent-look days of anxious tradgedy. (Warren Beatty, in the orderly role, easily forged ahead of such pros as Greg Peck, Mel Ferrer, Burt Lancaster, in the long-silent-look derby.) The only salvage note, and a small one, was that Jean Seberg as Lilith continued to show some talent as an actress, and considerable talent as a body.

Probable high point was the back-to-back screening of two films by veteran Luis Bunuel — two that spanned a 33-year career. It was the second Monday eve, a kind of 7th-inning-stretch moment. And though taste and enthusiasm, even among aficionados, were beginning to jade a little under successive viewings, this was not the case with Bunuel. Fact is the crowds gave his duo the heartiest approval — along with the "Hamlet" — of any; a tribute to both him and the Fest idea at its best.

The films were "L'Age d'Ore," his first — a 65-minute masterpiece of screen surrealism; and his latest and perhaps most finished work, Bunuel's adaptation of Mirabeau's famous novel "Diary of a Chambermaid," starring simmering Jeanne Moreau. "L'Age" was (is) total cinema — a collage that combined broad social satire, and personal revelation in stunning measure. The mood was antic, and scathing, by turns. Bunuel's inventiveness was endless. His camera "tricks," or fixes, kept on building — those small surreal film explosions that seemed to be occuring not on a screen, but in the viewer's own recall of some private dreamworld. "Diary" by contrast was almost straight filmmaking — but the air of brooding menace, the sudden splurges of violence, the shafting social comment (as well as political comment; in this instance, on the nationalist-fascist Leon Daudet movement, in France of the Twenties) — all of these typical Bunuel stamps were present, and were fused beautifully. As we say, this could be his most finished film.

Of the 15 or more we viewed, several besides the above were worth a mention. From Sweden came the work of a new, young director named Jorn Donner — a dandy little amoral tale of free-love confronted by — and here's the switch — the need for a relationship at once more conjugal, and less free. Aptly called "To Love," this one starred the dark, Ingmar Bergman sizzler, Harriet Andersson, in the role of the young widow who wants to remain free; and the vital young Polish star of "Ashes and Diamonds," Zbigniew Cybulski as her lover. From England, a powerful short war drama called "King and Country" — the depiction of a World War I, behind the lines atrocity — a young soldier "deserts," is tried and found guilty, and shot — all of this directed brilliantly, sparely by Hollywood expatriate Joseph Losey. Tom Courtenay, as the Cockney private, the victim; and Dick Bogarde as the Captain who defends him, came through with performances no less brilliant. This black and white film was, beyond a doubt, the "shake-up" entry and sleeper of the entire Fest. And from Italy, a sprawling tale in the Antonioni mode called "Before the Revolution." As it turned out, the director Bernardo Bertolucci was the stripling — at age 23 — of the Fest. His talents are large, though quite often the hand, but not the heart of the Antonioni style was at work. The young director, as with practically all the Italian social realists, showed he could handle a broad pulsing theme — e.g., the decline of an aristocratic milieu, under the impact of radical social cum political changes.

Finally a quick report on two others which for us earned the prize — in one, two order — of "Well-mounted Bores." The first was a soap-opera-lavish color film of the Cyrano stripe, "Cyrano et d'Artagnan," directed by 75-year-old Abel Gance, and played by the two leads, Jose Ferrer (the Cyrano, natch) and Jean-Pierre Cassel, with the brio of the Marx Brothers doing a masque on the old Academy of Music stage. Which isn't bad, except that Gance was playing it for real. The second was "Mahanagar" or "The Great City," directed by the renowned filmmaker from India, Satyajit Ray — and we're in a definite minority, but for us Ray is a master of the obvious, a titanic builder of filmic monotony. We took 90 minutes of this 125-minute tale (set apparently in Calcutta and relating, according to the program note the trials of a ". . . young wife, who takes the daring step of going out to work in the shocking world of lipstick and sunglasses . . ."), and then found ourselves squirming out of the darkened Philharmonic Hall — a bit guiltily — but with a ringing inner voice telling us, "Enough — enough — enough."

Certain overall impressions stand out. The Film Festival idea for New York is, unequivocally, a valid one, though we'd have expected more films of an experimental nature. At that the 1964 programs were a sharp improvement over last year's when, presumably, the Fest directors sat still while filmmakers palmed off some very bottom-of-the-can films. We'd question too whether the travertine-and-glass showcase that is Philharmonic Hall is the best spot for such festivals. Too often the bigness of the affair engendered a nightly atmosphere of social, rather than artistic "inness." Not that there was a paucity of the latter spirit. Indeed the very atmosphere of the showcase brought on, conversely, all manner of cinema academics cum mystifiers. For example Godard was on hand for a mass press interview and, as happened with other directors as well, in the same glass and sun-saturated setting, he was bumped often and severely by windy, très silly "in" questions; on "form," "motivational purity," "the rhythm of dissonance" and more; bits and pieces out of the portmanteau of the growing film literati.

A certain amount of this, perhaps, is good. Or at worst, indifferent bad. But film should not be handmaidened to the ornately social, or the obfuscatingly verbal. And Philharmonic Hall seemed to engender both in excess. The danger is of course that the "packaging" stuns the senses to what's inside — the film itself. Film pups can magically — $4.00-a-ticket, US-premier magically — become sudden handsome borzois in this kind of setting.

Nor did Fest Director Amos Vogel, himself, help matters when he declared in his overly gilded program remarks: "The striking success (sic) of last year's First New York Film Festival at Lincoln Center both reflected and contributed to a new (sic) cultural reality in New York: the belated and triumphant acceptance of film as a high art . . ." This is both inflationary and misleading. Presumably Vogel himself has been on the moon this past decade, and has missed the long succession of Bergman, Antonioni, De Sica, Fellini, Nouvelle Vague films that, in the majority, surely qualify under the heading of "film as a high art." It need only be added that these films, and the large pools of perceptive New York audiences that suported them, predate the Fest idea by some few years.

Finally we'd like to know how Vogel and Roud could square the high aims of the Fest with the inclusion of a battery of small Fairchild Screens — all of them deployed like so many electronic peepers, on the promenade outside the Hall — and all of them offering continuous showings of such films "as a high art" as Andy Warhol's "The Kiss," "Man Eating a Peach," and "Man Shaving His Face." (Or maybe it was "Man Shaving a Peach," and "The Kiss Eats Up a Man.") This bit of marathon kitsch posing as an avant garde entry titillated few of the customers, so maybe the joke was on the overanxious directors themselves.

1964

View From The Bottom of the Chair

(after seeing "A View From the Bridge")

I am A. Alfieri Tribunal, honorable Brooklyn waterfront lawyer who has seen many things. But none so violent as the fate of Eddie Incestia, one of the best of men. Lollapalooza dockwalloper, good attentive husband, caring stepfather, bowler among bowlers.

Before I plunge into the recital of Eddie's decline and fall, I must cry to the heavens that Eddie's tale is a Greek tragedy in modern dress. As you shall see, ATTENTION MUST BE PAID.

Eddie's day to day routine, while not heroic on the surface, had the élan of your true hero. He looked at his fellows with sharp eye, which meant he had leadership potential. Now and then he smiled, but through a troubled face, which meant he knew life's ironies.

And his fellows — they knew that Eddie knew. Smile or sharp eye, they knew that Eddie knew that life on the waterfront was — well, different. Rough — but unspoken rough. No running to cops with your troubles. Nor to womenfolk at home. Only when the boom hit you, then you spoke up. To the union delegate, no one else.

If Eddie's home life was seedy, it was *true* seedy. Railroad style flat, sturdy no-filligree furniture. On the bedroom dresser was a handsome wedding photo, token of an earlier nuptial blooming. And there was the living room chair — ah, that chair. Some days a man couldn't lift that chair by the leg with one hand. Not even a man with the muscular power of an Eddie.

Was the restraining hand that of some classic god? A god of wrath with a message for Eddie that wasn't coming through? But I'm running ahead of my story . . .

While Eddie was facing his daily moment of truth on the docks, at home were two womenfolk who meant everything to him. They were his wife, Beatrice, a true homemaker but fading in beauty; and his apple-cheeked ward, Katie Puratani. Since the day Bea's sister passed away, leaving Katie practically a waif in life's bosom, Eddie had been most protective of her.

But now the girl was full-grown, one might even say, overly nubile. And rather of an independent turn of mind. She wanted to break out into the world, get herself her first job. She acted funny in other ways, too. Took to admiring her pretty face in the mirror. Wore seductive clothes. Danced around the apartment.

And she walked wavy, a blind man could see that.

Meantime, in the hold of a tied-up freighter were Bea's cousins from the home country. They were waiting for nightfall, when they would be sprung by Eddie. (The brothers Mario and Rodolpho Submarine, two anxious stowaways who wanted to start a new life on the Brooklyn waterfront. Eddie had agreed with Bea that the Submarines would stay with them, at least for a time.

After Eddie led the Submarines home, a touching reunion took place. The women outdid themselves at the Agamemnon supermarket. And later over the hot stove. Happiest of all, but with Eddie looking on suspiciously, were Katie and Rodolpho. They hit it off beautifully. The boy could sing, oh that bel canto voice! And not just "Santa Lucia," he could also handle "I'm Gonna Buy a Paper Doll . . ."

And his looks! Open-faced, handsome, bushelful of wavy blond hair. All and all that first night was *grande. Simpatico.* For the Submarines, for Bea, for Katie. As for Eddie, he sulked behind a wait-and-see posture.

161

The weeks that followed were tense ones. All because of Eddie's runaway temper. He took to baiting young Rodolpho. What kind of a man was he, anyway, Eddie kept saying. Singing on the docks like a canary. Buying those *cha cha* records. Showing Katie how handy he was with a pinking shears.

Worst of all was Eddie's jealousy. A storm raged in him every time Rodolpho took Katie out on the town. And poor Bea had to watch all this, her heart cracking a little. Because — well, she wasn't *sure*. Was Eddie really lusting after the girl? She refused to believe *that*. Still there were numbing doubts. For the plain fact was — Eddie had made no love to Beatrice in many, many days. Not even when she *pleaded* for some of the oldtime affection. Mother of God, maybe it was *true*.

There came a sorry night of anger for all. Eddie was determined to prove two things — that Rodolpho was maybe a little gay, and that he wanted to marry Katie only for the citizenship papers. The five were sitting around the living room, nicely *en famille*, when Eddie sneaked a challenge to Rodolpho:

"Wanna box a little? C'mon . . . You're a big man. Show me the dukes."

It was a spectacle. Eddie all but flattened Rodolpho. But then it was Marco's turn. Good trusting Marco, who had nothing but love for Eddie. Now he would show the bully! Without a word, Marco bent down low and raised that living room chair, raised it high above his head. And gently brought it down again.

You already know that Eddie failed that crucial test.

He sought me out shortly after. His manner was strange, kind of shifty. Why, he wanted to know, could nothing be done to stop the match between Katie and Rodolpho. Legal-wise, of course. And with years of ancient practice, mine as well as history's, sitting on my shoulder, I told him:

"Eddie, they have a *right*. Love is a law, too."

Anger coursed in him like a swift stream. He paced the dark corners of my office. He pumped his fists together. And he repeated: "You sure nothing can be done? By the law?"

And again I said: "They have a right. Get it out of your mind. Better still, bless them."

But he would never do that. The jealousy worm lived in him deep.

Take the Eddie-Rodolpho kiss. How I brood on its meaning. (As a classics' student, I can do no less.) How strange a parallel with past ritual kisses, all of them ending in tragedy. I feel a chill in telling it.

Katie and Rodolpho were alone one night, in Katie's room. The air was sweet, intoxicating. Though worried by Eddie's hostile stance, they spoke about marriage in warm tones. Then Eddie stormed into the room. He took one look at Katie's half-furled skirt. It was a look of surprise that changed into a scowl. And behind that look was the message: "*This* is what comes from walking wavy." As he turned from Katie to Rodolpho, the scowl changed to a hissing smile.

Said Eddie in a rage: "C'mon lover boy, I'll show you how."

He grabbed Rodolpho by the arms. He locked the young man in a powerful embrace. And he crushed him with *the kiss*. The shameful kiss. The taunting kiss. The lascivious kiss.

I brood hard on its meaning.

From here my story races on. Madly obsessed with the thought of losing Katie, Eddie committed the one inviolate act that sealed his doom. He broke the waterfront code. Told the Immigration cops about the brothers Submarine. He did so as if in a sleepwalk, for surely he was by now pursued by the Furies.

Eddie's end came about with all the passion and wonder of — well, a Greek tragedy in modern dress. (Did I say that earlier?) In a scene ominous with shadow and drenched in neighborhood lore, he faced his accuser Marco and demanded apology. Right out there on the fabled cobblestones. In full view of a keeping, ethnic audience.

"Restore my name, Marco," Eddie shouted with pain. "Tell these good people you lied about me . . . My name, Marco . . . Restore it!"

Marco's answer was a shower of saliva full in the teeth of Eddie.

The faceoff was swift. Two bailing hooks were thrown into the circle, from out of nowhere, (Or were they from the gods on high?) For long minutes the men were locked in those two crescents of glinting steel. Thrust and parry, parry and thrust. The clangor of those bailing hooks, set against the rise and fall of those keening voices, made a strong impression on me. It was classic *to the bone*.

Marco soon forced Eddie to his knees. His terrible eyes accused Eddie. "You are a pigeon," Marco taunted. "You broke the code. You have lost your name."

Indeed he had, Eddie's name was like ashes.

He rose from the gutter. He took a dozen steps backward, away from Marco and the crowd. His leather jacket draped him like the robe of Oedipus. And like that great King, who gouged out his own two eyes, Eddie jabbed the hook violently into his belly.

And so I come to the end. I have often wondered since that awesome and tragic day: Was Eddie really Italian, or was he Greek?

1965

Kurosawa's "The Lower Depths"

In commenting on Kurosawa's "The Lower Depths," (U.S. premiere at the Bleecker Street Cinema), the film reviewer who reveals the shattering last line is equal, in my judgment, to the fink who tips the boss to an impending strike plan. This happened at least once (Jonas Mekeas in the *Village Voice*) and the point is that no line in recent films, or play, story or novel, has so purging an impact.

Kurosawa traps the viewer in as bleak a cul de sac as he's going to find. This includes Beckett's ashcan, Albee's park bench, Gelber's dope pad, Sartre's no-exit place. All of these are Elysian fields next to K's mise en scene. Compared to the way he works, with flesh and spirit, and totally from the inside, the others seem to be working with erector sets.

Sit back in your soft seat, he seems to be saying, and as a reward for the two-hour attention you give my modest effort to screen a half acre or so of hell on earth, I for my part will see to it that not a tear remains, not a drop of blood that does not congeal into dust, not a hope or laugh that does not harden into a final statement of defeat.

All rolled into that last line.

Did Kurosawa have more than an inkling of O'Neill's "The Iceman Cometh"? There's this benign Hickey figure who comes in out of the void. (From the outer and larger void, to the inner one, as in a set of Chinese boxes.) He takes three square feet of squatter's space and, to each in turn, he offers drops of Buddhist treacle out of a bottle labeled "Hope For The Damned." A beautiful foil. Or is he? When he takes it on the lam once again, apparently to avoid the cops for some unnamed crime, pain returns to the others.

No defense needed here, I feel, in revealing a gem of a line on old benign one's disappearance. Trying to figure out why, one of the damned says, and I paraphrase, "He got hot heels." There are more such throughout.

On the O'Neill speculation: my hunch is that something more subtle than a mere borrowing is going on. Whether Kurosawa did or did not know of "Iceman," there is strong evidence of cross-pollination, both in mood and idea, between Gorki and O'Neill. So that if K was indeed unaware of "Iceman," how explain the appearance of a Hickey figure other than by the magic of pollination.

Final word: Go see it. But leave the bon bons, Hershey bars, Fritos and or the rest of it home. For wormwood is what you are going to have to swallow.

That Touch of Kitsch

Easily the best Hollywood answer to the French nouvelle vague, British working-class angry, Italian dolce vita decadent, is a highly successful type of film that can be called "The Park Avenue Never Was." There have been three so far; "Pillow Talk," "Lover Come Back," and "That Touch of Mink." All have been box office smashes. And they continue strong, according to *Variety*, on the re-release circuit. Of equal if not overriding importance is their potential in the area of America's image.

Where the foreign product can only lacerate an audience's ego, the Hollywood "never was" is coolly and professionally designed to float them on a cloud for a two-hour visit to *Kitschland*. Here they won't find zombielike lovers in search of identity in mossy Bavarian castles; defrocked concert pianists in search of identity in the purlieus of Pigalle bistros; murderous French beatniks in search of identity who shoot the *poilu* in cold blood; Midlands duffers in search of identity who punch time clocks and noses, on their way up to marrying bosses' daughters.

The "never was" is made of less bloody stuff. In its impeccable pursuit of ersatz, overdose of chic, too too frail preciosity, the genre is in fact markedly bloodless. Nowhere this side of Madame Tussaud's will you find characters with more plaster of Paris contour than in a "never was." That is a sealed guarantee.

Certain staples are required for a "never was." First you must have actors with the lived out look. They are the walking embalmed of Central Casting. When a love scene is called for, they have at it with all the passion of honeymooning fruit flies. And their comedy turns are invariably the comedy of the lockjawed double-take. The male lead usually calls for Cary Grant or Rock Hudson. Both are high-octane models in Petrocelli suits, with just the right touch of camp in their slouching ennui.

The "never was" heroine can be none but Doris Day, whose acting range runs the gamut, from flowing Vermont maple to Campfire marshmallow. Doris's most winning ploy is the passionate pout. It comes short, medium and long. Her second best talent is the way she flaunts her choppers. She can bare teeth with more abandon, whether in anger or ecstasy, than anyone on the lot, up to and including Burt Lancaster. As to the Doris Day femme fatale image, the image is often a technicolored mirage.

Support roles for a "never was" must be chosen with equal care. Because no audience can resist Cary's and Doris's charismatic emoting for too long, the secondaries must pop into the scene now and again as foils cum buffoons. A subtle balance of tin and brass is needed here. Two dandy examples (from "Mink") are Gig Young and Audrey Meadows. Gig of course is all out tin. And he's the all-American flat tire, who wishes he had the tensile strength of the punching bag. Gig's best ploy is the head tic, which he learned from Woody the Woodpecker. Audrey has the brass, and it is brass right out of the Revere foundry.

Vital to the success of a "never was" are sets, decor and costumes. All must be abundantly High Gauche. In "Mink" Cary, who is a millionaire in something or other, works in an office acres wide, loaded with Renoirs and Matisses, pregnant with Itkin's best (furniture). Doris is a comptometer clerk, Audrey an Automat sandwich girl. On the job they wear flaring organza costumes. The style is Cassini Proletarian. Away from the job they room in "House Beautiful" digs. The digs are crammed with pink and gold ornaments. Here the style is, interchangably, Raucous Park Avenue or Park Avenue Raucous. The girls loll about in At Home Cassini garb.

We come to the so-called story line of a "never was" (story line hell, it's a closed circle of suffocatingly "in" wheezes). The script jockey is one Stanley Shapiro, and he commands $250 Thou' per flick. Shapiro candidly told Bosley Crowther that he learned wisdom and wit from a great comedian. He revealed that the comedian, whom we shall call Fred Osmosis, taught him ". . . how to tell a joke . . . how to write a straight line . . . and, above all, he taught me how to accept and appreciate another writer's ideas . . ." (Alas, no residuals for the comedian, he's dead.)

On his very own, Shapiro offers fillets of fractured Freud and filberts of kewpie doll Kinsey. He is long on sight gags, short on sagacity. His sex encounters — if that's not too strong — are more come-on than a library full of "Lolitas." The chief impression of a Shapiro crafted script is that of a eunuch giving hot chase to a transvestite and, when they collide in each other's arms at the finis, the two go off for some passionate rounds of potsie. (Potsie, not *pot*.)

In a "never was" you get a plethora of what used to be called payola; and may well be mere harmless freebies since the reform set in. (But don't wager on it.) This is a species of name and product-dropping; and "Mink" is as chock-full of names as a page out of the Yellow Book. Reform will be observed and none will be dropped. Suffice to say that in one pearl-studded sequence alone no less than three payo . . . oops, freebies make the scene.

As to the American image that shines through a "never was," 185 million of us are beholden to Hollywood for the aura of dead calm in a bomb bomb globe. There is our world, and theirs (the foreign film's). Ours: Cary and Doris gawking at each other dreamily. Theirs: A Paris beatnik doing in a poilu, after which he takes his girl merrily into the hay. Ours: Cary and Doris cruising each other like happy guppies in a fishbowl. Theirs: A half dozen seedy assignations along the Via Veneto. Ours: Cary and Doris boy-girling to the altar, unscathed. Theirs: A defrocked pianist driving his femme to a fifth-floor jump. And so on. All our heartland frother. All their existential gore.

The beauty part is that virtue does pay, and handsomely.

Theater

Look Out Broadway, Living's Gonna Get You

Le Living consists of 34 gut-and-play theater nomads, built around a kind of Olympic flame of inspiration emanating from a hawkish-looking Julian Beck and a wraith-like Judith Malina. After a four-year exile in Europe, they hit the beach, on their return to the States, at the Brooklyn Academy of Music, causing a perpetual motion of audience frenzy. At the heart of it is the feeling that Le Living can't be boxed into a system — any system — of critical nitpicking. The fact is that one's workaday frame of esthetics seems to buckle at the hardedge, and the only escape is to the stormcellar of re-examination. Audience response shows that it can be a painful process, or joyful, or cynical, or evangelistic, or hateful. It is seldom indifferent.

The 16 performances brought on a richness of confrontations — actors goading audience, audience goading actors, audience goading audience. The group's set piece for making confrontation at its most frenetic is *Paradise Now.* The title is of course supremely ironic. While there is no mistaking Le Living's passion for change, the approach is mostly by way of the verbal harpoon to the audience's craw. Abrasive slogans come raining down from both sides of the proscenium. Before long the theatre is a domed reactor for flying pinwheels of controversy.

> ACTOR: "To be free is to be rid of the state."
> VOICE (from audience): "To be free is to give me back my money."
> ACTOR: "To be free is to be free to eat."
> VOICE (from audience): "Anybody special?"
> ACTOR: "To be free —"
> VOICE (from audience): "— is to fuck in front of your mother."
> VOICE (from audience): "To be free or not to be free."
> VOICE (from audience): "Freedom is horseshit."

169

VOICE (from audience): "If you're a horse."

It is a form of speaking in tongues, and the special genius of Le Living is that it throws a line of infinity to an audience by way of loosing hidden or surface or open hostility, play, rebellion or whatever that might break the bank, say, of conventional mediums like Broadway theater, television, the *New York Times* — and, most surely, the prudish-pornographic *Daily News*. What gets sprung in the process is the Pandora's Box of our politics, our madness of the cities, our captivity to Mad Avenue, our posture of religion, our sexual aggressions and regressions. And we become free to say anything, at least within the domed space of the theater.

Along about the third of *Paradise's* more than four-hour span, the Le Living cast go into the aisles, and become actors-fish in the sea of the audience, guerrilla style. They are almost bare to the bone, little cloth patches covering breasts and genitals, and the audience response to their snakelike movements, and to their intimate "I-thou" chatter, is an open-ended mix of mild shock, creeping pleasure, and little pockets of hostility. An example of the latter was the man with hippopotamus girth and growling voice — a long-time actor and teacher of actors — who had posted himself at the rear of the orchestra, during one performance of *Paradise*, and was greeting members of the cast as each came by. "You are beautiful, kid," he would say to each one of them, massaging their backs with a hammy, roving hand as he spoke. Then he would look at each sorely and growl, "But the Living Theatre *can't act a shit.*" Before long several from the audience jumped into the argument. There were cries of "Fuck acting!" and "Down with ego trips." Later the hippo man carried the battle into the street — locking horns with a shaggy and strong-voiced member of Le Living named Steven Ben Israel. Pretty soon one got a sense of where the real battle was at — a gut battle between an alarmed greaser of the skids into the Broadway system, and an outrider revolutionary actor type with more than an itch to punch that system silly, and for the count. Finally it was the fat man who lost his cool, glancing a light blow off Ben Israel's chest as he (the fat man) lumbered onto the theater bus for Manhattan.

Alarm might also have been the spur that sent another theater man — he of the New York Shakespeare Festival — out into the night after little more than an hour at the same performance. On the same evening a woman in tailored outfit kept rising from her orchestra seat and was demanding in a voice laced with rage that everybody "Sit down in front!" Her exasperated shouts — after one standee at the stage apron had shot back at her, "Stand up in back!" — sounded like those of a loyal Broadway theater-goer who was not about to attempt the sea change from Shubert Alley into the rough and tumble of guerrilla antitheater. Further along pretty near the entire cast was drawn into the vortex of booing and counter-slogans coming from a bunch of St. John's University students who were there not so much to see Le Living, as to "pledge one of us." They too bailed out into the night, en bloc, having zapped the carnival mood a little, for about one hour running, with some rather mild Conservative Party hobgoblin juvenility. And there were the two youthful shorthairs from West Point, who were dressed in civvies, and who had come down to see *Paradise* "after checking out the scene in the Village Voice." One of them revealed that he and his buddy had started a movement at the Point against compulsory chapel attendance — and that seemed about as far-out an act as the evening would come up with.

While all of these were in the nature of personal happenings, the main thrust of *Paradise* is for a collective response. The audience was invited — and many hardly needed prompting — to flood onto the stage and do its thing. *Paradise* thus became a kind of aphrodisiac for the theatrical unconscious. Actors and nonactors linked up, intersected, stomped the stage, went into seances of "Om" chanting, or the nonactors merely vibrated in place while Le Living performed. (A good deal of what Le Living does smacks of a conscious savagery, or of a kind of ritual bloodletting in dance, derived mainly from what looks like the Aztec and the Egyptian.) There was also the chance — it seemed only a hairtrigger away — that the activity would debouch off the stage, and out into the open. Deed, in other words, would follow word. At one point Julian Beck shouted, "There are 1700 prisoners in the Atlantic Avenue jail, a short distance from here." It caused a stirring in the audience, and someone in the orchestra cried, "What are we doing *here*." As it turned out the bridge between word inside the domed space and deed outside of it never was made. What was made was a symbolic bridge of sorts — when at show's end several of the actors in the near-nude (and it must be the Yoga in them that makes them immune to a Brooklyn midnight chill) led the audience outside "To liberate the street." It was the last impasto stroke on a theatrical canvas of Gully Jimson largeness, and even the two cops on the corner seemed to be getting the vibes.

No so, alas, the lady critic of *The New Yorker*, who wrote of *Paradise*: "The acceptance of all this bushwa by the audience was almost as fatuous as the stuff itself . . ." Maybe, poor girl, *her* bourgeois was showing.

1968

The Beard and the Muff

As everybody knows by now, Michael McClure's titillating one-acter, "The Beard," has a daring finale: under an umbrella of dimming lights, the play's two characters indulge in an act of cunnilingus. Billie the Kid does his thing, and golden-girl Harlow chants "Stars, stars, stars . . ." And the Hallelujah chorus rings through the house. As performed at the Off Broadway Evergreen Theater, it looks like the real thing, and may even *be* the real thing. This has led to some very uptight critical response, and even to some refusals to carry ads on the play. For example, that bible of show business, *Variety*, denounced the play in the kind of pucker-lipped accents one would expect to find in, say, *Springfield Republican*. "Bad taste," they said. And they said it straight. That bible of *bad taste.* And that very correct journal of Eustace Tilley, *The New Yorker*, turned the playhouse down cold on advertising. We've made a survey of some of the out of town coverage of "The Beard," and we find that the frankness and unbuttoned candor of these comments are in sharp contrast to the *Variety* and *New Yorker* flaps. Here are some of the out of town comments:

"Mouth to cunt resuscitation . . ."
— *Hartford Fortnightly*
"Muffdiver's holiday . . ."
— *Boston Blatt*
"The 'Messiah' gets it in the mouth . . ."
— *Providence Liberal Conservative*

"Like a drink of heavenly nectar — Harlow's . . ."
— *New Haven Trumpet*
"Pleasurable as an all-day sucker . . ."
— *Cape Cod Mugwump*
"Billie licks Harlow. Harlow sees stars. Audience licks
chops . . ."
— *New England Nonce*
"One man's bad taste, is another man's ambrosia . . ."
— *Scarsdale Pimpernel*
"When you get past the smell, you have it licked . . ."
— *Hog Island Call*
"Billie digs Harlow's cuisine. Goes big for hair pie . . ."
— *Tarrytown Gourmet*
"Home is the hunter, home to the bush . . ."
— *Westchester Watch and Ward*

Our own view of this harmless little roundelay of sex —
this fugue-like cuntata of the stage — is that it tells where it's
at in the geography of censorship. The cunnilingus bit got the
play busted in the City of Saint Francis, whereas in the City
of Fun it doesn't raise a pimple on an elephant's hump. And
here we think is one proof that Mayor Lindsay may well be
numero uno hippie of New York — he conceivably wouldn't
have to look far to attempt a bust of the McClure concocktion
and yet he just doesn't seem to be interested in busts. We're
talking of course of censorship busts, not women's.

1967

Repertory Is as Repertory Does

One repertory company, that of the Lincoln Center for the
Performing Arts, did (and did in!) Georg Buechner's *Danton's
Death.* The second, the Royal Shakespeare Company, did a
play (and did it brilliantly) at the Martin Beck with similar
historical impact, the contemporary Peter Weiss's *Marat/
Sade.* And herein lay the polarities of privately sponsored
repertory — in the first, a theater that is as clotted in imagination as it is overstuffed and over-press-agented in its search for
approval; in the second a theater of hard discipline that, in
the three-hour span of each evening, was a time bomb in the
lap of Broadway complacency. A bomb that exploded.

In the calamity of the first, Buechner's surging play was
smothered in the new establishment practice of making art

not necessarily for art's sake, but rather for the sake of good public relations. The theory seems to be that you can draw splashes of great drama, opera or dance merely by waving a magic wand of millionaire patronage. Thus was Lincoln Center built; thus was the $10-million Vivian Beaumont theater made; and thus were the services of Blau and Irving, as co-directors of the company, attained after the earlier failure of Kazan and Whitehead. The establishment, in its housing, functioning and public image-making, glitters like the gold it sprung from. The art so far, and sadly, is of a dim leaden hue.

That the theory may be wrong at its core, is what is most disquieting for Lincoln Centers are proliferating with sorcerer's speed across the country. In the case of Blau and Irving's first effort, the establishment was ready with its main strength. A bountiful cast, cleverly mobile sets, frilly as well as gutter-soaked period costumes, lighting and original music score. All of which were eloquent in their detail, and eloquently beside the point as packaging for a play that refused to come alive. Nor does it pardon the company to say that *Danton's Death* is flawed, or unplayable. (Orson Welles and his Mercury group, for one, laughed that one off the boards years ago.) If anything, it is and remains a major test for any theatrical intelligence sharp enough to cull its curious appeal, to make it work in terms of its passion, stunning flights of metaphor and, most crucially, its dark search into the heart of political terror.

In the Peter Weiss play, as performed by the Royal Shakespeares under the direction of Peter Brook, you were in the grip of just such a theatrical intelligence. The work itself — with its long Brechtian line, and its stark and spastic overtones of Artaud's theater of cruelty — would predictably have mounted terrors equal to Buechner's for the first named group. Not so the London-based company which went about its sure business of using play, theater and audience as a unity wherein cameos of shock and visceral truth were made and unmade in stunning measure. You entered the Martin Beck under a full glare of lights, and curtainless stage, with aisles and boxes used as extensions for the action — and lo! you were from the first only dimly aware of the line of separation between worldliness and the unworldliness of stage.

So true was this apparitional gain to the main thrust of the play (Weiss himself has said, ". . . the whole world and the whole of politics is a sort of madness . . .") that you began to feel a kind of liquification, if not liquidation, of any hard notion you may have brought into the theater of what truth *is*. The experience was an unsettling one, but a vivid one as well, imposing its own stamp of theatrical probity. The night we saw the play, a preview night with an audience that needed no prior critical touting, this audience seemed to be one tight knot of squirming, gaping involvement. Indeed a few timid ones squirmed their way out of the theater, long before the final minutes of the three-hour "ordeal." What this seemed to confirm, most of all, was the power of the play to work directly to the viscera. Or as we say, liquification to the pit of the audience's being.

When this same thing (the exodus) happened on opening night, but on a hundred-fold scale, director Peter Brook was quick in his response to the press. He called the predominantly black tie audience. "The worst ever . . ." He likened them to a "brick wall," and went on to say, "It was as if they were hurrying to get the right table in the restaurant." Revealing too was Brook's further charge that they had not been emotionally involved with the play. He put it this way, "It was as if there are perhaps a thousand people in this country that we are talking about specifically in this play and a good proportion of them, say 800, were there on opening night." One might conclude from this — too much black tie and not enough viscera.

Oddly enough, *Marat/Sade* is tricky but not abstruse, either in its staging or content. The full title of the piece, in fact, is the thumbnail of all that needs to be known. The title goes, *The Persecution and Assassination of Marat as Performed by the Inmates of the Asylum of Charenton Under the Direction of the Marquis de Sade.* The spine is a series of interrupted dialogues — between Sade as an inmate in the flesh, and Marat as performed by another inmate. Weiss's strong talent for both historical and contemporary exegesis comes over beautifully in these set-tos (nor is there any doubt that it is the contemporaneous bite of the piece that drives the black ties to the exits). There is razor edge balance here — between Sade's satanic but cool pessimism, and Marat's burning but near-despairing calls for revolutionary change. For the rest Peter Weiss makes use of an interlocutor who speaks in salty, Brechtian couplets; a quartet of circus-like clowns and harpies who chant their barbs with cabaret abandon; and the frenetic chorusing of the other inmates, who serve as a kind of raw and wrinkled skin for the body of the drama.

So rich is the Royal Shakespeare Company in versatility, from mordant comic turns to mordant dramatic buildups, that you found it difficult to separate individual from ensemble. Mention should be made of Ian Richardson's harrowing Marat; Patrick Magee's corrosive Sade; Glenda Jackson's trapped and tortured Charlotte Corday; Clifford Rose's epicene M. Coulmier (asylum director); Michael William's tacky and salty Herald (interlocutor); and John Steiner's furious and campy Duperret (would-be lover of Charlotte). (All, incidentally, repeated their roles in the highly praised screen version.)

The principal players like everyone else are of course hopelessly insane, but see how close and how often they all come to catching us by the tail of our own sinking sanity. To put in this way is to state the real measure of this towering theater piece — and the measure of our indebtedness to author, director and company. Would that we here in New York, the great Diners' Club-Lincoln Center hub of the arts, could millionaire our way to this kind of theater.

1967

New Wave Off Broadway

A bracing new wave has firmed the Off Broadway theater scene in the past couple of seasons. First splash was "Viet Rock" (at the Martinique), which had the mixed fortune of drawing enthusiastic preview audiences, and then, of subsiding into premature closing two or three weeks after being guillotined in print by that one-man Committee of Public Safety, on Broadway, the gray lady New York Times's Walter Kerr. "Viet" was mounted by an ensemble that rates considerable watching — Joseph Chaikin's Open Theater, on evidence a healthy, turned-on (to Thespis) successor to the Beck-Malina Living Theatre, the latter of which was foreclosed by U.S. tax hawks five or six years ago, only to show up in Europe where it has churned audiences into putties of appreciation of what an avant, roasting and chancy theatre can be.

The piece had its flaws, but the sweet smell of Broadway marshmallow it was not. Megan Terry at age 28 is a lady playwright with a hardedge view that scorns the conventional. In "Viet" she had laced (or more likely, lashed) together a series of quick-paced sketches in which frenetic body movement, acerbic lines of satire and bawdy parodies of rock music combined to make a kind of post-Brechtian masque — an American Au Go Go, really — of our Vietnam involvement. Not the least of its virtues was the way it built a frame of reference for, in the first place, the G.I. and *his* "place" in Vietnam. In both senses, moral and geographic. And that it didn't come up Green Berets opera, but something closer to a moral and physical gangrene, turned out to be an identity problem more for critic than audience.

More a boxoffice winner is "America Hurrah," which opened at the tiny Pocket Theater only days after "Viet." That "Hurrah" was and is a "hot" ticket, as well as a highly-praised production, places it in the category of "That's show biz" irony. In point of fact, "Hurrah" came out of the same workshop as "Viet," both having evolved from Open Theater methodology, a hard regimen of calisthenics cum depth-acting cum actor-writer collaboration. Pantomime — that once oh so gentle sport! — figures too, often with the hot directness of a blowtorch. Author Jean-Claude van Itallie, who like Miss Terry is still only in his 20s, has fashioned three short pieces, all of which turn up stones — so to speak — that reveal some pretty wriggly specimens of the American experience. IBM-type interviews, head shrinks, subway robotism, meat rack surgery, motelling — are some of the topics. And if the aim is quite often deadly, the joy in the ensemble work makes for a special kind of theatrical uplift that — one would guess — is the essence of good satire. Even gray lady cheered — but then, as between metaphorical theater and old debbil "agit-prop," the former allows for *distance*. (Ah that precious distance!)

A third part of the wave — Gunter Grass's "The Wicked Cooks" — suffered the fate of audience uneasiness, very likely, in face of a Kafkaesque theater piece that demanded more than just "sitting it out." At any rate, the result was quick expiration, at the hardluck Orpheum Theater, and more's the pity. The Grass work, which should be read as allegory, despite the author's demurrer, has a seamy army of cooks looking — with menace, and wild-eyed porkiness — for the secret recipe of a perfect soup. They are cooks, to be sure; and they are, to be equally sure, all the timeless mobs who hunger for "perfect" answers. And there's the mysterious Count — a persona that could be read as the artist, also timeless, who's at war with the mob, and its "solutions" — who pretends he has the recipe. Some arcane mumbo-jumbo here, about a certain "gray dust." When the Count is finally cornered, he recants (there is no "perfect" recipe, none) and he shoots himself. The play ends with the cooks, delirious as ever that the recipe *did* exist, going on a wild pursuit of one of their own, a kind of maverick cook named Vasco (for Vasco da Gama?). Vasco, they are convinced, has inherited the Count's secret. (And if we're off in a nuance, here and there, author can hardly sue. The name of the game *is* allegory, after all.) In sum a difficult piece, but a production that had constant flashes of rawboned shock, plus those bizarre turns of surreal humor that are Grass on his best. As for gray lady, when he wasn't clocking the action like an olympic decathlon, he was condescending it out of mind.

The fourth play — Norman Mailer's adaptation of "The Deer Park," his 1952 novel — had the atmosphere, in previews and on the rumor vine, of a Madison Square Garden fight of the year. Old Norman had trained sharp for this one, to hear some of the puffy-eared hipsters tell it. Ten years of jabbing, cutting and bleeding assault. And now, it was a fight to the finish, against a tough novel that would take the count (at the Theatre De Lys), in a meteoric attack of "existential" theater. Mailer had corralled a mob of movie deadbeats, and put them down in a tinseled, hyperthyroid setting — the Desert D'Or of the novel — where they performed, so to speak, sexual (homo and hetero) and political and psychological lobotomies on one another. The surface action — all supposedly taking place in the mind of Sergius O'Shaugnessy, an egocentric and talky-poetic hero surrogate of the author — spooled along in a series of 88 cinema-like scenes. Some were no more than flash dialogue bits, others were more extended confrontations, in which flesh and egos are lacerated to — at times — a scream. Well, the decision from one corner was: Entertaining, existentially dopey, and a little bit old-fashioned. But entertaining it *was*, and the fans weren't tearing out the seats. Where the piece succeeded, in pretty near an evening-long tattoo, was in Mailer's expertise at catching the Hollywood line, the boffo, the embroidered cant, the inflated sentimentality. Not since Nathanial West, and in a softer key, F. Scott Fitzgerald, had anyone roasted those chestnuts to such a turn. And the direction served to a"t" — now brisk and untethered, now full of a kind of lapidary posturing. The latter, sometimes known as *schtick*. Only when it was in bondage to its nether mood, its ersatz Tennessee mood, did "The Deer Park" bog down. As when Marion Faye (a real hurting pimp-faggot of a character) parades his degeneracy, we hadn't seen such a show of baroque iron balls in years. Rip Torn in the Faye role; Will Lee as Teppis, a gamey MGM type studio chief; and Hugh Marlowe as Charles Francis Eitel, an aging gloomboy of a director, all did well by the leads. All in all a swifty of a main bout, and one which found gray lady approving, if from a somewhat nasally-aloof plateau.

Barbara Garson's "MacBird!" (at the Village Gate, jazz-den turned into playhouse) is the very plumed crest of that wave. A full-fledged New Left satirist at age 26, Mrs. Garson has seen the Shakespearean present, and it works. And what has she wrought? For one thing, she's taken the thane of Cawdor and, by deft theatrical transmogrification, she has made him into the politico-scamp of Texas. But more — she's read the whole Scottish tale of assassination and remorse, bloody power struggle and sea of private guilt, as a fantasia of American politics of the '60s. And her treatment cuts deep, not so much by specifics, but by its nerve-ends awareness of a foul and pestilent air in our politics. Hence the argument that Mrs. Garson has "loaded" her explication, that she has made of Macbeth's crime a cloak that drapes too easily onto the shoulders of the President, is an argument that misses. Not MacBird's crime (which in any case is never flatly stated), but his raging ambition, and the smog of violence it inspires, is the motor of Mrs. Garson's play. Actually her vision is uncompromisingly anti-pol, and MacBird is in some ways no more than a pathetic climber to the lofty tower, where the Ken O'Duncs reign. As this works out on stage, the lowerdog gets our sympathy, what little of it can surface, as much as the other way around. And the ancillary roles — the Earl of Warren, the Egg of Head, the Wayne of Morse — are grist to the same mill. She buys none of them, and this makes for a certain audience pain. An instance of the play's sheer *touchiness*, was the intermission remark that went: "I like it

179

enormously, so far, except for what she does to Adlai Stevenson (Egg of Head). That I find a bit unfair." Partisan theatergoing, a la mode. There were of course some weaknesses, both in direction and play. For one thing the pace was too headlong, as if, say, a pantry raid by children was in progress. And the play was undercut, here and there, by other bits of juvenilia. As when Ted Ken O'Dunc sneaks a look at, and then sits down on, the throne chair while brother Robert's attention is elsewhere. Cuteness, and at times over-the-line preciosity, was the result. As for the text, Mrs. Garson has indeed captured, with brio and sharp parodist's ear, scads of rhyming couplets, soliloquies, rhetorical firestorms — they are all there. But she has, perhaps, made her borrowings too broadly: here a line from "Hamlet," there one from "Richard the Second," and so on. No doubt the temptation to crib, so hard to resist, tends nonetheless to make a raven's nest of the Bard. Finally a short note on Stacy Keach, a relatively unknown actor until now. The way he plays the role of MacBird, you can be sure that a star is born, brilliant and risible in the highest. (So come on, gray lady man/Loosen up and cheer/This one/A century will run.)

1967

Three for the New Scene

Three more or less farout entertainments helped light up the Off Broadway scene in 1968. The three were: the hippie musical called "Hair," a rock parody version of "Hamlet," and a mixed media celebration called "An Electric Christmas." All were aggressively irreverent and boldly experimental, in varying degree. Let's begin with the musical, which launched the New York Shakespeare Festival's new — and gemlike — theater on the lower East Side, the ponderously named Florence Sutro Anspacher Theater (of which more later). Described as "The American Tribal Love-Rock Musical," "Hair" made a strong bid to capsulate a hippie idiom and make it work in Broadway musical terms. And that in part was a hex, maybe even a contradiction.

The hip idiom worked, as did the costuming, most of the big production set pieces, and the general thrust of the music. A good deal of new sound, and new bouncy posturing (the latter, in a musical comedy sense), came through with a wallop in "Hair." The composer was Galt MacDermot. The book and lyrics, by Jerome Ragni and James Rado, went all out for a new "thing" that was light years beyond the old moon/June thing. For openers there was "Red, Blue and White," a number quite capable of biting the ass of the most marathon of flagwavers, and maybe even making him feel gleeful in the end. And there was "Hair" — a full-company number that sang the defiance, insouciance, narcissism, and more, of the whole gestalt of you know what. There was a be-in number, done in slow pantomime, with short bursts of Hare Krishna chanting, and some larks of blowing, all told as inventive a piece of musical theater as we've seen On or Off Broadway. Where "Hair" slipped a little, and went soppy (it happened here and there), it did so because it hadn't cut the Broadway umbilical cleanly enough. Laments went on lamenting; number followed number too much in a rote seesaw pattern — now a love ballad, now a whiz-bang production number, now some comic "business" (for business's sake) — and finally, the whole company went jugular now and then; went that is after the audience with that "Let's bring the house down on 'em" attack that is the bane, and the bore, of Broadway. The overbalance was probably due to what was best about "Hair": its youth, and youthful ambiance. The other side of which, and no crime here, was a straining to be lovable and "on." All in all "Hair" was a theatrical freakout and breakout, and a box-office success. It was moved from the small Anspacher, to the much larger Cheetah digs, where the audience was invited to remain after the show, and partake of the rock doings, at no extra cost. Which sounds like a hippie version — does it not? — of the square's "One for the road." Final note on "Hair" is both ironic and money-in-the-bank: It's now the hottest ticket on Broadway, in its third incarnation.

The second production was "Hamlet," or a rock parody thereof. And we give points, with no sense of split loyalty to tradition, to anybody witty and daring enough to tear down, and then schmaltz up, the Bard. The trick in effect is to lard "Hamlet" in comic terms and not make it come up ham. And the risk, to coin a phrase, is of course awesome. For be sure of this: There's more existential humor, living parody and antic joy (as overlay to its quintessential tragic mood) in the original, than is dreamt of in all the hyped conceits of some lightweight, and hense misdirected, director. That the piece was produced by the Shakespeare Festival — and was in fact a successor to "Hair" at the Anspacher — and that it was directed by the Festival's top brass, Joseph Papp — all tended to give it a kind of Brand Name authority up front. The piece had authority, yes — but it was the authority of a muscular karate brawl, with frequent grunts and bellyrolls all over the place. (Too much Hellzapappin and not enough hellfire comedy.)

Anyway, Papp conceived a mini "Hamlet" of about 100-minutes' duration, with no intermission. And with short blasts of rock music and psychedelic lighting. Call it (to change metaphor) a verbal toboggan ride, a fulltilt theater experience that bruised, as well as tickled. Certain of the bits that tickled come to mind. As when Hamlet, in the guise of a *Puerto Ricano* janitor, and while hunched teeteringly over a rubber trash can, declaimed the *To be or not to be* in the racing sing-song of the East Harlem *barrio*. Or when the ghost of Hamlet's father wearing longjohns and a Wagnerian horned helmet spoke his vaporous lines while swinging from a roof trapeze. Or when Horatio was on stage, garbed in striped uniform more fitting for Leavenworth than Danish castle, the words "STATE PRISONER" stencilled on his back. Or when Ophelia strode the boards, in Judy Garland-Palace Theater tights, black top hat and swallowtail jacket, and even the strut. Or finally when Papp skedaddled the cast all over the house — you could never tell but that you'd be sitting twofers with, say, Ophelia — and that was a fate devoutly to be wished, she was that lovely a lass.

As for the acting and or mugging — the entire cast was spirited enough, and indeed professional enough, but we'd still like to know what "Hamlet" they thought *they* were doing. It would have been an interesting poll. Martin Sheen played the Hamlet role; and April Shawhan, the Ophelia (and mark us, she'll be up for grabs very soon). Perhaps mention should also be made of "Rossencraft" and "Guilderstone" — as one example of those hyped conceits we spoke about earlier. And a word about the Anspacher, which is named for a Festival benefactor (one of the names of the Festival game is gelt). The theater was built from the shell of old and unused Astor Library — a superb if miniature example of rescue from the jaws of obsolescence. It has a high glass ceiling, sharply raked seats, three iron runways in the stage area. Two sets of Greek columns give the house an Apollonian air, but the play's style that evening was all-out Dionysian.

Our final report is on the mixed-media show, "An Electric Christmas" — performed twice at Carnegie Hall and easily the most experimental of the lot. The format had an oddball link-up: New York Pro Musica (12 medieval and Renaissance specialists) cheek to jowl with the Electric Circus's rock group, Circus Maximus. They shared stage left on Carnegie's wide proscenium. Two other ingredients were a light show and an "Electronic Music Synthesizer" (we got that last from electronic composer Morton Subotnick, who thought it should be in "caps"). The light and synthesizer operators were deployed on stage right. Both shows had SRO audiences, but not necessarily oddball audiences. It was more like long-hair meeting up with long-hair — a good many college kids and hippies, and large numbers of Carnegie regulars, both taking a cool but receptive stance, as of: "Okay, prove that it works."

As we came down the Carnegie aisle for our seat, the synthesizer was tracking short runs of Gregorian, those chaste and somber devotionals, whose quality (a kind of lulling sing-song) somehow evoked prayer and lushness both. The live part got under way with Pro Musica doing canons and ballads from its wide repertoire of 14th Century and after. They were in good voice, and their playing — on such instruments as lute, recorder, viola da gamba, etc. — was equally good. Pretty soon the lights people joined in, and their thing was more artsy than psychedelic: rich splurges of pointillist, some Jackson Pollock style takeoffs, some deep-color mutations with the feel of say Philip Guston. Last — and we think we have the order — was Circus Maximus, whose electric twang and rock beat — the "now" sound — roused old Carnegie with shivers of tension.

All present and accounted for. The mix was hitting the fan fully. Synthesizer — which looked like a triptych of telephone switchboards and measured about 6 ft. by 6 ft. overall — with a series of bleeps and rumbles, and then a 10-minute composition of electronic sound, the effect of which was not unlike Honegger's famous railroad opus, "Pacific 231"; lights, with a swiftly changing display — a Buddha image, a set of amoeba-like designs that could have been Miro, a

woman-chasing-man silhouette right out of James Thurber —
which bathed the entire stage area, and the dress circle
nearby; Pro Musica and Circus Maximus, doing their turns,
interweaving old and new, with hardly a pause in between.
All of this in what to us is the best sound box in the U.S.:
The redstone lady on West 57th Street, Carnegie Hall.

The closing number — on a program that ran to about 90
minutes, with no intermission, and that might be a trend:
"intermissionless" — was worth, as they say, the price of
admission. It was a duo performance, one group backing the
other, by Pro Musica and Circus Maximus, of the 14th
Century chanson: Guillaume de Machaut's "Douce Dame
Jolie." Pro Musica was first, and gave the song a "proper,"
meaning classically pure, reading: it touched you with just the
right balance of euphoria, and gray hints of sorrow. Barely did
Pro Musica's last notes expire, when the rock group picked
up the song, transcribing the former's limpid French, into their
own pop-American (the title line came out: "Sweet lovely
lady"). Pro Musica's John White put it: "Our music and rock
are similar . . . the rhythms are strong and vital, the
harmonies are crisp and clear, and there is much improvisa-
tion." And that's where it's at — old and new, the bridge, the
loom of art.   1968

The American Place Theater

This project, located in the heart(!) of New York's Hell's
Kitchen, may light up our drama like an old-style Fourth
bonfire. Having seen its first production, two plays by Robert
Lowell with the working title, "The Old Glory," I can only say
that any word this side of "superlative," would be the hex of
the inadequate. But first I'd like to quote them: "The APT
exists to foster good writing for the theater," and "Our name
. . . is meant to suggest something about our way of life . . .It
has been taken from Alfred Steiglitz's 'An American Place
Gallery' . . . where, in small compass, grew so many of the
major talents of our time . . ."

Amen to the intentions! Twice amen for the delivery! The
first of Lowell's pieces, an adaption from Hawthorne's story,
"My Kinsman, Major Molineux," is a light and bantering
masque; a kind of street-side tug of war of Yankee-British
loyalties, in prerevolutionary Boston. On one viewing only,

184

the piece seems to work more as a pantomime, than as meaty dramatic fare. Nor is that meant as a pejorative; there is so much that is pleasant, and eyefilling; so many small details of a peculiarly "native" bounce, that I found myself constantly on for director Jonathan Miller's large bag of tricks. As for author Lowell, his focus here seems a little blurred; the piece never quite peeks above, looks higher than, the simple, rag-tagging moments of "Yankee, or Redcoat? Which side're you on?" ale-room japery. But there are those bon bons of pleasure; the miming, the stunning costumes; the now-and-then cuttingly funny lines. I wanted more — author, director, cast.

The second is Lowell's long one-acter from the Herman Melville novella, "Benito Cereno." If the writing in "Molineux" was done with a tuning fork, Lowell in "Cereno" went to work with a surgeon's scalpel. The drama is lean; full of salty, wry humor, in its early development. Lester Rawlins, brilliant as Captain Delano, is a seafaring poster (come alive) of Yankee tropisms. He walks the deck of his sailing vessel, spyglass at the ready, and lays low every hoary provincialism of his buttoned-up mate, John Perkins, played with scarecrow tightness by John Ryland. These opening minutes are, additionally, the purest Melville, Lowell giving a loving, rolling lilt to whole, rich passages of seascape description that, except for sea-haunted O'Neill, have not been matched in our literature. And the pure theater here, of playing those rolling, incantatory lines in a style of mock classicism, shows director Jonathan Miller at his best.

No theater I have seen, in years, can match the counterpoint working out of the themes of surface servility, on the one hand, and sheer turnabout terror on the other. The detail is rich, tingling. For example — there is a moment, two-thirds of the way, where I felt my blood literally curdling; a moment where Delano, who clearly is the *last* to discover what has happened on the slave ship, removes his large feathery admiral's tricone and brings it slowly down over his face. The before-and-after of this miming gem, with Rawlins' every feature changing from a kind of bland condescension of all things foreign and sloppy on the high seas, to the beginnings of a sweating (*real* sweating) realization of what has in fact taken place — this before-and-after is of the nature of a dramatic core, an intelligence, that I for one have rarely witnessed. 1965

Black Poetry Is

The cast was tossing poetry-filled bombs not gasoline ones (a case of black power in the shape of poetry power) from the open stage of the Delacorte Theater in Central Park. The program was "An Evening of Negro Poetry and Folk Music" and it was long, often stirring and humor-filled. There was audience power too in the record crowd of over 3,000 — with hundreds of non-ticket-holders bunched at the two end gates of the oatmeal-bowl playhouse. They were alert and talky as they waited for the eight o'clock go-ahead. Once inside some found what few unfilled seats there were, while others spilled into the aisles and made do with the lowslung wooden steps for seats. As good for viewing as the regular ones, though not as comfortable.

From the moment the eight actors and singers — plus the three musicians — made their entrance, there was a sense of a theatrical treat in store. And beyond all, there was a gut feeling that art — which on this night would consist mostly of traditional and modern poetry and song from the Negro repertoire — was at least one equalizer in a black-white storm of hurt passion, guilt and unappeased wrong. The tight-fitting audience, a good third of whom was non-white, was an audience not unaware of the embattled world outside the Delacorte's sylvan and peaceful setting. But so upbeat is this setting — with its flapping Elizabethan flags on the rooftop, its fine darkling symmetry of open sky and glade and pond and trees, playhouse stuck in among them — that one could hear not a murmur of discord, for the light and blending note of bright things ahead.

The performers came on almost in a lope. It was a happy lope, judging from the way each one looked the audience over, eyes in a near twinkle, much the way a miser would look over his pile of gold. Roscoe Lee Browne, director of the program, who played a kind of Leporello kibitzer to the cast's Don, led off with a wry crack or two about the weather. The political weather, that is. And the immense poise of this actor — a combination of slightly aging Puck, and deep-throbbing stage presence — was immediately winning. He introduced the cast, each of whom bowed and then sat, all forming a kind of musical-chairs effect across the stage, with Browne seated a little forward from the others. They were —

Amanda Ambrose, slim and regal looking, in white linen gown; Leon Bibb, trim and ready as a welterweight, wearing a dark blue suit; Gloria Foster, handsome and womanly, and handsomely attired, in turquise dress; Moses Gunn, also in blue suit, flecks of gray showing in neatly-groomed, short beard; Ellen Holly, youthful and pretty, dressed in black; Josephine Premice, who gave off glints of the clown and sophisticate, both — and who wore short black jacket over black-white gown; and Cicely Tyson, restless and fine boned, smooth as beaver in body-hugging green. And the trio of musicians — Bill Lee, bass; Stuart Scharf, guitar; and Floyd Williams, tympani — who sat a little above and behind the cast, on stage left.

It was a long but never tiring program — an absorbing mixture of protest, ghetto laughter, remembrance and some rousing take-offs on white song. Amanda Ambrose got things going with her camp version of the Irish toora-loora lullaby, after which the old sod can hardly be the same. Then came a darker note with Cicely Tyson's reading of Paul Lawrence Dunbar's "We Wear the Mask" ("With torn and bleeding hearts we smile"). Leon Bibb was at his very best in several folk songs — among them were the traditional " 'Buked and Scorned" and his starkly beautiful rendering of "O'Shenandoah." In the latter Bibb scored with an icy passion, in such interpolated lines as "O'Shenandoah I love your daughter" and "She said I was a dirty nigger." Moses Gunn's voice and presence were by turns commanding and bitingly pithy — in readings from poets Robert Hayden, Arna Bontemps, Ray Durem and others. Josephine Premice untorched the traditional "Careless Love" torch song — she belted it across with a kind of warmed-over night club sogginess that made the audience howl, and had the other performers holding on like a scenic railway ride. Gloria Foster and Ellen Holly were in fine contrast — the former strong and clear, and the latter softly silken, in both solo and duo readings. Roscoe Lee Brown was at all times himself — as anchor and performer he moved, read his lines and ad-libbed with wit and professionalism. And with a voice of pure fright — as in his reading of a lynch scene from the works of Richard Wright. The musicians were effective in their background roles — in the background, but hardly vanished.

There were two sets, upwards of 30 pieces of poetry and

song in each, with a short intermission in between. Among the other poets represented were — James Weldon Johnson, Langston Hughes, Gwendolyn Brooks, Calvin Hernton, Helene Johnson, LeRoi Jones, Countee Cullen, Myron O'Higgins and Ted Jones. Almost three hours of the sweet, tart and burning essences of a people's art, performed on a mild summer's night. During those hours, it was as if Watts and Newark and Detroit had never happened. Just a bad American nightmare. And during those hours one was reminded of Joe Louis's (remember Joe, that "credit to his race"?) famous crack on the eve of a fight, when he said of an opponent, "He can run, but he can't hide." Backlash whitey can run, but he can't hide, from the humanity of black poetry.

1968

History into Choreography

Daniel Nagrin is a dancer — and a theater presence — seized by an idea. Several years ago he read, with gradual but deepening interest, the great war book of ancient Hellas: Thucydides's "The Peloponnesian War." Nagrin let the book sink in, and confesses to a sense of revelation, as of cold light traveling toward us from a dead civilization, but still powerful enough to resonate meaning for our own time.

The result of his reading — and of his search for what might be called choreographic witness — is a set of dance cum theatrical impressions of stunning, and deeply disturbing, impact. Using the text as a sort of wrapper, Nagrin has conceived a mixed-media, inside the warp of which he dances, and acts out, a veritable shower of brilliant, and at times pain-inducing, epiphanies. The stage is bare — and the house dark — for a full ten-minutes before Nagrin appears. Meantime the taped voice of Frank Langella, softly modulated and almost icily abstract, gives us Thucydides's text. There is a chill in the words, as if one were trapped not in the history stacks, but in moments of violence that sit on the lid of one's conciousness. An ancient text, and an icepack out of time for our fevers.

When the lights come up, Nagrin is seated on a chair on a bare stage. His posture is stiff, and he's wearing a boxlike gray suit out of the 20s, all American Edwardian in aspect.

The first of an evening-long series of musical tapes, always played in fragmented swatches, floods the hall. It's the national anthem, a warbly Bing Crosby version, and then several others. Nagrin stands, bolt upright. His strong features go soapy, as he moves his lips to the song, felt hat held tautly over his breast. There is a rigid — and quietly insane — formality to the incident. When Nagrin flops to the floor, doubled-over in collapse, the meaning of the piece is immediate. He is working us over at the nerve-ends of our entrapments, speaking to the horrors of our self-made prisons, where even so bland a thing as la Patrie — pushed far enough — can drain us of our reason.

And so the liet motif is established. Each tableau begins in the prosaic, quickly descends into the insane, and ends in the agony of death.

Of the dozen or more pieces, some others are a parody of Swan Lake, a frenetic Dance of the Hours, a headlong Russion peasant dance, and a campy Fred Astaire takeoff. All, in a way, so many Venus fly traps, *before* the traps are sprung. What follows, as in the Swan number, is a skidding into physical pain; or, as in the Hours number, a descent into Hitlerian fantasy, wherein madness, and later, the intervention of a kind of death's-head agony, take over. The shifts, abetted by the jagged musical line, work over us like a species of water torture, Nagrin's evocations being step-by-step choreographic drops on our skin.

Other pieces — call them Goya grafted to La Ronde — are a G.I. and his rifle, man meshing with gun, at the finale, in crazed violence; a triptych parable of death, Hitler and the Pope; a pedantic — and lunatic —lecturer; and a transvestite study, at once touching and funny. Surely there's pain in all this, but Nagrin's technique is beyond mere grand guignol, and he draws us in — by wit, by pathos, by occasional pratfall — the better to draw and quarter us, at the gut level of our emotions.

The sound track offers a dense mixture. Besides the earlier fragments, there is the voice of Al Jolson, who comes over in a kind of nasally nostalgia; bits from Gluck's "Orpheus"; touches of Gregorian chant; a smooth "Sheik of Araby." Also jazz and electronic, by Archie Shepp and Eric Salzman respectively. Both assembled the tape, and it's a brilliant job. Costumes, which Nagrin changes into on stage, are by Sally

Ann Parsons.

And the text, weaving in and out. Words out of time, but no less a cool litany of disaster for now. "Though they (Athenians) were once good, they now have turned bad . . ." "So quickly does action follow decision . . ." "So both sides claimed a victory . . ." At concert's end Nagrin, dressed in classical robe, stands at the rear for some quiet talk with the exiting audience. It's as if he's witness to, and at the same time closing a ring against, the danger implicit in that haunting text. *Take my hand for we must do at least that on the lid of our collective danger.*

At the Cubiculo, a small handsome building, once owned by the American Legion. The cube shaped playhouse is open-staged, has high brick walls painted black and white, seats about 150 in raked rows.

1969

Galleries

Hamlet Clown, Larry Rivers

Larry Rivers has grabbed New York's daily critics, camp-following jetniks, amorphous "let's go to a museum" midcult legions. A pretty roundhouse garb, any way you figure it. At the usually staid Jewish Museum, which opened a massive retrospective of 188 paintings, drawings, sculptures and prints, the SRO was on frequent display. The critical claims were most extravagant, for example, the Herald Tribune's Emily Genauer, who swelled her column with the hardly modest word that Rivers had arrived as top American artist today.

At that, Miss Genauer may be half right. If there are top and bottom among our current painters, Rivers can qualify for one, as well as for the other. He is a wildly uneven craftsman — quirky and strong in some areas, utterly raw and abrasive elsewhere. It appears he's emptied his workroom — daubs, experiments and misfires, as well as the surer, more heroic pieces — onto the wall of a large and generally selective museum. Which raises questions — for him, museum, and viewer. As the case is, the viewer can only recoil from what is worst, and hold that against what is best. Thus does Rivers go; he bear-hugs you with pleasure from one wall, he sets you back to muttering from another.

Let's take it the way the show unravels. In the main floor galleries are ten large canvases, all with pale white background, and all of which seem to chase one another in a game — bright, mostly — of pop-goes-the-paint. You feel, looking at one after the other, between blinks of the eye, that the artist is trying for more. But he settles for a kind of "fill in the titles" expressionism — painterly murmurings, in a way — that is less than you want. Typical is one called "Europe II," which displays Rivers' penchant for the vignette, the more on a canvas the merrier. Five or six hazy, pastelly figures are put together in a kind of abstract pie. The mood is playful, and yet a somber note creeps in. As with most of these, you somehow must bite into it with a wide gulp, or it will resist you. A more ambitious canvas in this group is "The Studio." Here he goes almost all-out figurative. "Studio" is an admirable work — elaborately busy, kaleidoscopic, near-splashy and bold in its color-sureness. And yet an underlying inertia, a mood of langour, shorts the piece from being full-tilt heroic.

Rivers comes across stronger in "Last Civil War Veteran," "Next to Last Confederate Soldier," and "Dying and Dead Veteran." These put a pall over the small, second floor gallery they are hung in — a tribute to Rivers when his aim is unflinching. As statements they are powerful threnodies. Passionate pain and suspense hang over them. By turns, the brushwork is bold and eerily quiet. De Kooning's influence is present, but Rivers is off on his own deep search here. Next to his pop side, which merely tickles you (if that), these tear at the flesh. They are in a tragic mode, as opposed to a heroic one. The heroic is best shown in the large "George Washington Crossing the Delaware." Completed in 1953 when Rivers, at 30, was soaking in two such disparate streams as Bonnard and Hans Hofmann, the Delaware canvas is perhaps his most famous. And it could be — there is no law against it — that popular taste and critical acuity merge here. The work is muralistic in scope, admirably controlled in its muted, autumnal color patterns. There is mystery, too, in its half-submerged Washington figures — on a white charger, or elsewhere, as he surfaces out of a mist to make the crossing, or in a half-dozen other vignette-like parts.

Thus far — Rivers at his best and near-best. The schism occurs with those paintings that can be called kooky, on one level, and near sycophantic in the concessions to camp, on another. Examples of kooky are three or four chalky nudes (on the third floor), repellent in their manikin-like blandness, that hit you like some kind of circus side show. Apparently for kicks, Rivers has stenciled in anatomical direction signs, e.g., *pubes,* for you know where, *ginoccio,* for another place, *capezzolo,* etc., etc. In one of these pieces he goes Berlitz on us, switching his letterings to French. The gimmick shows up in yet another place, called "Celebrating Shakespeare's 400 Birthday (Titus Andronicus)," a bloody mélange of female torso, severed hands and ripped-out tongue. And, of course, the gratuitous labeling of these parts. Supposedly, this is Rivers' surrogate in oils for the bard's parable of terror — and it doesn't work. Indeed, if all these are put-ons, then the joke is foremost on Rivers. The humor (what else?) is tacky, the waste is obvious.

Camp is as good a place to end as any — and here we come upon the one canvas, by far, that drew the SRO sibilant "in" comments, near-shock among the midcult aficionados. The medium-size canvas, a nude of Frank O'Hara, can best be described as the artist peeling down his subject to his genitals. The stand-up pose is rather stodgy, veering to coy, in the way hands join in a kind of cupola on top of head. For a passing wink, no doubt, Rivers has put his model in unlaced ski boots. (Which makes the canvas, say, only nine-tenths a nude.) And the shock? For that, here is the word of a knowledgeable (male) museum buff: "It's all in the way Rivers paints the *member*. Male nudes must be limp, *never more*, in that spot."

Part of the problem might be: Is there an artist more Hamlet-clown-prone than Larry Rivers? He seems to echo this when he says, in a program note on his "History of the Russian Revolution,"an upended leviathan that crowds a whole wall: ". . . [This] is the greatest painting-sculpture-mixed media of the 20 Century, or the stupidist."

1966

Dialogs at the Whitney

a tape recording

SB: Bernard Weinrib, you call your piece "Three Aerial Forms." Flight of course is very much with us. But I don't get your drift. Your creation looks like sections, mock-ups, bits of fuselages that add up to a mood of "something" in flight. Okay, that's your creation. Your sculptor's right to fashion his material. And my right as a viewer, is to wonder whether your piece is not in fact an artistic "dive" (not a flight). For example, your note reads: "Lent by the Chemical-Plastics Division of the General Tire & Rubber Company." That bothers me because the stuff and guts of it seem to deify the sponsor, the Great God General Tire's corporate and products' stance. This is a trend I for one deplore: Artists being new-waved by the plastics-neat "outlook" of the GGGTs. "Functional," you may say, "plastics are part of life." And I say, "I want more; more *art* and less of what looks like dodads off the workbenches of the General Tires."

BW: You are square.

SB (*squarely, on to the next*): And you Marisol. You (and God?) must love you. You make so many of you. Replica of Ford car. Likenesses of Marisol in wrap-around sunglasses, cigarette holder clenched between teeth; Marisol as child, ribbon in hair; Marisol sporting man's hat, all three wood figures squeezed into jump seat. Up front, Marisol as Marisol. Next to her, at the wheel, a mock-up of young Negro; his photo pasted on wood. The entire ensemble (the family bit — get it?) bland as buckshot. Now, wouldn't you do better, with this kind of child's play, in the windows of F. A. O. Schwarz?

M (*curious*): F. A. O. Schwarz? That gallery, I never heard of.

SB: George Segal . . . At the Sidney Janis last season, you grabbed 'em with your Marquee assemblage. Stirred 'em to a point where, so to speak, they had riots in the head. ("Segal's stuff's got a good future book in pop," I heard one pearly-stickpin guy declare.) Along comes your "Figures on Rooftop." Two prone plaster-of-Paris figures, on *real* roof sheetings. Moth-eaten blanket under one, *real*. Rotary roof vent, *real*. (The artist, as scavenger?) Oh yes; man and woman sunning themselves, I guess. An agony symbol of city living? *Look at the poor ciphers, so helpless in their isolation.* Or, *How frenzied is their attempt at escape, from the many-millions' swarm.* In any case, the agony is a sausaged agony. Plastered ready-whip agony. You're giving us a feedback of norms. Next step, automation.

GS: Your putdown makes me shed tears, on the way to the bank.

SB (*moving on*): Ho ho, Bruce Conner, you want to scare us. Boys, girls and old ladies. Scare us with your gothic horror, called "Couch." Your reject (first thing that hit me) from a Salvation Army warehouse. Mangy skeleton reclining on rotted love-seat. That's it, your piece of "sculpture." Late Late Show Hitchcock. Or, Santini Brothers find Dada. Do you have a trucker's license?

BC: I have license.

SB: And Claes Oldenburg, conjurer man in the world of Happenings. (Just once, can you make "Claes Oldenburg" happen?) At the Whitney you have a thing called, "Soft Wall Switches." Unequivocally, the "putting us on" piece of the show. The pure no-nonsense con of the thing, is a poetry all its own. Three foot square section of chalk-white canvas, with two hamlike (canvas) switches growing out of it. Hence, Soft Wall Switches. Non-art, non-language, non-communication. For sure, tomorrow's connoisseur's masterpiece.

CO: Thanks for spelling my name right.

SB: (*moving to corner object; a low whir issues forth*): Sheldon Machlin . . . *Yeah yeah yeah* . . . This piece, this bauble of yours . . . *Yeah yeah yeah.* You call it "Cadence." . . . *Yeah yeah yeah* . . . Groovy, a juke box thing . . . *Yeah yeah yeah* . . . Row of (plexiglas) discs, mounted on a roller . . . *Yeah yeah yeah* . . . Spins 'round and 'round, like the real McCoy . . . *Yeah yeah yeah* . . . Only trouble is, I'm waitin' around for hours, *and no Beatles* . . . So it's *No no no.*

SM (*cooling it*): Beatles shmeatles, I have my buyer.

SB (*quickly, now*): John Chamberlain's "Kandy Krunch." Squeezed in mass of — auto fenders? Toylike in its lacquer-bright colorings. Seems like a cross between F.A.O. Schwarz and an automobile graveyard. *That's* it; part of a bad lot that went awry, in the auto crusher machine. And William King's "Business Man." Burlap sacks, supported by thin metal strips. Almost-good, posturing fun. But kids do this sort every day, and no one accuses them of being sculptors. Richard Stankiewicz's "Untitled " (out of mystery, or confusion?). Innards of an Oldsmobile Rocket engine; pushed around, welded into a steel mush. Could be out of the same crusher machine as Chamberlain's.

JC, WK, RS (*all together*): You're square square square.

SB: But take a piece like Jose De Rivera's "Construction Number 87," a twisting shoot of finely-wrought stainless steel, with more sculpture-in motion feeling than all the motor driven dodads put together. Or Peter Agostini's daring "Samurai 1400 A.D.," a suggestive, grape-cluster-like head, with a rich patina of old-green bronze. Or Isamu Noguchi's "Black Sun;" totemlike carvings, volcanic and surging, on a rounded form of gray-black granite. Or Leonard Baskin's "Apotheosis." Flat-backed, sharp-beaked, mythic. A bird of wood that, in the company of pops, looks as ancient as Mayan. Or, just good Baskin. Better square, than nowhere.

1965

To Look at Bonnard

If the Metropolitan Museum is NY's art powerhouse, the MOMA (Museum of Modern Art) is surely its main substation. No gallery can generate more juice—often having the effect of a pleasant surge for art lovers — but at times having a reverse effect, e.g., that of a hot burn at the heart of their sensibilities. The latter happens when fashion is the spur — when in essence penthouse values of what is chic, rather than art values of what is craft, determine the choice. And the first — the pleasant surge — came across recently, when MOMA opened a large and significant show of Bonnard canvases, prints and drawings. To their credit, and as a mark of their professionalism, let it be said that the Bonnard is right up there with MOMA's memorable retrospectives of Van Gogh; and of Picasso in past years.

As roving NY correspondent, I had planned to attend an afternoon press showing — on a Monday — and then found myself stranded miles from the Modern. So I missed the press one, and opted for a second preview, scheduled for that same night, which turned out to be a "black-tie, invitation only" affair. I showed up, more's the pity, in non-black-tie garb. I was wearing gray sport jacket, dark gray slacks. My tie was a gray-black-yellow rep, set against a button-down striped shirt. Seeing the droves of hi, middle society pouring through the glass entrance — the fleets of limousines emptying at the curb — the big white invitation cards held at the ready — seeing all this, I hesitated and thought, "Don't buck the odds."

Two days after the preview opening, I went back for a good first look. No parade, no social cakewalking. The artgoers moved as if in planetary motion, with the Bonnards on the walls the drawing sun of their attraction. The largest part of his work did indeed have that cataract quality of color, of light; a quality as near-blinding figuratively, as a direct look into the sun itself.

Typical were "The Palm" and "Tugboat at Vernon." The first — with its riot of green hedges, vermillion-orange-yellow flowers, vague womanly figure at the center — and, inklings of a tropic bay, top of canvas. And "Tugboat" — smaller in scale, thicker brushwork. With the same luminous intensity of color, of light. Gauguin came to mind, fleetingly. If anything

Bonnard is more the master of mosaic — a superb colorist for whom prisms, shadings, pastel tones, are virtually beginning and end of a total canvas. And thus a total experience.

An even better example of the "total" Bonnard, in color terms, was the large "The Brothers Bernheim." At first glimpse the canvas almost repelled, due to its flat-plane surface. But then the very flatness came alive, as a sheetlike reflector of the room's explosive light, its color vivacity. All the elements — the stolid business men (or art dealers?), the facing desks they're seated at, the sprawl of paperwork — added up to a clean, painterly, cinematic effect. At once bland in subject "Brothers" nevertheless was a stunning example of the Bonnard colorist world.

But color, that explosive glory of Bonnard's, is not his sole virtue. In a sense, it is the aromatic "mist" off his canvases. Another side is his nudes, of which there was a roomful. All of them partake of a strange, disturbing split, a tension, a duality. Perhaps one way of describing this is to say that if color is the "mist," then his nudes give off, additionally, an aroma of innocent "lust." Hence the duality: The nudes are temporal (that *lust*), and they are holy (full of innocent distance). Strangely, all seven or eight canvases in that one room were, quite literally, sloppy and sculpturally awkward. As figure canvases they seemed almost bland, uninteresting. But Bonnard's genius for shimmering color, for a sun-washed lustiness, gave them all a redeeming, touching quality.

And there was "Grapes," a small oil that almost exposes Bonnard at his simplest; his way of getting to you, on little, was shown by the "trick" of surrounding a fruit bowl with grapes — a bland, ordinary device by itself — with a thick oozy field of red-violet color; frenetic and eye-stopping at once. No comment would be complete, finally, without reference to "The Croquet Game." It is safe to say, and with no trace of pompousness, that this middle-size oil is a monument among all the riches of impressionism. Again, there were evocations of Gauguin, in the thick-palletted greens; and of the Japanese print world, in the sensitive-subtle facial details of the players. The canvas was an endless joy of variety, painterly drama. In naming the show, "Bonnard and His Environment," the Modern pays tribute to a total artist who made his own world of color and beauty.

1964

Edward Hopper, Poet-Painter of Loneliness

Three hammer-blows in three successive months on the soft head of popartistry: that's what has been happening lately in the Midtown art world. First there was the sleeper, and thinly attended, "American Masters — From Eakins to Pollock" show, at the Arts Students League; then came the stunning Pierre Bonnard retrospective, at the Museum of Modern Art; finally the Edward Hopper Exhibition, at the Whitney Museum, a retrospective of mammoth size that, literally, overflows the three large floors of the Whitney.

Edward Hopper of course lends himself to solo flight, admirably. The consistency of vision, the dogged pursuit of theme and mood, are richly evident in this important show. To state this mood would seem to be simpler that to limn it, to sound its depths. (His paintings look so *easy!*) At any rate I can try a few words here: Hopper's canvases are the representation of objects, places, figures and nudes that are trapped in tranquil, though not always splendid, isolation. And this is merely the labeling of it. The *taste* of his works, the ingesting of their uncompromising craft elements, is its own biggest reward.

Where to begin? With 74 oils, 62 water colors, 21 drawings and 27 etchings, dating from 1908 to 1963, the task of putting down some notes, on Hopper's life work becomes Herculean. In but a single, hour-long tour I myself near-filled a small, spiral notebook. Perhaps then, a direct transcription of these notes would do best.

The oils — at random. "Lighthouse Hill." The purity of light and shadow — washed, almost, of all distortion — gives a feeling of the airless, brooding world of De Chirico. "Corner Saloon." This is one time where Hopper seems "tuned-in" to the Ashcan School — John Sloan, specifically. The dramatic overtones, here, are in interesting contrast to his usual, understated tensions. "Lighthouse at Two Lights," and "Early Sunday Morning." Two striking works that, in their lofty isolation, evoke a theme of beginnings; a theme that Robert Frost might have been expressing, in his late, totemlike line: "The land was ours before we were the land's."

"Road and Trees" (1962); "Sun in an Empty Room" (1963); and "Sunlight in a Cafeteria" (1961) — all of them late works that seem flawed, to some degree, next to earlier Hoppers. The mood of isolation remains; but the figures, as in "Cafeteria," are a bit stilted, like mannequins, with no real pull towards the center of Hopper's private world.

Are these "tired" canvases, tired by repetition, worn out? ("So what," one is tempted to say, "at ages 79 to 81!") And then comes a 1960 oil, "Second Story Sunlight" — the aging artist has a trick in his bag, still! Here is Hopper at his brightest. The washed white bungalow, vivid and subtle. The blonde young girl, with her washed "American" looks. And the gothic-featured lady. Both sitting together, and yet worlds apart. All the detail in a surrounding trap, a forest, of vivid green trees. A vision, a painterly vision, of aloneness!

Two more canvases. "Nighthawks" — 1942 — the "famous painting." Triangular, wedge shaped street-corner coffee shop. Man seated alone, man and woman seated together. Counterman, "adrift" in his own private limbo. And the eerie, dark-light tensions, on the outside — juxtaposed with a slice of a red-brick corner building. All lending a vivid, three-dimensional effect. Equally famous — "Early Sunday Morning" — circa 1930. That one-story, storefronted, red-brick "poem" of the American suburban drabness. All of it caught in the trap of Hopper's purest vision; his miracle " extracting" process. (A word on that, in a moment.)

And, three or four more oils. "East River" — an example of Hopper's middle (1930) and most striking period. The morning light, just beyond the somber tenements, looks literally afire. "Railroad Sunset." The isolation motif — as vivid an example as any. A lonely signal house, half in shadow, half out. And a long, tapering band of orange, fiery-orange, sunset. Lovely, yet with a sense of a flawed vision. (Or is the flaw in the viewer? A recoil perhaps, from too sharp and constant exposure to the total work of a poet-artist . . . who shows us *our own* isolation? Long question, long art.) "Moonlight Interior" (1921-23). Strange, almost way-out Hopper. Nude, with poetic, blue-blurry, romantic tone. The woman, kneeling, ready to plunge into bed. An astral feeling, or "current." The blown-out cotton drapes, at the open window, seem to move with the night breeze. Has overtones of Edwin Dickenson, the midnight-touched, and near-forgotten painter allegorist.

It is a brave art, and an eyefilling one as well.   1965

Ashcan School — Si;
Campbell Cans — No

That buff-colored eminence on West Fifty-seventh Street, The Art Students League of New York, has assembled a formidable show: "American Masters from Eakins to Pollock." On a street that has fobbed off the whole school of Katzen-jammer pop purveyors, here's the 87-year-old League quietly putting forth 25 works by as many artists — works that wouldn't be found dead, because of their surging life and brio, in the same company as the Warhols, Segals, Marisols, et al.

The artists have in common the fact that all have either gone to school, or taught at the League, at one time or other in its often meaningful history. That the show is thinly-ribbed, with but one work by each artist, is a weakness that's hard to deny; but it's a weakness of appetite gone unslaked. The show is also a bold comment on the depth of response we feel from works of the American School, a road that has pulled us up short and perplexed at a junkyard stop of Campbell soup cans, marquee assemblages and advertising galoot dieties posing as art.

Let's start with Thomas Eakin's shimmering "Home Scene," a mother and daughter compositional masterpiece that, for all its surface placidness, catches holy fire because of its surprise tensions. Though the work is solidly traditional, it is veiled in such sure tones of mood dissonance, as to give one the feeling that Eakins is the beginning of our maturest art.

Next there's George Bellows' famous "Dempsey and Firpo" knockout canvas, with its naive appeal and romancing viva-city. To Bellows a fight is a fight is a romance-splurge, and not a cathartic goose for novelists gone bone-dry in subject matter. Bellows' canvas rewards us, and never more than now, for all the eye-strained hours we've endured reading the depth-bombing nonsense of the boxing hipsters, Mailer, Schulberg, et al.

And there's John Marin's vivid semi-abstract seascape "Casco Bay, Maine" — a precursor of the best of our own time — Kline, Hofmann, Guston — and of course, the early Pollock. From this canvas one can make a small essay on the theme that nothing's really new in art except the audacity of recurring talent. Close by the Marin is a George Grosz canvas,

a main-dish of gallows humor called "The Crucified Ham."
This intriguing work seems to put considerable distance
between the nightmare savagery of Grosz' Hitler period, and
his relatively calmer American period. And yet the thought
lingers: Could he have been putting us on? Maybe that distance was not so great after all, for Grosz the artist.
And maybe the little old ham was, metaphorically, the
same old tortured human of his earlier canvases. The demonic
brushwork and the riot of rich color is what's unsettling about
the work. This fevered style, so typical of Grosz' overall
output, was his own very special — and bitter — genius. On
another level it's a gallows kind of humor from a man who
might have been seeing dripping barbecues for the first time,
where once all he saw was bloody barricades.

There's Max Weber's buoyant "Adoration of the Moon,"
a four-figure gem of Hasidic joie de vivre — the four top-
hatted, bible(?) toting ancients in passionate discourse —
on what? Why the starkly luminous disc is up there, in the
first place? And for whose glory — God's or man's? There's
Boardman Robinson's "Entombment," a powerful, neo-primi-
tive canvas that masks a highly sophisticated draftsmanship.
And from among the sculpture, an Easterner-gone-cowboy's
glowing and starkly realistic tribute to the West, Frederick
Remington's small bronze "The Mountain Man." Works by
Borglum, Epstein, Hassam, Kuhn, Kuniyoshi, Luks, Marsh,
and others, complete the show.

The *New York Times'* Stuart Preston, in "wonder why" of
the month, wondered why the show was needed at this time.
So we'll tell him: To wipe New York's face clean of the *hoo
ha* art of Flushing Meadow, on the Southeastern perimeter,
and the popartistry in Midtown. It did just that for us.

1964

Art Scene

Robert Motherwell's retrospective at the Museum of Modern
Art cut the mustard of critical pros and cons like no show in
years. His large canvases and paper collages for most were
no more than mammoth hieratic doodles. One or two others
called his work heroic and or full of mythic connotation.
Roughest comment was that of the daily critic who said — as

between Motherwell's canvases, and his tireless verbalizing on his work, there was little to choose — both were equally inflated.

The Alberto Giacometti show at the same place drew nothing but raves. And large adoring crowds. The leanness, iconoclasm and sheer verve of most of his canvasses and sculpture, and the wry, mocking humor of some — added up to as total a crowd pleaser as any show in recent years. Which raises a teaser, so to speak: "Why the easy rapport? Doesn't his work typify the whole midcentury bag — alienation, lostness, Kafka, Camus? It could be that the mirror image is one of laughing for want of tears, at least in part.

School of Paris — Paintings From the Marx Collection. Making it a triple, the Modern opened a small show of "Forty-five capital works of painting from one of the greatest private collections . . . of works of the early part of the century." Well, not so small. And the operative word from the museum's release is "capital."

The beauty part for us; See how a Braque ("Seated Nude") begins to look like a Picasso; a Picasso ("Still Life With Plaster Arm") like a Braque; a Leger ("The City") like a Juan Gris; and a Gris ("Still Life With Playing Cards") like a Leger. Also, works of Bonnard, Matisse, Fresnaye, Dufy.

Larry Rivers in a large retrospective at the Jewish Museum — 188 canvases, sculptures and prints. Opened during a Newspaper Guild strike, which could have been bad, but the *Herald Tribune* opted out of its publisher's agreement, which was good for Rivers: Trib's Emily Genauer (to a tripled readership of 900,000) called him top American artist today. We call him a wildly uneven craftsman.

Pop, Op and now comes Yes art. In a Madison Avenue postage-stamp of a gallery, the Fitzgerald, a group of canvases, constructions and collages — all more or less in the familiar Brilloed, Campbelled and Coked pop iconography. Where the Yes comes in, and where this stuff differs from the popsters, we have yet to figure out. (Soon as word comes from Miss Susan Sontag, we'll let you know.) . . . The MOMA, in what could be called an attack of the bends, yielded up its movie auditorium to discussions and showings of avant film. The eight-day gig had the umbrella title, "The Independent Film: Selections From The Film-Makers' Cooperative, New York." Featured were full-lengths, experimentals, shorts and

rushes. From Bruce Conner, Stan Vanderbeek, Gregory Marko-
poulos, Kenneth Anger, Robert Breer and others. Breer's was
called "Eyewash," a fair assessment (we'd say) of his and
half dozen others. Still this is a big breakthrough, and now
let's separate the pros from the shakey-camera nudiks, stop
calling it a rutty "underground," and swear Jonas Mekas to
silence for just 24 hours.

1966

Oskar Kokoschka: Unstoppable Octogenarian

At 80, Oskar Kokoschka is doing a landscape painting of
New York, high in a midtown building. The commission was
given during the recent Marlborough-Gerson Gallery retrospective called "Oskar Kokoschka — An English Birthday
Tribute," a show of remarkable range and power that includes
68 paintings, 57 water-colors and drawings, and a selection
of recent graphics. Take one work alone from this important
show, and the guess of what Kokoschka might be up to in his
New York canvas becomes staggering. It was a landscape
called "Berlin 13 August, 1966" and the view from a middle-
distance was of a phenomenological turmoil of post-impres-
sionist color, trapped in a skin of Turneresque shimmer and
beauty. As to "Berlin's" impact, the mind reeled as from a
vision of apocalyptic fury; but in the next moment a change
seemed to occur that was like the beholding of a New Jerusalem, the artist having offered up his own sense of order
and continuity from a mosaic of the blood, fire and raped
steel of a walled city. One would guess that Kokoschka's New
York can be no less: a Janus city of turmoil calmed by the
light and order that a visionary artist can give.

And what an artist he is! His search takes man with brush
from that insane turmoil of the immediate, to a serene end-
product of painted canvas that resolves itself in — how else
to say it? — a life force. Kokoschka moreover expresses this
in a stormy eclecticism that calls up most of the leading
European movements of this century. Over and over again
the force asserts itself in the startling series of city landscapes, the almost caged beauty of the portraits, the mood of
mystery and tension of the allegorical pieces. The stamp of

Kokoschka is a stamp of hard, at times almost brutal, idiosyncrasy — yet by a miracle of line, color and inner vision, his art becomes transformed into a statement not only of an artist's experience, but of a recognizable time, place and mood as well.

Mood of course is a Kokoschka staple. Obsessive, changing or elusive, it always seemed to drill its way from canvas to eye, as in the tracking of a dream or nightmare profile by day. In three early portraits — "Professor Hans Tietze and Mrs. Erika Tietze-Conrat," "Portrait of Peter Altenberg" and "Portrait of Lotte Franzos" — a note of pain was softened here and there by a water-colory transparency of brushstroke, giving a kind of wispy gloss to studies that were sharply delineated, as if Van Gogh had been crossed with Whistler. Another early portrait — "E. Ludwig," subtitled "The Blind Man" — had the same sense of a split mood, the features done in massive, granitic strokes of deep greens and blotchy blood-reds that more than suggested a tragic study, yet one that had a kind of midnight dignity in the pose. Lighter in texture and mood was one of several portraits of Alma Mahler (call her, for a pun "Alma Mater," for Kokoschka obviously went to school to this rather stormy subject, both in terms of friendship and Eros). This one dating from 1913 had a soft and tinty effervescence, with a frozen Mona Lisa play of a smile; the face was round and childlike, yet very much womanly, with a touch of the spooky that made you want to wink. And in the portrait titled "Nancy Cunard" from the period 1914, a mood of masklike rigidity was contrasted — and hence softened — by an absolute freedom of background color — pastelly blues, grays and purples — all of which had the effect of dark and somber thoughts, encased in a wild, free-form riot of brightness.

No less striking in mood were the landscapes and cityscapes — such as "Dolomite Landscape" from 1915 and "Dresden, Neustat V" from 1922. In both the first — a Cezannesque study of thick greens and blues, a deep wash of moonlight and stark chalky mountain peaks running in a high outer rim; and the second — which was more in a Cubist vein, and remarkable (once again) for its bold brushwork and color, Kokoschka imposed a sense of myth that in one degree or another characterized all his work in this genre. Two more city-scapes: "Paris, the Opera" from 1924, Dufy-like with a busy, frenetic movement, playful yet strong; and "Prague: View from Moldau Piet," a piece from 1936 that had glints of Turner, crossed with Renoir. In the allegorical pieces, most of all, one could see Kokoschka's enormous range, a range that appears to be unstoppable. Typical were two paintings that spanned a 57-year period — the 1909 "Death and Angel 1" and the 1966 "Saul and David" — the first with its soft dreamlike tone being a release into a kind of understated expressionism, and the second with its brilliant coloring and strong brushwork being — similarly — a release, this time into a gutsy, songful and edgy post-impressionism all at once. (Kokoschka on "Saul": ". . . he has a tremendous grudge against his age . . . He cannot grasp the fact that he is now eighty — as I am . . . (And) like David who is standing behind him in this picture — it seems only yesterday I was eighteen . . .") There was finally that single painting (isn't there, always?) of which one would like to have said: "Just wrap it, please. I'll take it as is." It was a late (1963) and rather small garden scene called "Grapevines," a rich collage with a depth of summery abundance right out of — and perhaps surpassing — the world of Bonnard. In sum one might say that if Picasso overturns movements, Kokoschka restores and adds his own peculiar genius to them.

Kokoschka has said of his work: "My paintings are really a personal diary of my life" and "For me the real miracle is life, not art." To that he added: "And you can only have art if you see, really see, what life is." Which is of course a trinity — self, world and work.

1967

Take Me to your Architect

We have passed the site (the newly arrived Huntington Hartford Gallery of Modern Art, at Columbus Circle) on our walks — gazed at it from the windows of Broadway and Fifth Avenue buses — stopped by at night to see it aflame in all its neon-white purity. Now that the stone flower is in full bloom, we'd like to reveal a little game we've indulged in — privately — on all those shakedown tours of ours. Call it a game of architectural charades — or, for those who prefer a working title, a game of *Essence*. It goes this way. Name ten pictures that come into mind, as you are looking the building over.

Here are our ten:

1. An ice house, Venetian
2. An anti anti missile silo
3. Tomorrow's hotel for visiting penguins
4. A bunker, for a last stand against the Martians
5. Jimmy Hoffa's Alamo, if Bobby makes it in '68
6. An IBM punch card in stone — see the frieze of punch holes run wild — on the building's borders
7. New York's Midtown Champs Elysees, terminating in a jai ali court
8. Son of Coliseum, out of Philharmonic Hall
9. Rich man's culture crypt, or Woodlawn on the IND
10. Package deal: Caracalla Baths — Playboy Club.

And, as a bonus and or alternate:

11. Real estate periscope on Central Park: "Wow, Charlie, look at all those untapped acres of grass and trees . . . *Doin' nothin'.*"

If the East Side's new Pan Am gargantua has been called a "club" (and we assume the word is meant to convey a weapon; rather than, say, a bunnies' and playboy's fun house), the West Side can now match them club for club.

In spades!

1964

Music

New York Sound goes Classical

As I approached Central Park's Sheep Meadow, from Tavern on the Green's macadam roadway, I could catch the plaintive strings — from a good half-mile away! — of Beethoven's "Eroica" Symphony. The first of a trio of concerts in August — free and to be repeated in the four other boroughs — by the New York Philharmonic was in progress. The bandshell, a miracle erector-set of Fiberglas planks, far reaching acoustics and frosty-white lighting, set up and broken down in a five-hour crash, looked like a tiny white cavern in the black distance. The downfield scene was brilliantly lit and vaguely apparitional, against a dark forest of trees.

I scaled the benches on the West Walk, and made my way forward to the crowds. They were spread out — or sprawled — in a wide circle that closed ten feet short of the shell. Sheep Meadow, big as three Yankee Stadiums, lies beneath the biggest patch of open-sky in Manhattan. People had been coming by for hours before the 8:30 concert opening. There were dating couples with picnic baskets, young marrieds with one, two or three kids in tow, East Side executives (junior grade) and office girls toting bottles of wine, singles from the neighborhood with leashed dogs or cats, all staking out on blankets, or canvas folding chairs, an interregnum under a fading sun that was more Chautauqua than Midtown.

The huge crowd of 75,000 was a relaxed mass of listeners now, as Leonard Bernstein led his players on, not so much storming as walking his way through the "Eroica." Always a conductor with a choreographic bent, Bernstein's style was handsomely suited to the big outdoors. His phrasing had sweep and clarity, his beat was precise and (a switch, for him) was even a bit too calculated. Ideally one wants in this towering symphony, to have architecture, but not at the expense of "soul." In any case, he was getting assistance from the audience here and there, in the form of a sudden obbligato of sound from a child, or a low half-bark from a dog. The peak of excitement came, as it happened, after the intermission, when Bernstein mounted a performance of Stravinsky's lush and volcanic "The Rite of Spring," a performance that had the huge audience near rocking with pleasure. His stress on the piece's dynamics, on its rich and gutsy syncopation, got over to one clutch of youths to a point where Bernstein's baton had them, literally, dancing on the park green. (Doing a Midtown frug, to Stravinsky's "primitive" European modern.) All in all it was a "30-in-one" concert, as someone had called it, meaning, the record crowd was the equal of 30 Philharmonic Hall audiences.

The attendance for the second concert, one week later, was "kept down" to a mere 40,000 by threats of rain. Lucas Foss, a taller and less choregraphic Bernstein, took over the podium for that set, in a program that featured Mozart's *G Minor* Symphony and, in what turned out to be the evening's popular treat, Marian Anderson reciting from Lincoln in Aaron Copland's "Lincoln Portrait." There were ominous streaks of lightning, along with a rumble or two, after which the clouds did open. But it's in the nature of these concerts that New Yorkers, not otherwise known for their love of rain, will wait out anything this side of a monsoon, and the gamble paid off this time. Ten minutes or so after the first light showers, which began during the Mozart and caused a halt, Foss came back on the podium. The crowds, all but the handful who had left, came out from under umbrellas, blankets, newspapers and trees, and greeted Foss's return with a cheer. Luck held on through the Mozart, and later, right on through the Lincoln piece, the regal presence and performance of Marian Anderson turning out to be added reward for the management's, conductor Foss's and, most of all, the audience's chancy patience. (When Miss Anderson repeated the Lincoln at Brooklyn's Prospect Park, a few nights later, it was during the hours of serious Negro-white clashes only a mile or two away, in the East New York section of the borough. It might be said of that night: Art is long, life is short *and angry*.)

That gallimaufry of a musical stew, the Brahms Piano Concerto No. 1, was a good juicy fare to end the series with. Rain had washed out the concert, on the previous evening, and the quick re-scheduling had caused a falling off in attendance — to, once again, a mere 40,000. Everything else though was big — not too surprising of course in so elongated a piece of romanticism as the Brahms. Rudolph Firkushny, at the piano, and Alfred Wallenstein, on the podium, had combined forces to produce a rousing finish to the series. And if this is not New York City's most ambitious and most alive pop culture scene, it surely fits the bill until something more grand comes by.

1967

Aging Infant

What can one say that's new about *this* symphony?

The teaser insinuated itself as I sat back at Carnegie (mid-orchestra, outside aisle seat, best for conductor profiling) and listened to the opening bars of the Beethoven "Eroica." I wanted to check out this one, led by spare, aging Leopold Stokowski and his own (for what, the 20th time?) pick-up orchestra (which he's named the "American Symphony"), with some memorable "Eroicas" I've caught in the past.

There was the prime performance of all, some years back, which is etched in memory with the sharp cutting boldness of a Rembrandt print: That of Arturo Toscanini putting the New York Philharmonic through golden hoops for 45 minutes of sustained, brilliant, fire-consuming music making. Toscanini, who stood on the podium a lithe five-five bantam, the magic of his hands working over the heads of his players like a very wand of Promethien fire. His music lush, but never soapy; diamond pointed, but never chipped; lyrically haunting, but never keening.

In more recent years, there was Herbert Von Karajan and the Berlin Philharmonic, in the same hall. This was a reconstituted B-P, risen from the ashes of past great ensembles under such as Furtwangler and Fritz Busch. The tone of the Berliner's "Eroica" was one of almost absolute purity, but with an emphasis on command and precision that to me was disturbing. It was as if the players, over and above what the conductor was doing, had it in mind that the paragon work was theirs and theirs alone. That no note, no passage, could be done other than from some fixed past; that the score was a mathematics' graph, rather than the warm and dramatic markings of musical genius. All in all, I expected the entire ensemble to rise, at the finis, lower their instruments, click their heels — and salute their maestro, von Karajan.

And so to Stokowski, the aging infant with the aureole of white hair. He is our local marvel, is Stokey — always listening to his very own voice; a peculiar voice that combines showy, almost saucy, lushness with a broad, though never aloof, seeking for classic lines. If he took the opening movement (that movement that seems to look out at the world, at the heavens, with the very eye of a Galileo; and which gives off those near-stacatto, jaggedly beautiful glints of musical lightning) a little too amiably — it may have been a case of an old symphonic hand measuring a new group's staying power.

And stay they did. Right on through that taut, startlingly worked-out, and thorough, Allegro; the sad, affecting, but always manly cries of urgency, of the Funeral March; the Jovian bolts of play, of gods cavorting, of gypsies frolicking, that is the Scherzo; and the miracle of the Finale, with the mystery of its dominant statement: a little country dance that becomes an elegy — and, further along, the yearning return of the Funeral theme, for the merest shadow of a looking backward; then, in the movement's final exhausting recapitulation, the development of that little country dance into a full-blown chorus, an explosive paean, of affirmation.

It was good music, offered at the full by an always-interesting conductor, no matter his age, and his predominately young charges. Nor was the eye anything but pleased at the sight of a good two-dozen lady instrumentalists.

1963

The Philadelphians

"After this one, you can put Lenny Bernstein in the *ashcan*!"

The putdown from a Carnegie Hall galleryite, at once so defiantly rude and acidly partisan, pretty well summed up, if a little invidiously, a brilliant and pulsating reading of the Sibelius Second Symphony by Eugene Ormandy and the Philadelphia Orchestra. Capping an all-Sibelius evening, the performance brought on wave after wave of heartfelt bravos. A tired but smiling conductor and his 100-odd players took, all told, a half dozen calls. Only the lights-on prevented more.

Of what elements is such music made? Let us begin with

the obvious note that the Second is a work that is grooved —
there is no other word — for popular appeal. It is large-
souled, spacious, hauntingly lyrical. If it has few surprises (in
the sense, say, of the more private mysteries of a Mahler
opus), it can nevertheless claim for itself that quality of drama,
or organ-toned grandeur, so typical of Sibelius' big works.

Here the north country master rides, as it were, two
musical steeds to the far reaches of symphonic inspiration.
One is the Nordic — a wild nature-driven animal racing along
to the full play of woodwinds, horns and tympani. The other
— a handsomely plastic Pegasus that soars to the lyric turns
of massed violins and velvet-toned cellos. Primitive "country"
values ride in tandem with romantic "Tchaikovskyan" ones.

If one may continue, on the excuse that this is a non-
professional's report, with metaphor: Ormandy's way with this
symphony was that of the sculptor. He gave careful weight and
balance to each element, molded the work to Olympian finish.
His approach was the timeless one of the classicist, but it
was never stilted. And what of Bernstein? We bring him in
because that galleryite may, after all, have something there.
One has seen him (at his "choreographic" worst) do this very
kind of symphony, unlike Ormandy, with all the slapdash
abandon of the atelier bohemian. Globs of wild color here,
drippings of keening sentimentality there.

You pays your money, and takes your choice.

For us there was the added pleasure in the way the hall
"sounded." We were high in the wing of the top tier, standing
for the most part, looking down the wide canyon of parquet
and ample stage. It was a rare treat; no tuned-up roof baffles
(and what do they add except aural bafflement?) needed. Not
here, in a hall that for sheer acoustic honesty cannot, we
believe, be matched.

Indeed, we will press the point: After a hundred different
maestros, from Bernstein to Klemperer; and a hundred different soloists, from Cliburn to Milstein, have had those baffles
moved hither and yon, to suit their individual wants — the
Lincoln Center hall will still not come up to the sweetness,
pungency and sheer velvety excellence of sound this very
queen of music halls "makes."

Nor does it hurt that you don't have to dress, to go to
Carnegie out of *Town and Country* or *Gentlemen's Quarterly*.

1964

5 Manhattan Descants

Manhattan Descants

The memory of big, bluff and deepvoiced Ed Blair, Tennessean and former Wobbly troubadour, who for years major-domoed some real swinging Sunday afternoon poetry readings, on this spot — the memory of Ed is not absent. We are on the long open Gansevoort pier, about a stone's throw from the White Horse, for another Sunday session. And they gather like pilgrims. Chaucerian bards in sandals, lady poets in calico, an oddball in gold vest redolent of Madison Av. They read in piping voice. Poems of protest, lyric pieces of melody and mood, staccato lines that are the very tracery of unsquare Greenwich Village. The river — flat, generous and glinting North River — flows at their backs. Scows pipe their own sea chanty as they glide by. Big ocean liners move downstream, soundlessly. And as the river is the highway of the world, just so are the poets' lines the voices of the world, moving outward on that Gotham-mirroring North (or Hudson) River.

The scene shifts to a leafy, triangular wedge — St. Mark's in the Bouwerie's mini graveyard. Night of jazz under the stars. Audience of jazzniks, neighborhood children, teenagers high on nothing but *the scene*. The music-makers sit and stand in the round. Tenor-sax-with goatee riffing sweetly. Mr.-piano-keys diddling, ever so lightly, those keys. Bassman and drummerman — the one strumming on gut, the other jouncing his sticks off the hard, tight skins. The notes soar, hang high in the leafy trees. Cool summer breezes carry those notes down Tenth Street, past the narrow galleries with names like Aegis, etc. A young miss done up in ponytail, sleepy but fighting it, plays a phantom London Bridge. She loops her small body under the relaxed archway of her mother's body — the latter standing tall in cotton blouse and Bermudas, pliant as bulrushes on the wind. And deep — six feet deep or more — below the footstones of several church elders, who lie buried in St. Mark's graveyard, one can almost hear the rattle of bones — the happy *give* of skeletal remains to the beat of those keys, skins and gut.

And this scene. Seated on a bench in 42nd Street's Bryant Park, William Cullen looking down his bronze nose solemnly, more judge-like than bardic. This is a piece of real estate! Tree-lined walks, stone benches for checker players, an acre or two of manicured green lawns. Italian oldtimer garment workers, killing time between piece-work dates in shops nearby, play some rapid but very tight games of checkers. The signs read "Keep Off The Grass" but pigeons don't; they squat in congress of tens, twenties; and they preen feathers under a high noon sun. Lunch-hour concert — a recording of "Tosca" — people coming by with easy stride — as if they've shaken off the business armature of the day. Secretaries, slim and evenly tanned in sleeveless dresses, sit down crosslegged with Chock Full O' Nuts lunchbags in laps. Haspel-draped salesmen with tache cases, or outsize envelopes that bulge with silk swatches of their trade, do the same. Two children — sister and brother, blonde as cornsilk — busy themselves doing dissections on some patchy leaves they've gathered up. They work small fingers up and down the blanched veins, the browning surfaces. First probings into nature's secrets? And the sun pours down a myriad of slanting beams, through long colonnades of shade trees. The music, if it doesn't stop the clock, the marching mercantile clock, does suspend all thought of time *for now*. The songfilled moments are all. Bryant Park is sealed from grating buses, and lurching cabs only 100 feet away. Maria Callas's Tosca — a big, big voice. Suddenly, the high rise of that magnificent voice stirs the children, invades their probings. They let the leaves fall away, fall from their hands in a slow arc to the ground. And they approach their mother who sits on a bench nearby. Trio come together, in a nestling rapport. Sun-drenched, song-drenched noontime in Bryant Park.

Scene four. Blithe strains of Mozart, shot through with instant fireflies, at an evening's chamber concert in Washington Square. On the north quarter, the aloneness of that heroic Arch, and its twice-life-size General Washington stone figures . . . Magnified now in the eerie-pink wash of flood lights, to that *nth* degree of presence that is the stuff of dreams. In the same sweep, the Arch is companion to a long, low contour of Georgian '90s elegance. Two blocks of red-brick, white-archway houses that is the stuff of Jamesian novels. South, too, the eye catches period piece beauty. In the form of that tawny, high towered, Venetian touched house of worship — Judson Memorial Church. (Where worship is many-faceted. God's script, the arts in all forms, are offered equally.) The outdoor concert draws a "gallery" of young couples, bodies lean and relaxed in Levis and slacks, who stretch out on the flattened lawns that surround the music stand. And out-of-towners en famille who make a turn in the road. From noisy MacDougall Street coffee house, to outer circle of listeners. The audience is diffuse, and it is one. Night music is the gatherer.

Massive and high-quality Philharmonic concerts on Sheep Meadow — 70,000 symphony moonlighters at the crack of a baton; "Coriolanus" at the oatmeal bowl Delacorte Theater in Central Park; live dance band at the Harlem Meer; Bread and Puppet Theatre in neighborhoods, around town; music ensemble on Riverside Park's cinder track, hard by the Hudson; folk rock concerts in Tompkins Square Park; big jazz jam in Bedford Stuyvesant. Pockets of beauty for eye and ear; in the free city of the arts.

1967

Search & Destroy

One of the tougher issues in the New York teachers' strike was that of "unruly" students. Naturally, everybody got into a semantics bag over that word "unruly." What's "unruly" to teachers may be nothing more than "doing my thing" to students. Anyway the union claimed the problem could best be solved by giving "teach" more say in the area of classroom discipline. And so it went — the problem was not, and still is not, solved.

Maybe the military shows a way out. Make the "unruly" schools (and we all know *those*) battle areas and offer teachers in those areas 20% battle pay over the base, as in the military. This doesn't necessarily mean that what's going on in certain New York school districts is comparable, say, to what's going on in Vietnam. Still, if it's fair to give the G.I. that extra 20%, why not the teachers?

But even if we concede the wisdom of battle areas, there remains one more delicate problem. Given her new role of classroom disciplinarian, the teacher will inevitably take on some of the posture of an occupying army. Ghetto parents are aware of, and have given hot voice to, just such fears. Nor can it be ignored that black power academicians have also voiced such fears. All of which points again to Vietnam, as a possible solution. Where teachers ride the kids hard, as if they (the teachers) are on some kind of schoolmarmy search-and-destroy operation, the kids and parents should be allowed — indeed, should have legal right — to act the part of a parent-junior Viet Cong.

1967

The Waiting Game

Want to see grass roots bureaucracy at work? Do jury duty in a civil court in New York. There is little that can match it for wasted motion, wasted dollars or fractured time. Our jury system — and I speak from bitter experience — is a bog of quicksand on the path to justice.

I put in eight days recently, each day packed with hours of dull waiting. Only twice was I in any way close to getting on a jury. Nor does it reveal any secret when I say that both cases, in retrospect, were far short of being momentous.

Come along with me, on my first day. The New York State court-house on Foley Square is its own monument to waste. In the main-floor rotunda, 20 elevators await you. Manned, not automated. And it's a toss-up that I'll get an elevator all to myself — it happened to me several times. All this for a five-story edifice full of hidden offices, catacomb-like mezzanines, dank circular hallways. Yearly maintenance in this Hexagon-on-the-Subway could probably put both Governor Rockefeller and Mayor Wagner into orbit around Venus.

After running the gamut of two information-booth men and a starter and assistant at the elevators — and still not being sure where I'm headed — I get to the jury room on the fourth floor at 9:30 a.m. The room resembles a union hiring hall, a capacious place with long benches and bad acoustics. Murals of Old New Amsterdam deck the walls. I count a corps of 14 or 15 clerks and four uniformed court officers ready for the day's routine — plus an SRO complement of about 250 prospective jurors.

A man standing at the table microphone runs the main show. Roll call starts at approximately 9:45, is not over until 10:20.

A sideshow activity is hearing deferment pleas. This involves the talents of four clerks seated primly behind a waist-high barrier. They listen, no frequently, doodle with pencils. *An emergency? . . . We may go along with that . . . Will six weeks from today do?*

Smiles are traded, and a few handshakes. This morning a dozen or more citizens are excused. But no fear. The dent is soon mended by the IBMs and roller card indexes.

There is a flurry of interest as Mr. Croupier goes to his drum for the first panel selections of the day. By now, it is minutes past noon. Taste buds are beginning to tremble at the thought of lunch. The babble subsides as he cranks the drum and picks dozens of jurors' slips from it. Between roll call and panel selection, there is a two-hour hiatus during which the most occupied person by far is the tall, graying court officer whose head is buried in a book of law — perhaps he's learnin' while earnin'.

Thirty or more names are called, mine not among them, "The rest of you," intones the caller, "are excused for lunch. Be back here at 2 p.m."

Two days and many newspapers, paperbacks and weeklies later, my name is finally picked. Again it is a noontime call, so I lose the gamble for a long lunch. About 40 of us are put in a group. We are ushered to a third-floor courtroom, empty and broodingly silent for the moment. We sit at the back benches and read the gilt inscription that circles halo-like on the wall above the judge's chair: "In God We Trust."

Finally several people emerge from the judge's chambers. A second court officer hauls another drum, smaller than Mr. Croupier's, to a table. All group around the drum. They face us and one man comes forward. He's the jury clerk. He introduces two attorneys. One, eager and oozing palmanship, is the plaintiff's counsel. The other, full of stern efficiency, is defense counsel from an insurance company.

We are told that the case before us involves a man in his 30s who, while riding his bicycle on the upper West Side, back in April, 1958, was knocked down in traffic by an automobile. The suit is for $10,000. After the clerk takes 12 names from the drum, each is announced and seated in the jury box. The seats are temporary, to be sure. These people must be quizzed by attorneys before making the grade.

No experience I can remember on land, sea or in the Army can match the five-hour session that follows.

Like lint pickers in a Seventh Avenue fabric house, counsel take turns picking us apart. *Ever ride a bicycle? Ever drive an automobile? Ever in an accident? Work for an insurance company? Relative? Believe a person has a right to ride a bicycle on New York streets? . . . Within the law, of course? As a woman, will you lean one way or the other in your sympathy?*

Etc. Etc.

They dismiss nine of the 12 jurors between them. After the drum is rolled for nine new names, the interrogation crunch goes on. Along around 4.30 p.m. weariness gives way to a glimmer of hope. It appears that the right combination of Solomon-pure citizens has at last been found.

Suddenly the defense attorney hesitates. He wants a conference.

Jury clerk and two lawyers huddle to a side and confer in low key. No backfield, with seconds remaining and touchdown needed, could look more unstrung. The clerk comes out of the huddle and paces six steps to the jury box. He announces, with an impatient shrug, "You are all dismissed. Report back to the Jury Room at 9:30 a.m. on Monday." (Eventually, I believe, the case will be settled out of court.)

On Monday the waiting game resumes. The jury room is more SRO than ever. I count roughly 275 jurors in that room. At $6 a day, these people are collecting over $8,000 on the week. Figure it out on the year and you can send the City Comptroller (who foots the bill) on that Venus jump with Rocky and Bob.

Nothing happens to me that day, and I exchange notes with a dozen fellow jurors. Of that dozen, only two have sat on actual cases. Both had no chance to render judgment because, in each case, plaintiff and defense settled before the trial's end.

I later discover that about 100,000 citizens a year, in Manhattan alone, get jury notices and, though some may be automatically excused, the great bulk of them go through much the same obstacle course I am describing here. Add those called in the other four boroughs and — don't get me wrong, I firmly believe in the jury system itself but not its abuses — what a waste of man hours!

This seems to be the usual mode; build a paper structure of panel calls, winnow the panels down to 12 and an alternate; and, after days of testimony, arbitrate.

Tuesday around noon the entire room clears on Mr. Croupier's crisp announcement that, due to a mid-week holiday, all jury duty is suspended until 9:30 a.m. Thursday. On the way out one juror confides, "Still time for the first at Aqueduct." He scoops up a tabloid and tears out the handicap page. My envy is roused for a man who has found National Purpose.

Two days pass. I recall that in three jury-duty terms over a six-year period, I have yet to render a verdict. I begin to exhibit the Roger Maris syndrome — if they won't pitch to me, how can I bat out a clean one? Then my last chance comes. Mr. Croupier calls my name and I join 35 to 40 others for a new panel.

We're escorted to the same third-floor courtroom. Sitting on a side bench is a tall, strapping man who is suing the city for $10,000 (easily the most popular figure) in a negligence case. Plaintiff claims that two-and-a-half years back, while pushing a loaded dolly on Sixth Avenue and 24th Street, the wheel got stuck in a rut and the load overturned on his foot. It's his contention the city is responsible for the rut.

Seated alongside plaintiff are two teenagers, who are witnesses for the injured party. Both wear zoot suits, their hair is tousled. They are deep in comic books.

The drum is brought in and around it crowds a new cast in old roles — jury clerk, counsel for plaintiff and defense, court officer. Clerk makes his introductions and rolls the drum. I succeed on the first call. After 12 of us are seated in the jury box, the questions come in a ripple of good cheer.

We gather from defense counsel that a subtle element is present in this case — the city. We are assured that while the city can be sued ("just as you or I or any corporation") we sitting in judgment must purge ourselves of any prejudice — "for or against the city."
gracefully curving 40 feet or so. It had twin screws and moved at a soundless 10 or 12 knots. The craft was steered in an odd way. All

Five hours and 10 excused jurors later, I meet my Waterloo. I can only guess why I have been dropped, but a strong guess it is. After a rather windy talk on the duties of citizenship, given by defense counsel, I remark (upon being asked for *my* opinion): "We are all responsible for good citizenship, when you get right down to it."

I am invited off the jury box forthwith. The last words I hear before our decimated panel leaves the room are plaintiff counsel's pearls to the 12 jurors and their alternate who have thus far made it:

"We in America have a fine system of law, the best in the world. Let's keep it that way."

He says it by rote. What I can't buy is the condition of waste in our civil courts. Two main factors that seem to conspire here are: 1) overweening lawyers whose use of legal cant is surpassed only by their misuse of jurors, and 2) court personnel who have a vested interest in numbers games.

On my final day of jury duty, I wonder on this: It it any different in Pocatello, Des Moines or San Francisco? I must find out (I tell myself) before the next jury notice is popped into my mail box.

1964

The Pizza Eaters

42nd Street is the street of sighs. On the storied midway of winking marquees, and happy strolling innocents, any bright thing can happen, any dream can become a reality. No street in the vast New York grid captures so much charm, displays such an uncorseted èlan. It is Allah's garden, and Elysian fields, the tourists' Shangri La all in one. (Detractors are not to be believed.)

Let us go there, and see for ourselves. It is a mild outdoorsy night, a big yellow moon slants a Halloween face in profile to the street. Happy crowds gambol along, east and west. New York bluecoats patrol (harsh word) the midway in twos. Their steps are feathery, their shiny young faces are benignly approving. They swing nightsticks, but with the easy motion of a conductor leading a Strauss waltz.

Ah look now! Two young men, lean and to the 42nd Street manner born, dismount their motorcycles, place them up against the curb. They are the image of medieval knights in modern dress. Tall and sinewy in faded blue Levis, heroic shoulders draped in glistening black leather jackets. Their gestures are flip, precise and nervous all at once. For the moment they stand silent as a movie poster, taking in the happy ambience as if destiny sent for them. They begin to disrobe, successively, huge white bubble helmets, Cinerama wide goggles, big leather gloves.

The friendly bluecoats, passing the spot, greet the knights with broad toothy smiles. "Welcome to 42nd Street," they call to the visitors, "the street of sighs." The young heroes respond with ramrod nods of their now bared, and blond-topped heads. They call back to the bluecoats, "Thanks for the warm welcome, fuzz. Glad to make the scene."

And so we follow our heroes, as they seek wholesome adventure on the street. They pass under the fire-frosted marquees, which they study with a serious air. The movie titles,, for our two young men, are the winking epitome of the good life — the very tracery of high culture, romance and drama that drew them to 42nd Street. "Godzilla Terror in Zombiesville," one title reads. The companion on the same marquee is called, "Rock 'n' Roller Avalanche." Our knights continue the journey, handsome faces creased in mild disdain, as they return the worshipful stares of the young maids — who are also seeking adventure and beauty on the street of sighs.

Two of the maids saunter over, at perfume-smelling distance of the spot where our heroes are deployed. They hesitate for a couple of seconds — sheer modesty dictates this. Then the maids flash our heroes M. M. smiles. The attempt at a Monroe effect, besides the smiles, is present in the tight jeans, spun-candy hairdoes, peekaboo blouses. Bosoms thrust out maddeningly, derriers loom like sudden hills on a panhandle. (Both are studies in content trying to escape form.)

Our heroes try to maintain their cool, but the palpitating scenery is having an effect. Slowly their sullen aloofness, their granitic stares turn to . . . *interest.* They look each other in the eye, then gaze at the maidens with a wan curiosity, as if to say, *What's your offer?* Ah the hyacinth aroma of 42nd Street romance, it begins to rise like a mist. The bolder of the two maids, sensing the moment of truth, calls out seductively: "Care to bu-*uy* us a pizza?"

And so the cherubs, fawns and doves of Times Square togetherness are joined. Our youthful four, light-stepping lovers clasp hands, and proceed to the neon-flooded King of Pizza parlor. Meanwhile the pair in blue, having made their one-hundred-and-nineteenth patrol (harsh word) of 42nd Street, east and west, are now approaching the parlor. They are full of light-hearted bonhomie, for the night has turned up nothing but sweetness and companionship on the street of sighs.

For a moment the two blues pleasure themselves with watching the crowd, which in turn is watching the pizzamaker as he flings his doughy discs to the ceiling. When the blues see our four pizzaeaters happily chomping away, just inside the King's large picture window, they offer one of their special "All the world loves a lover" benediction smiles. "How nice to see a scene like *that*," one bluecoat declares. The other nods and replies sorely, "Yeah, what's all the talk about pushers 'n' hopheads, faggots and dykes, and *trouble*some characters. Not on our loving turf, nothing but *nice*ly folk gather here." And off they go, into the salubrious night, shepherds of the 42nd Street flock.

As for our two knights and their ladies — when we last see them, they are mounting motorcycles for a spin into the romantic eventide. Motors are gunned up high — and what a roar those two-wheeled iron horses make! The ritual roar of the Times Square field of valor. The knights seal down helmets, adjust Cinerama goggles, tighten big leather mittens over hands. And they zoom away — the maids stapling their bodies, their thrusting bosoms, to the ironfirm backs of our heroes.

That is the street of sighs.

1965

Crafty People

The Hudson River marina, at West 79th Street, is a kind of Macy's of boat docks. All sizes and shapes are accommodated — from an incongruous but seaworthy junk, to a large pleasure-dome on water owned by a grocery heir. In between are production line Chevs and Fords of the drink — dozens of Owens's and Criss Crafts that, in the busy weekend traffic, stage their own nautical version of the East 42nd Street Barnes Dance.

A surprise even for these waters showed up not long ago. A miniature ocean liner named the *Bremen*. The hull was a sleek, you could see of the captain was shoulders and head, which stuck out over the flying bridge as he handled the wheel. Functionally the "liner" was perfect. Esthetically it wanted for nothing as a handsome replica of the once mighty North German Lloyd Line's *Bremen.*

We were told with pride that it was powered by two 38-h.p. diesel engines; duplicated the *Bremen* down to its 3,225 portholes and windows; took its West German hobbyist inventors ten years to build.

As the craft moved from the dock, a consort of two small inboards moved with it. Their decks were crowded with cameramen, who clicked away with rapid-fire impatience. (It could have been Miss West Germany they were shooting at, and maybe it was the *new* Miss West Germany.) In the making were television footage and newspaper photos. Many of the watching crowd were German-speaking. All were charmed and mildly curious. Some made sounds not unlike a child's musings on seeing an unusual toy.

As we looked on the scene, we were struck by a teaser. We could only applaud this fine talent for miniaturism, and found ourselves dwelling on the thought: "What if they did all things in miniature? What if the *herrenvolk* itself, or at least its top brass, came in miniature? What would it mean to the world?" Our fancy took shape and we began to speculate on:

- The Krupp works in miniature
- The German Wehrmacht in miniature
- Herr Conrad Adenauer in miniature
- General Adolph Heusinger in miniature

We went farther back — to the 'Thirties and 'Forties —

- Adolph Hitler in miniature
- Joseph Goebbels (a raging shorty to begin with) in miniature
- Hermann Goering (this would have been difficult) in miniature
- The German Luftwaffe and SS in miniature
- Auschwitz and Belsen in miniature

The little *Bremen* was moving downstream with its party and was soon lost to the eye. This was the start of a two-month good will tour along inland waters, including stops at Buffalo and Washington, D.C. Eventually it would piggyback to its home port on a real ocean vessel. We wondered if there might not be a small (but hardly miniature) moral tale in this nautical oddity. A tale of a defeated war imp who grew to be a giant via the piggyback ploy.

1964

The Giants of Old

Bye bye Polo Grounds — we sing your praises in memory. The Mets have moved their gear out of the center field clubhouse, and will open the 1964 season in Queens. The twin-decker green oval, pantheon of such mighty names as John McGraw, Frank Frisch, and Rogers Hornsby, is being torn down. The hallowed park will give way — plank by plank, seat by seat, pillar by pillar — to sunlight and open breezes pouring down from Coogan's Bluff. No more the sight of those proud National League team flags — multicolored and scalloped at the edges with a recumbent "V" — as they flapped away on the rooftop.

My first memories of the great Harlem ball park go back to days when baseball was seen in the flesh, rather than as a game of gray wraiths disporting on a 21-inch screen. How often I made the journey to see my beloved Giants (and how new it was each time) on the shaky Sixth Avenue El, the five-car Polo Grounds Special groaning along the serpentine tracks, the last Bronx station (West 167th Street) fading from view — and the rising excitement as the train spanned the Harlem River bridge.

High over the water you could often see a racing shell pulling away from the Columbia U. boathouse, the young bronzed oarsmen churning the mocha stream with powerful, rhythmic strokes. But, moments later this was forgotten — there was the ball park with its soldierly array of pillars, horseshoe rows of green seats, and the wide sward of the outfield. "Polo Grounds — last stop!" the conductor shouted, and the words were like an electric eel on my back. I raced down two flights of wooden stairs to the bleachers' section, digging in my pocket for the reassuring "feel" of my 50-cent piece.

True to my partisan calling, I got into my seat a good hour before game time. My heroes were practicing in the field, or belting long drives from homeplate. In center field was the valuable Lefty O'Doul, a fielder with the jetlike speed of a Willie Mays who roamed far and wide, making over-the-shoulder grabs just below the bleachers, after which he'd tip his cap in response to our cheers. Other stalwarts of the pennant-winning teams of the '20s and '30s included chunky Mel Ott, the home-run specialist whose batting style was a cocked right foot, succeeded by an explosively clean follow-through.

The field general was of course the great John ("Jawn" to the press) McGraw, baseball's "Little Napoleon," whose genius was praised in tones of reverent awe. Was he not the supreme tactician of a game far more urgent than the Mussolini-Ethiopian war, the Great Depression, or any other "problems of the week" posed by civics teachers? I watched his every move, every bit of strategy. With his silver-maned, leonine head poked over the dugout's top step, he'd crook his finger in a signal to, say, O'Doul. O'Doul would then shift position; and seconds later, sure enough, the enemy batter would loft a fly ball right to him.

That was the kind of baseball our Giants played, and we played right along with them. Our great "Mac" was doing his job from the bench, we were doing ours from the bleachers. It was management in tandem for the full nine innings.

But the days of splendor are gone; now the scene of the triumphs is going too. Goodbye, Polo Grounds. May the new stadium of the Mets over in Queens prove worthy of your fine tradition.

1964

Bronx Cheers for a Sparkling Fourth

What was an old style Fourth of July like?

A good place and time for the query, at least *my* good place and time, was the Crotona Park area of The Bronx, in the '30s, when youthful Hank Greenberg used to smash impossible home runs on a makeshift diamond, we kids cheering from behind a battered screen.

"Fatso's got three boxes of five-inchers, maybe more. His uncle ran them all the way from Mount Vernon. Not a cop in sight." So began the rumors of hidden fireworks, all of us toting up our contraband with the high hopes of ordnance generals.

In those days the police made a big show of raiding neighborhood candy stores for illegal Fourth supplies, so there was an air of bravado to our game. It added to our fun — and to our stature — when all the bluecoats could find was pink sparklers, or minuscule paper bullets for cap guns.

The secret stuff was something else again, like those five-inchers of Fatso's. For these we relied on the older fellows, cool ammo runners all of them. They used to pile into open cars and race for Yonkers, Mount Vernon or City Island, where they found the coves for a fast purchase of bootleg fireworks.

Sure, prices were high, but our runners made light of it with a sporting nod and a sage, "You pay for what you get." They would stock up on "big stuff" and bolt for home.

For days before the Fourth and as entré to it, pesky half-inchers would burst all around us. They seemed to come out of nowhere, as from an army that had us under siege from away off. The wormy red teasers were strung in two even rows of twenty. We called them, a little disdainfully, "Chinese."

226

A more telling name would have been "janitor baiters." We used to fire them and then toss them into dimly lit hallways in one arclike motion, using a good deal of stealth on the way. Gleefully we waited for the explosions, which had an added fury because of the narrow passageways. If the janitor's pursuit was speedy, our flight was even more so.

The Fourth came around in blazing sunlight; bad weather just never seemed to happen. We downed our breakfast in gulps, and raced into the street for a look at new vistas. It was the flags that made the difference. They hung in crisp hand-laundered elegance from drab apartment windows, or were tacked fast to drooping porchfronts. Those porchfronts, set back 20 feet or so from cobblestones of somnolent Park Avenue (in the 170's), added up to a wedge of village green on the broader tenement canvas. The effect was of a midway of cheer and patriotic witness.

Now the big stuff was going off in angry barks, perfuming the air with a smell of sulphur that meant battle to us. We whiffed the danger. As for Fatso's five-inchers, they were indeed real enough. After warning us to keep safe distance, he began to plant one of the monsters in a manhole cover. He was careful as a sapper wiring plugs of dynamite to a bridge.

Finally happy with the angle of the five-incher, he bellied up to it caterpillar style and fired the wick. The wick hissed menacingly, even while a sweating Fatso was neatly capping the huge red 'cracker with an empty Crisco can. And he got out of there fast.

The taut volley hit our ears with a "powwww" and rocketed the can a good fifty feet skyward. We let out a " Look at it go!" roar each time Fatso reprised the stunt.

Most of the heavy cannonading took place on Park, where the deep ravine of the New York Central tracks ran through our neighborhood like a pass to a foreign border — "way up to Canada," we used to fancy. We practically "owned" that street which, except for occasional forays of tired-moving Fred M. Schildwachter & Sons ice wagons returning to their stables (at 175th Street), lay in a borderland quiet almost entirely shorn of traffic movement and police patrols.

Fourth revels came to a busy crescendo in Crotona Park, our green and hilly backdrop to tenement row. The bandstand area which we used for our top secret meetings was decked out overnight in bright showers of confetti and tricolored streamers.

The park fireflies for that one evening danced to the tootings of a small band, about a baker's dozen in number. The musicians ooompaaad away for all they were worth, a shine on the buttons of their dark blue tunics, beads of sweat giving a pickled-in-brine cast to puffed faces.

They played John Philip Sousa marches, if not with a lilt, surely with a heroic blaring of horn and pounding of bass drum. The sky was aglow all around us with green, devil's red, and purple clouds from bursting rockets, pinwheels, starfish and Roman candles.

A series of Fourth images would cross our fertile minds from out of the night shadows and foaming colors, as vivid and run-together as in an old stereopticon. We could "see" wintry Valley Forge, its snows, bonfires and stacked muskets. Or Paul Revere on a flying steed, racing down New England's cobblestone streets. Or angry patriots dumping tea into Boston harbor. The locomotive of history rushing forward on the track of our inner eye.

After the park there were special Fourth treats waiting for us at the candy store. (Appropriately enough, the store was located on Washington Avenue.) But first our parents would check us out for our normal complement of eyes, ears and limbs. Swift purchases of pink lemonade and charlotte russe with holiday trim (the ruby red maraschino cherry) followed.

The Fourth was our bonus day, above all others.

Parable of the Books

From the beginning, it was as if some affliction had come down among the people. Millions who depended on the seven or eight daily newspapers which told of spies in the land, with room for legs and bosoms, comics, and some good murder somewhere — these millions sucked the air and sniffed skyward, as for a portent of doom.

For the newspapers had vanished (due to a strike).

The people gathered at the usual places. They stirred uneasily and waited. In the rain, in the cold, when the sun shone — they gathered at news kiosks, at local candy stores, at roofless stands along the curbstones. *No newspapers.* And still they came.

As the days passed, as the nights darkened over the city, the crisis deepened. Hollows developed in the cheeks of the millions, brows became deeply furrowed. Balm was offered in the form of extra helpings of dot-dash news over their radios. Sadly, this gave them little ease. Their ears had become atrophied to anything that wasn't Perry Como, Mashed Potato-Bossa Nova, Tennessee Ernie Ford — and the commercials.

As for television, the millions strived nobly. They indulged a crash diet of Sing Along With Mitch, Easy Ed Sullivan, Jumping Jack Carson, Late Show and Late Late. But relief would not come. The void was deep.

A cry, "How can we go on without our newspapers!" was uttered. "Lord give us our daily violence, our Walter Winchell poop, our Dorothy Kilgallen froth," echoed another. And so they went (early and late) to the usual places, seeking the Wall Street Openings, the Wall Street Closings, the Seven Star Sports Extras, the Early Birds, the Late Cities — seeking the bold headlines of spies in the land, the legs and bosoms, and some good murder somewhere.

Still the newspapers were gone.

And in desperation, many reached out at the familiar places for some standby diet. They rummaged over girlie magazines, adventure, assorted slicks, horse racing dailies, business journals — *Anything!*

Then a strange thing came to pass.

Someone among the millions rediscovered a book store. He had wandered into the place as if he were a lost desert wayfarer suddenly come upon a cool oasis.

A book was purchased by him.

And he read it.

Like a revelation, it struck him that life could go on, with or without the newspapers at the usual places.

And more! He felt a sense of joy in reading the book, an identity with his fellow millions, who were sucking on air and sniffing skyward. Little of this joy did he ever experience in his newspaper.

And like Moses come down from Mount Sinai, this one among the millions took the book to the others. Soon these others made their way into the book stores. They purchased books and they read them.

Thus did the crisis break.

No longer did they feel the loss of bold headlines.

1963

Easter Stroll

I came out of Carnegie Hall, the ending chorus of Bach's "St. Matthew Passion" holding soft, lasting sway in my ears. *Hearts turn to thee, O Savior blessed. . . .* Sweet music and kingly metaphor combined in a truth men could live by. Or out of a crown of thorns, a tiarra so bright that it burns into our awareness for always.

Merged with the crowds, I headed down Seventh Avenue. Curious that as I came step by step closer to the Times Square glow of neon, leaving behind the Carnegie audience, the flow of walkers took on a new cast. Measured first of all by boisterousness, by holiday ease and noise.

A couple emerged from a Chinese eatery, the girl sighing repeatedly, as if she was a burping baby once again. At the same time she patted her stomach with dainty strokes, proof of her happy satiety. They tarried a while in a huge shadow, thrown off by the shaft-like magnificence of a new hotel skydrome called "The Americana." (Miami's "Tomorrow" hotel kaplunked right onto the New York skyline.) Hugger-mugger and play over, they moved south with the flow.

At the stage entrance of the Winter Garden, the weaving crowd surrounded a tall elfin-smiling man who was attempting to get to his parked limousine "That's him — that's Ray Bolger. . . ." The refrain spread, the crowd locked the man in even tighter. Pieces of paper and programs, a business card or two, were extended to within inches of the man's lovingly sharp nose. "*Paleeze,* Mr. Bolger, sign mine. . . ."

Palpable on the night air were the rustle of Saturday-night finery, and perfume oozing from hair-do's high as guardsmen's shakos. As I advanced farther into the neon mists, I was caught in slow-moving streams of people emptying out of movie houses. For an arrested moment or two, a gray mood was on them. It seemed to match the gray of the marquee titles. "The Day the Earth Caught Fire." "Cape Fear." "Experiment in Terror." "Judgment at Nuremburg."

The mood changed rapidly, once the crowd got into the Broadway mainstream. From a gray silence, to an antic (colorless) garrulity. Getting a good play was the suggestion box. "Let's go find a place to eat." "Let's look in on the Funorama." "Let's watch Fascination." And they moved forward, jostling one another, moved toward the Times Tower with its circular ribbon of lights, its winking news on the march. WORLD AWAITS KENNEDY GO AHEAD ON TESTS. . . .

If the crowd hardly took notice of the lights, it did slow its pace to take notice of something going on just north of the Tower. On the jutting triangle whose only business is an All-In-One recruiting shack, there were five or six persons standing vigil. Some faced one way in the chasm, some the other. They were silent. They held picket signs, either aloft or pinned to the ground. *We Are Utterly Opposed To War. Peace Is The Only Shelter.*

And judgment was swift, at least among the more vocal of the crowd. These came forward to oppose the triangle of silence — with shouting. "Take your message to Moscow." "You some kind of nuts, or something." After which they bent straight ahead for Forty-second Street, the winking news going round and round above their heads. . . . WORLD AWAITS KENNEDY GO AHEAD. . . .

1962

"Nice Place for Kids, But I Wouldn't Want to Eat Here"

First it was the beef and chicken pies, two ultra dishes of the Automat in-group. One day the deep dish had a new contour. It was less deep, with a 10c hike to boot. We said to the friendly manager: "You have a new beef pie dish. Small on the bias. Right?" He answered with no effort at all: "It is your imagination."

Another time we opted for the "15c-Beans-Reduced-10c"; and discovered it was 15c once again. Purée soup (more purée than soup) made an overnight jump of five cents. From 20c to two-bits. The spiral continued with vegetables. All of them, including former 10c-ers like spaghetti, carrots, macaroni, rice, zoomed to fifteen cents. Next came the mystery of the shrunken bread. The kind they use for 70c peekaboo roast beef sandwiches. Suddenly it was about one inch short on four sides.

Latest flash. An across-the-board hike of 5c on those showcase sandwiches kids love to play with. (They play with showcase *and* sandwich.) There's bologna or salami on white. Two palefire slivers of meat caught between two chalky slivers of bread. A quarter for the turning. . . . And so on (and up).

One regular blamed it on Billie Sol Estes. Another said — Automat's a nice place to take the kids, but I wouldn't want to eat here. A third opined that since they got smart and went public (*sic*), you could hardly tell them apart from Schrafft's. And a fourth chimed — look at Ivan in far-off Moscovy, the trouble he's having with his meat and potatoes.

1962

The Death of Benny Paret

Benny "Kid" Paret, the prize fighter, is dead. A little over a fortnight ago he took his last shelling, twenty-eight straight blows in a neutral corner, an exhibition of morose savagery witnessed by homescreeners from Maine to California. Sobs have been sobbed, *editorial* obeisances made, in all the home press. From the gray-lady *Times* — up, down and through the middle — to the juvenile retch-throated *Daily News*. And decent enough outrage-letters have been written, enough of them maybe to float the "Kid" off to a better hereafter.

But nowhere in the press has there been a line on one pre-fight aspect that helped set up a fatal climate. The vendetta prose of the sportswriters, who were assisted in this by the fight managers, no doubt, and also no doubt by the publicity hawks at Madison Square Garden. For days before the event sports pages were coming on with gore about opponent Emile Griffith's new-found determination to send Paret to kingdom-come. Griffith's manager was wet-nursing over the gore, and the Garden was happily stirring it over. An Eighth Avenue chef-d'oeuvre in the making, none have been better.

Meanwhile, the prize-fight aficionados, holding nightly court at the Broadway Automat, cigar stubs deep in their teeth, were reading those sports pages and swapping hopes, as a kind of dessert with their gone-tepid cups of java.

"This one's gotta be a 'lock'," was the message, "the big dough is on Emile." And the final irony is that Griffith himself, a clean fighter and fine young man, got caught in this noxious buildup that made him into a killer for an hour — from 10 to 11 p.m. of a Saturday night. With eight or 9,000 "fans," minks, moutons and black silk ties among them, on their feet and yelling for more, more, more lethal blows.

There is a vast gulf between guts and gore. Geographically, the first is very often to be found inside the ring, the second almost always ouside of it. As for the sobbing press, they have an opportunity beyond any to do something about the prize fight game (misnomer for racket). They can refuse to cover, write about, take advertising for, all professional boxing. If they would do that, their sobs would no longer sound like those coming from a crocodile swamp.

1962

Look Ma, No Elephant

There is a new kind of Republicanism on Manhattan's West Side. Call it "Look ma, no elephant" Republicanism. Not only no elephant in sight. No Republican label on any of their placards, signs or handbills.

The name of the candidates are prominent enough —

Richard S. Aldridge (Congress) and Pierce Paley (Assembly) are plastered on store fronts, building signs, streamers. Riding with the names are tier on tier of announced good intentions. West Siders are assured of the whole package. From better housing to rent control to . . . well, we know the pre-election package by now. It is all there. As bulging as Macy's Thanksgiving parade announcement.

But no elephants. Not even a bald eagle. And no Republican labels.

Also, there is this very white drinkmobile. Looks like an outsized ice cream and popsicle dispenser on wheels. Lots of bright campaign stuff in large lettering on the truck's carcass. It is Aldrich's campaign truck. Tools up and down Broadway or Amsterdam Avenue — *dying* to make friends. As the man behind the mike says: "*Do* step up for a free orange drink . . . *friends.* Come on over and say 'hello.' Dick Aldrich wants to meet you."

At Broadway and 73rd Street, the drinkmobile was getting a pretty fair play. People were stepping up, reaching for drinks, downing them neat. The candidate was shaking hands. Palming away a baker's dozen to the minute. A handsome six-footer with porcelain smile, Aldrich looked better than fair at togetherness. He struck you as being capable of discussing "issues." Appearance-wise.

But let's face it — when drinks are flowing, and friendship's in the making, issues can wait. At least it went that way for 30 minutes or so. Then someone demurred. Seemed a bit churlish — but what he wanted to know was: "Are you trying to buy votes with a free orange drink?"

The mike man took up the rude challenge and in hurt voice said: "We are here to make *friends* . . . It's a warm night and we feel the least we can do is offer you a friendly orange drink . . . Like if we came to your door — to every door in the great dis-ric' of 200,000 families — we would expect you to say 'Do come in, do have a drink, it's a warm night.' We would expect that."

He paused for his hurt to settle, then rammed home this final word: "The man who asked that question is of course a Democrat. Probably a reform one at that."

During all this, Aldrich was minding the store unperturbed. He shook shook shook hands. "Hello, I'm Dick Aldrich," his voice stenciled away. "*Your* candidate for Congress." He was neatly bilingual, when opportunity arose. In a kind of upper-form Spanish, he reminded all south-of-the-border voters that he had spent "17 years in Latin America."

At the ten p.m. curfew the mike man made his final political announcement. Composure restored, he told the audience: "We will be coming by again tomorrow. And for the remaining campaign weeks. So do remember — FRIENDS — we want you to step up and say 'hello.' Mornings, from 7:30 to 10 a.m., we are at West Side subway stations . . . Come by for a *free* cup of coffee and doughnut. Evenings, it's orange-drink-time. Good night and bless you."

1962

The Art Searchers

In the Junior Museum wing of the Metropolitan Museum of Art, the children are the show stoppers. Curious, avid, appetites aroused, they race at each canvas with arrowy speed.

Several stand before a Dong Kingman semiabstract called "South Street Bridge," a splashing, high-good-humor cryptogram of New York's harbor, bridges, docks.

A mother of one of them pipes, "Can you find the Statue of Liberty?" The half-dozen in her care scramble over the work, fingers inches away. Soon comes a shouting reply — "It's *there,* hidden among the tugboats!" — from a blonde, bobbing pony-tailer.

The others chorus her find with joy.

They next surround a Mark Tobey tempora called "Broadway," a lively expressionist kaleidoscope of New York's theater district. The woman urges, "Can you pick out the connecting street lines?" Again fingers race over canvas and voices ring out.

When you leave the Junior Museum and wander through the Met's wider areas, innocence is left behind. In its place you find the SEARCH.

And what is that?

The SEARCH is the practised technique of museum goers (other than children) who fall into the "What-Am-I-Here-For?" school and proceed *not* to find out during a three-hour (average) tour.

A recent unofficial survey (the writer's) revealed that 98.55% of Sunday museum goers (other than children) are SEARCHERS.

Let's zero in on two of the breed.

A mid-twenties' couple stand at a polite remove from the rich alabaster marble Aphrodite on the main floor. The goddess is off in a corner by herself, red velour backdrop and plants of fern setting a rich scene.

The couple exchange tight smiles. They display viselike control. Moments before they read the wall footnote on Aphrodite: "Ancient marble copy of a lost Greek original by a follower of Praxiteles about 300 B.C."

With that footnote as guide, they *ought* to feel impressed. They come closer. Again the tight smiles. Their eyes narrow; a decision at last! "What's the mystery," says the man. "It's a nicely turned slab of marble, is all." The words are almost belligerent, but the rising inflection betrays doubt.

The young man, who met the girl for the first time an hour before in the fountained restaurant, reaches into a paper bag and brings forth a giant doughy pretzel. He breaks it and both munch away on halves as they pursue an enigma. *Aphrodite what art thou?*

There are more traps at the Met for the now coupled off SEARCHERS — and for the Sunday thousands — on what must easily be the world's most hazardous obstacle course in the Arts.

The huge and heroic bronze of Emperor Treboniannus Gallus — Is the pose that of a warrior or statesman-orator? The showcase full of Degas dancing figurines — Why does the man spend so much time repeating himself?

Climax of the couple's tour is the Met's crowded main floor postcard counter where they each buy three "popular" numbers.

Other museums, other SEARCHERS.

A recent attraction at the Museum of Modern Art was the curious "Assemblages" exhibit. And was *that* ever rough. Our SEARCHER digs Cezanne, even Van Gogh, but oh the puzzlement of Assemblages. So a rapid peek and he wheeled from them as from torpedo tracks, a wise decision in view of the Sunday crush.

More promising are MOMA's film showings, downstairs photo gallery, main floor cafeteria. If the wind is right in that last spot, he will join forces with an opposite number (or female) SEARCHER over coffee-and.

The museum's outdoors beckon. On a bench hemmed by outsize sculpture our SEARCHERS talk ART . . . and beautiful friendship blossoms.

Safe harbor in heavy Sunday swirls is MOMA's penthouse restaurant. For members only. Weekends are rather quiet. But the spot jumps on calendar work days with "Regulars."

Theirs is a SEARCH for the menu first, art later. If time allows.

By no means a tiny group, the penthouse habitués give MOMA the distinction of being one museum where art is in running battle with the blue plate special.

One young Midtown executive put it: "This 'club' has it cards and spades over Sardi's East for luncheon dates. I closed three contracts here in the last week alone."

His record for the course is peerless. Seven months of more or less steady penthouse visits without once taking in a museum exhibit.

"I do the Westport shows when I get the chance."

Dialogue heard at a corner table one Sunday afternoon:

"She said, 'What is your position on modern art?'

"I thought on it for a moment and said:

" 'I stand about six feet from the painting and study it. If I like it, I back away a few feet more and study it again. If not, I walk off.

" 'That's my position on modern art.' "

1960

The Masked Marvel Revisited

I shot a few practice racks of pool, after a mild attack of nostalgia over the game. I was at one of those newfangled "Billiard Lounges" that have mushroomed on Times Square — and why they don't stick to the old "Pool Room" shingle, I'll never know. What hit me was the big changes — the emphasis on décor for one — that have taken place over the years. I stood ankle-deep in wall to wall carpeting. I played on a table that had the glossy chic look of Swedish moderne. My eyes swam over a canary colored top — the good green baize is going out fast. The lighting hung not *over* the table, but from the *ceiling*. Inlaid rollers for keeping score — in place of the trusty (the rack had to check with the buttons) wire abacus of old. And biggest switch of all — ladies' powder room.

Imagine how Mark Twain would feel, he who saw the game as strictly male. Surely he'd blister the notion that pool should be a gathering place for dating couples, and what's even more bizarre, a neighborhood pleasure dome for the Entire Family. Imagine the consensus at old line halls like McGirr's: "This is pool?" And for a clincher imagine a cologne scented lady putting chalk to cue, and then running off a clean rack of 14 balls, after sinking a perfect break shot in the corner pocket. Yes, indeed. Might as well try to imagine ace quarterback Y. A. Tittle performing a Swan Lake pas de deux with Moira Shearer on the Metropolitan stage.

It was a different scene in the 1930s, when billiards was only "pool." There was a long, low-slung hall called Dwyer's Academy, an upstairs shrine with tinted picture window that looked out on the Third Avenue El, in the Crotona Park section of the Bronx. We kids were poachers, not players. But we knew the map from the territory, knew it blind. It was a case of being chased, and chased often, but in the ringing words of General MacArthur of years later, it was also a case of: "We shall return."

Dwyer's had a progressive approach, they installed a baseball scoreboard and brand new ticker machine. The ticker's clack clack motion, and the clean hard sound of caroming ivory, fused in a kind of poolroom dissonance that was music to our ears. At World Series time they rigged up a dandy electronic diamond, a pre-univac that gave play by play reruns of the big games. It was close to four-stories high and hung from the red-brick facade of a nearby warehouse. The contraption looked like a glorified pinball, and it was as popular as it was rare. By game time thousands were jammed into Tremont and Third Avenues. All heads were tilted upward for a clear view of the board.

At the opening "crack" of the bat, a loud cheer undulated through the streets. It was an odd place for a "ballpark," what with clanging trolleys, honking automobiles and police on horses all competing with the crowd for space. The fans eyed the electronic diamond all afternoon, cheering or moaning as the case might be. What they saw was the jittery movements of toy batsmen, going from base to base — and the winking peregrinations of red (pitcher, catcher) and yellow (fielders) light bulbs which represented the nine defense men. If the toylike goings-on became a bit feverish at times, the confusion was of a happy kind, i.e., "Second only to being there." Best of all were double-plays (or triple, a rarity), hang-ups between bases, and attempted steals. On all of these latter plays, the lights danced around the diamond as if caught in an electronic version of blind man's buff.

A more intimate glory was Dwyer's exhibition pool play, Blue Ribbon affairs that featured top stars like Willie Hoppe, Willie Mosconi, Eddie Shaeffer, and others. All the vagabonds of the green baize circuit, who walked their talents from poolroom to poolroom, their pearlhandle cue sticks stacked in cases with the care of violins going into Carnegie Hall.

One was a rare curiosity to us, a shrouded gent with the nom de guerre "The Masked Marvel," whose table wizardry was second only to our embroidered myths about him. When Dwyer's posted its semiannual notice on the Marvel, we junior grade aficionados circled the date in red. On the eve of the match we gathered in Dwyer's narrow hallway, early and eager. A ragtail bunch of conspirators, we discussed in sotto voce how best to make our assault. Our plan was in two stages. We'd troop up the Everest high stairs, and, once we were at the summit, we'd lose ourselves — one by one — on the many-tabled terrain. The older fellows soon began to arrive. Using their broad shoulders for cover, and tailing behind as if on cat's feet, we infiltrated the scene of the match (at Table One) in good order.

Lucky for us, Dwyer's took a rather cavalier view of our presence, at least on Marvel night. A festive chatter ran through the hall, in anticipation of some good poolshooting ahead. Once the match got under way, we were spared the petty beefs as to our age, the "I thought I told you to *scram*" barks at our heads of normal times. An air of politesse, if that's not too strong, invaded the premises. We had our chance to watch, to savor it all.

We stood fixed in wonder, as the Marvel paced around the floodlit table, he silent as a bear. His black silk cowl had us in thrall. It was a one-piece oddity reaching down to his waist, at which point it was tied in a stringy bow. The garment was right out of a Saturday matinée movie thriller, or a Dumas tale of dungeons and mayhem, or a scene in London Tower of executioner ready to chop. (Marvel was a study in concentrated menace, even when he just stood around waiting to shoot.) He would stop pacing at one point, and size up the whole table of brightly colored balls. His eyes were two capsuled moons, alive with disdain behind the slits in his mask. It was his moment of truth — and ours.

The Marvel would then bend, or rather pounce, low over the table and begin one of his long runs. His stroke was steady as a metronome. It was an easy stroke, cue meeting ball with hardly a ripple of sound, topped off by the merest hint of a follow-through. For all we could figure, there was a touch of necromancy riding with every shot.

Match point — or 150 — would come all too soon. By tradition, Dwyer's reigning house man would draw the match with Marvel. But he'd turn out to be no whizz in those tense surroundings, for all that he was a sharp bread-and-butter player among his peers. As for the Masked Marvel, the mystery of that stalking figure in black silk cover, who handled his stick with educated fingers, would remain with us for days.

That was pool life, years before the current billiards togetherness.

Three decades later. Who was the Masked Marvel? Was he still around? I went over to McGirr's a few days after my practice session, hoping I might find someone who could fill me in. And I was lucky. After a couple of false leads, I was tipped about a man who seemed to have the definite Marvel story. He was a poolroom ancient, a short talky member of that disappearing breed who night after night haunt the aisles of McGirr's, where they like to recall in low voices all the flashy ghosts of past sporting events. From Ruth to Firpo to McGraw . . . The old man was taking in what looked like a routine snooker match at a corner table, he along with several other table superintendents. I asked him about the Marvel, and he ran the story down for me as if with total recall.

There have been several Masked Marvels over the years. The first and "bona fide" one was Irwin Rudolph, four-time world champion in the 30s and 40s, a stickman with the reputation of a "poolshooter's poolshooter." Exhibition pool money was pretty tight during the Depression, and Rudolph and his manager hit upon the idea of donning a mask while playing the nabes. Rudolph played fast one-night stands, for an even faster twenty or thirty a match. That's where the mask came in. It would not have looked good for the champ to show himself, not at those prices.

When Rudolph eclipsed from the scene, the Masked Marvel routine was taken up by others. My informant spoke of these latter Marvels as "Garden variety shooters with a burn on for some quick dough." He went on to say, "It got so bad after a while, all they needed was a stick, and a yard of black cloth . . . And zoom, another Masked Marvel was born!" And they still crop up on the pool horizon. He said he knew of a Marvel working Long Island halls as late as a year ago. He described him as "A short dumpy shooter by the name of Louis Something . . ." He summed up with a tribute to the bona fide Marvel: "You take all the so-called Masked Marvels who came after Rudy, there wasn't a one who could handle Rudy's stick in a blackout, let alone under poolroom lights." I buy that. The Masked Marvel of the evenings at Dwyer's could only have been Irwin Rudolph.

Night of the Warhawks

I was in my area of Broadway — the neighborly part, in the Seventies — when the confrontation took place. It was a raw evening forty-eight hours after the Kennedy speech on Cuba, the one which commenced the blockade. The street I was on is dominated, on its Broadway corner, by a sprawling apartment building, once elegant Quick rental squeezes and a frenetic turnover of tenants are the practice now. There is an around the clock drift, into and out of the building, of human flotsam — part resident prostitutes, part juvenile delinquent coveys, part Joes of all ages seeking contact.

Bottles have flown from windows of the building — ending in

sudden explosions of shattering glass that had no apparent target or cause. People have been injured, and the game continues. Following a pattern I've learned from past experience, I was giving this spot the widest possible berth. A young man was stationed on the corner south of the building. He was talking into a pencil microphone, offering the Democratic line on such issues as housing and Medicare.

As I turned south on Broadway for the subway, I made a short detour to within a foot or two of the young man. His only audience, and that by an accident of proximity, was a group of eight or ten male adults. They were standing under a candy store awning. In season and out the store was a kind of anchored headquarters for them. Over the years I had passed this corner on an average of twice a day. It was rare when none of them were around.

I waited for the speaker to end his peroration on, I believe, Medicare and then asked him if I could put a question to him. The effort had a touch of pantomime — my stopping, my turning toward him, my pause before I spoke, all done (as it were) on the fly. I was on my way to a downtown political meeting — a meeting of protest against the House Un-American Activities group at which the Cuban crisis, too, was bound to be aired. I was late, and I had no thought of tarrying. As for the candy store corps, they were barely in my consciousness.

Yes, the young man replied, he would be glad to answer any question. He then lowered his microphone. In a voice a little heavier than normal, I said: "Why don't you tell President Kennedy to stop threatening the peace of the world?" Even as I spoke, I was aware the question (or statement) had a harsh edge. *Who* was doing the threatening? What forces and emotions were welling up — hour by hour — that if not checked might well mean the doom of all? My question was harsh, but the developing mosaic of fiery ruin far harsher.

The speaker, using the microphone again, repeated my query verbatim, prefacing it with the words: "The gentleman wants to know . . ." As I moved on for the subway, now at a slower pace, I was alerted by a loud growl coming from someone among the candy store crowd. The youth hardly began his answer when the growler, a short barrel-chested man in his late thirties, came forward and took a stand between his friends and the speaker. He growled again, this time facing me clear, as I had by then halted and turned around. There was a distance of fifty feet or so between us. "Come back here — *bum*," he shouted. "Got no guts to ask a question and stay for an answer — *hannnh?*" The words rumbled from his throat, and the others cheered.

My first impulse was to move off again, but the short man's

stepped-up verbal shafting kept me rooted. Very soon, the rising din of growls, catcalls and sharp words, began to draw a fresh stream of onlookers to the scene. Most of them swooped in from the direction of the corner building. Though they made no immediate sign of doing so, they seemed ready enough to join the dispute on the slightest whim. Nor did I have any illusion which side they would choose. They were the rumble-prone prowlers of West Side streets, whose petty and violent outlawries were almost daily occurrences.

As I stood there hesitating, doubt and anger mixed in me. I also felt a small stab of — was it shame? I was caught in a switch; or, more to the mark, as if I'd been cornered after leaving the scene of an accident. Perhaps it was the irony of the clash, most of all, that kept me pinned down. No word or nod had ever passed between us until that moment. Now, suddenly, I was on the receiving end of some acid cries in the night. The candy store posse, whose agenda rarely went beyond the subjects of "broads," "gamblin'," "action" and "the *pitchers*" (movies), were manning the republic's ramparts in an hour of danger.

"Talk about the President that way — *hannnh*? . . . C'mon back and listen to the man's answer — fink rat commie. . . ."

It was barrel-chested, and now he was shrieking. He stood poised in a boxer's stance, feet apart and planted firmly, hands jabbing at the air as he railed away. The cheers coming from his pals were, it appeared, more in recognition of the brass of his performance, than for its "patriotic" content. In any case, it was clearly "them" — the pack — against me. The young man, who during the commotion had shouted into the microphone for order several times, finally gave in to the role of uneasy spectator.

"Yeah . . . We'll lynch *yuh* . . . do *yuh* hear it *good*! . . . C'mon back and face the medicine . . . We gonna . . . We like *ta* . . . lynch *yuh* . . ." These last cries came in the form of a jagged roundelay, each one of the short man's friends boldly chiming the "lynch" motif, after he himself had sprung the word. I waited for a lull and, when it came, I yelled to the heavy man: "I put my question . . . And I know his answer." I remained for a second or two more, and finally turned for the subway.

The rush at my back, which I half-expected, never came.

1963

Garbager Than Thou

The New York garbage strike was a ten-day siege, but it will be ten times ten before the insult fades away. For the Mayor, the towners by the millions, the metropolitan "image." New York is a 24-hour rack, that's never been more true. You leave your apartment, on a cold snowy New Year's morning and it's a toss-up whether busses/subways are rolling. A strike is averted, they are rolling. So we all won on that one — Lindsay, the union, the towners. But a few days later — taxis, milk delivery, garages. We get pinned to that rack. It's a talisman of the city tribe.

Now, it's the nitty-gritty of garbage. A case of where we eat, read our fat newspapers, dispose of our empty six-packs. Shit hitting the fan: the *very* image. And we build the landscape higher and higher, outside our windows. Landscape of the discards of "good" living Suddenly the manicured upper East Side learns about garbage. Before the strike, *their* mental set was sort of William Buckleyan, e.g., garbage is a Harlem syndrome. And the supermarketed West Side, maybe with a little less surprise, learns about garbage too. Only antiseptic Lincoln Center is proof against it. And in Harlem, in Bedford Stuyvesant, on the lower East Side, in the East Bronx, they all maybe laugh a little. *Look at honkie, tracking through his own muck . . . If it lasts long enough, they'll even get to see a rat race.*

And the union, the sanitation pros. They got the fan going, with a remarkable piece of (the) action. A noisy meetin' outside *their* City Hall, our City Hall, union boss DeLury's City Hall. They shout down DeLury, pummel him, tell him to hump off. "And you go tell the Mayor to hump off." Taylor Law, public responsibility. "Bullshit." The city's not a boss, in a strict capital-*vs.*-labor sense. "That's a lot of bullshit, we want our piece of the action."

Bright morning follows bright morning (at least somebody *up there* hasn't told us to hump off, not altogether). The landscape thickens. And the towners are heard from. They call in their views on the WBAI radio relay. For hours on end. Gleeful anarchists, chirping for *more more more* breakdown. Haters of Lindsay, the union, their own neighbors. *Grrrrr.* Or sweet voiced upper East Side lady. "Our side's cleaner. We use double-wrap cellophane bags. Place them on the street *carefully.*" And radioman Bob Fass. "What color cellophane, pink or baby blue?"

Six days, seven days. Elephant hills of garbage. And the Mayor is sleepless, talks passionately of "blackmail." Wants us all to go to Camelot. "We'll hold out, it's the principle, the law." Good try, but our jungle's not Camelot. And the Governor comes to town. Mr. Bland with a stiletto. Sets up shop in his private triplex on West Fifty-fifth Street, his capitol away from the capitol. Wants the mess cleaned up *his* way. Meaning, *any way.* Maybe he looks at the elephant hills, and

242

sees a White House dome. And the towners keep vigil by their home boxes. They watch the Mayor-Governor politego battle with catatonic eye, same as when they watch a shoot-'em-up. Ten days of it. The whole town playing garbager than thou.

And the rack's rolled into the wings, to be oiled for the next round.

1968

6 Lunalude & Londinium Day

Watch On the Moon

Astronaut Neil Armstrong was saying — from near 250,000 miles out — that he was experiencing drag in his walk on the luna firma, due to the part dustlike, part sand-sticky nature of the Sea of Tranquility, and even while he was reporting this, tens of thousands in Sheep Meadow were moving about in an Earthian drag, due to intermittent rains that were churning up the Central Park terra firma. The event was coming over live on three giant screens, with such side-show attractions as a half-dozen big helium balloons, which hovered overhead on a misty-orange backdrop, a monster sized inflated plastic bag, which was kept aloft by the ingestion of flame-fed gasses, a rock group that performed from New York City's Showmobile, and various ad hoc entertainers, like David Peel's lower east side rock group (who premiered a stoned moon number), or longhair guitar strummers, or a trio of Latin bongo players, all of whom use park acreage for their own versions of free-space tripping.

The moonwatch crowd's mood was neither awe-struck, nor overly calm, but somewhere in between the two. They cheered — warmly rather than noisily — when Armstrong took his first steps away from the module ladder, and they cheered again when the two astronauts planted the flag, this time a little more loudly, but still not noisily. One girl remarked she wished it had been the UN flag. When the President came on at around midnight, part of his conversation was blurred out by some medium-to-heavy booing, coming from all sections of the three wedge-shaped formations of watchers. (Luna module or used cars, his was still the accent of the pitchman.) Later still, when the two were back inside their module, the networks flashed to Neil Armstrong's home town, in Ohio, for a chat with his parents. One question — and it did sound dim-witted — was about Luna 15, put in that typically pre-judged way that is the habit of TV scribes, voice tuned like a club for a "You betcha" response: Did the Armstrongs think the Russians were unfair in their timing? And with not a moment's hesitation, Armstrong pere fell to with his answer: "I think they were unfair, no doubt about it . . ." The astronaut's mother, on the other hand, wouldn't — indeed, she said she couldn't — say.

And remembering back to Neil Armtrong's thought on the

matter — to the way the astronaut voiced his lively interest in whatever information Houston was getting on Luna 15's journey — remembering back to that gave you a small whiff of generation gap on the prairie. The older man, as if out of old memory, was sure in his response. But Neil Armstrong's monograph (on space) seemed to go light years beyond the prairie response: "One small step for a man, one large step for mankind."

1969

Londinium Day

My flight from New York was almost billiard-table-smooth, two short periods of turbulence marring an otherwise good journey. When the big BOAC jet landed at Heathrow Airport I came upon one pleasant phase of English handling of foreign visiters: the informality of customs. *Why are you here* and *What do you have to declare* are questions about as casual as *Do you take milk with your tea.* The man loaded for bear must find this approach heady, for he'd have to think while he waits out the line "Dig it, looks like I'll get past these dudes with my kilo with no trouble at all." But something in the eye of the very correct gents and ladies who check you out tell you that there's an X-ray checking your valises and a polygraph tracking your breathing pattern while you talk. Anyway I was passed through without even a look, though I'd said I thought I'd exceeded the cigarette quota by one carton over the allowed two (of American smokes).

Minutes earlier I overheard some remarks that amounted to the reverse side of the informality coin. We were bunched together waiting the arrival of our valises and baggage, and a matronly lady traveler back to England was telling the two airport baggagemen "You very well need a gun for protection when you walk the New York streets." Dimly it hit me that this was part of the ritual putdown of all things American and I was ready to file it as carbon-copy stuff when the baggagemen popped with their lines as if out of a prepared script. One put it in a kind of rolling Cockney that tickled my ear but at the same time the words hit me as pretty near obsessive and a bit self-righteous as he told the lady, "Want to run the world, they do, and can't do a thing right for themselves." I suppose what jarred me was the sense of dislocation. I was hearing all of this, was indeed saying some of it myself, at a hundred points back in the States, the difference being a not insubstantial one of the easily available snipe judgment from a distance of oceans, and the more difficult judgment one makes almost daily from one's home base.

The feedback of other, and more positive, first impressions soon took hold. I arrived at an early hour (6.30 a.m.) and had to fumble around with changing dollars into pounds, making telephone calls to the couple I'd be staying with, and getting from Heathrow to a house on Ladbroke Grove — all of which activity would not have been possible without the help (as they say at the Hollywood Oscar ceremony) of a lot of people. First was the call — an English telephone is perhaps not the world's most complicated instrument but the business of getting your half-shilling coin past the pips so the call can proceed is for a foreign hand an all-thumbs operation. And moving out from Heathrow into the great open circularity of London is a venture not without mystery for that same foreigner.

I got to Steve Dwoskin's and Liz Bennett's house a couple of hours later, after a double ride of big red bus and taxi with the meter of the latter pushing to 21 shillings for a long ride through low-contoured country of small homes and neat two-story factories very much like parts of Long Island. Both my hosts are involved in the London avant film and graphics scene and work goes on in their 3-story house until early hours of morning — so when I got to their door at about ten it was a case of Steve dragging out of bed when he'd normally be turning over for a second lap of sleep. But I wasn't alone in my interruption of Steve's routine, for on that first day, and on almost every day since, a constant stream of young film-makers, most of them students of his at the London college where he teaches, have come by for small talks on the scene, or to run off some new can of film, or to use Steve's combination office and workroom on the second floor to unravel some technical problem. The easy informality of the visits, exchanges and shared enthusiasm is a marked difference from what you find in the New York film underground.

My visit to London, and to Steve's place, was for the

249

purpose of seeing through the completion of a book of mine, the proofing, designing (done by Steve), printing and binding all going along in rather slow but sure stages, and under the roof of a typically small entrepreneur printer-publisher called Villiers. Second day here I found my way out to the plant, in the Tufnell Park area, by way of the Underground (a good half of whose dozen or so units cut out into some very verdant London aboveground), and I went over copy with the lanky, loquacious and highly professional supervisor, John Sankey by name, who assured me that the main problem that had come up with the galleys thus far would be solved easily; they had Englished my manuscript, putting punctuations out-side quotes, and spelling words like "fantasy" with a ph in-stead of an f, all of which would now have to be un-Englished. Mr. Sankey put it, "The man who worked on your book thought you were an English author." To which I was tempted to reply, "That no doubt indicates he's an American type-setter."

Meantime, I've been moving around London with almost crablike slowness, there being no other way I know of for a visitor to enter into its density, variety and peculiar sense of mystery. The latter word should I suppose be put in quotes, for on the surface London's persona is one of commerce, consumerism and heavy moving traffic no greater, nor lesser, than any other large Western city. But the mystery is there too — in the way the city beds down almost all at once, between the hours of 11 and midnight, lights going out in those lowslung, row-on-row three-family houses in a hundred small enclaves that make up the residential bulk of greater London. And mystery too in the way these enclaves (call them a hundred or so Greenwich Villages in form) go about their daily routine as if independent of each other, but are at the same time very much laced together by a language of under-statement that amounts almost to a code, and by a pace that seldom approaches the pushy. Of course there's the Londoner's penchant for talkiness, as an obverse of the under-statement, and that might be *the* mystery of all. Still, I find it's a talkiness that doesn't so much evade the subject, as work variations on it with a feel for the verbal that often as not seems close to manic, even while it falls on the ear most times with curious appeal.

Capsules of some scenes that have impressed me. The

Roundhouse, large shedlike enclosure abandoned by British Railways some years ago, now used by London hippie-rock-dissent groups. I attended a marthon rock benefit there and my notes read in part: "Hellplace for young British drop-outs, anarchists, heads, Oxford boys hurting to be outlaws, all wanting to freak out conservative taste; ecstacy seekers of a new day, using a space the fuzz and the bureaucracy frown on. Roundhouse is a double insult to the establishment: The kids are not only at home in just such a dingy environ-ment; they have made of this huge, iron-beamed, foul-air catacomb a space that allows them for a time to wriggle free of the Royal umbilical." Piccadilly Circus, nerve-center if not the actual geographic core of London, inner circle from which all the other circles seem to grow. Piccadilly is called "The Dilly" by young wanderers from all over Europe and America, who gather at the Eros statue inside the iron railing and groove each other's defiance of their middleclass backgrounds. Brightway of garish lights, signs that go in circles, merry-go-round of red double-decker buses, streets narrow and winding, with a constant parade of London and other English visitors acting as a kind of native chorus: All in all a pleasure-seeking nightalley beyond any on five continents. And there's Hyde-Park — where I could debate, after coming 3,000 miles, with an Arab, standing eyeball to eyeball, while others chimed in, all of us trying to make sense out of the Arab-Israeli mess. (The Arabs seemed to have all the passion; the pro-Israeli side all the facts.) And where a Belfast Irish Marxist, from the James Connolly Association, could not only argue the cause of Catholics in Bogside, but could get cheers from a largely sympathetic British audience. Speech in Hyde Park is of course free, but to paraphrase George Orwell, it's probably more free there than anywhere in the world.

I've saved for last, as an ironic coda to London-lady-traveler's bit about violence on New York streets, the scene on Portobello Road (a dark, narrow street not far from Steve's place), where one of 3 pub-crawlers throws a punch at a visitor's jaw, with no more provocation than that the visitor might have been walking a little too close to them, while on his way home after having a pint or two at a local pub. Bloke takes a swing at me, and it almost sends me packing, after being here but two days: *This is what I came to London for?* Some laughs at Steve's — after I related the incident — and